NEWBURY HOUSE SERIES

STUDIES IN BILINGUAL EDUCATION

Sponsored by

The International Center for Research on Bilingualism

Laval University

Quebec City, Canada

BILINGUAL EDUCATION IN A BINATIONAL SCHOOL
by William F. Mackey

THE LANGUAGE EDUCATION OF MINORITY CHILDREN
Selected Readings
Edited by Bernard Spolsky

BILINGUAL EDUCATION OF CHILDREN: The St. Lambert Experiment
by Wallace E. Lambert and G. R. Tucker

A SOCIOLINGUISTIC APPROACH TO BILINGUAL EDUCATION
by Andrew D. Cohen

BILINGUAL SCHOOLING AND THE SURVIVAL OF SPANISH
IN THE UNITED STATES
by A. Bruce Gaarder

THE AMERICAN BILINGUAL TRADITION
by Heinz Kloss

BILINGUALISM IN EARLY CHILDHOOD
Edited by William F. Mackey and Theodore Andersson

BILINGUAL SCHOOLS FOR A BICULTURAL COMMUNITY
William F. Mackey and Von N. Beebe

BILINGUAL SCHOOLS
FOR A
BICULTURAL
COMMUNITY

**Miami's Adaptation
to the
Cuban Refugees**

William Francis Mackey
Centre International de Recherche sur le Bilinguisme
Laval University
Quebec, Canada

Von Nieda Beebe, Principal
Caribbean Elementary School
Miami, Florida

NEWBURY HOUSE PUBLISHERS/ROWLEY/MASSACHUSETTS

Library of Congress Cataloging in Publication Data

Mackey, William Francis.
  Bilingual schools for a bicultural community.

  (Studies in bilingual education)
  Bibliography: p.
  Includes index.
  1. Education, Bilingual—Florida—Miami.
  2. Cuban-Americans—Education—Florida—Miami.
  I. Beebe, Von Nieda, joint author.   II. Title.
  LC3733.M5M3   371.9'7   76-57185
  ISBN 0-88377-068-7

Cover design by Wendy Doherty

This book was set in Souvenir on a
Compuwriter II TG by Gertrude Wilkins & Associates.

The photographs for this book are by courtesy of Dr. Von N. Beebe,
The Miami Herald, and the Public Information Office of the Dade County
Public Schools.

NEWBURY HOUSE PUBLISHERS, Inc.

Language Science
Language Teaching
Language Learning

ROWLEY, MASSACHUSETTS 01969

Printed in the U.S.A.   First printing: June 1977

Contents

Figures

Tables

PREFACE

Those who cannot remember the past are condemned to repeat it.
Santayana

The justification for this book is the assumption that people can profit from the experiences of others. In the field of bilingual education, this assumption may be particularly applicable, since in many parts of the world this type of schooling remains unknown. Yet, because bilingual education is part and parcel of the social and political accommodation of two or more ethnic groups, it would also be safe to assume that no two biethnic situations are entirely identical. The reason is that the degree of success or failure of any bilingual education program may depend on so many demographic, social, economic, political, and other forces. (For a checklist of these variables, see Appendix A.) An account of the experiences of others in coping with these influences presumably could be helpful to anyone wishing to apply, modify, or improve any one of the many types of bilingual schooling. This study was undertaken in response to a demand for such an account.

The Miami experience had already become known as one of the most remarkable and successful experiments in bilingual schooling ever undertaken in the United States. Teachers, administrators, educators, and academics had come from all over the world to visit the bilingual schools of the area. The ramifications of the local educational problem, were far too complex to be assimilated during a visit to the schools. There was a need and a growing demand for some sort of structured account explaining the whys and wherefores of this remarkable innovation. It is such an account of how bilingual schooling evolved in this bicultural community that we have attempted to supply.

It became evident to us that the evolution of bilingual education in the area was essentially a case of sociolinguistic ecology, and it is within this perspective that we have framed our description. Ours is not, therefore, a psychometric study of the advantages and disadvantages of bilingual education based on comparative samples from one or more schools. Such evaluative studies had already been undertaken within the school system. The study presented here is an account of how an entire community responded to a pressing sociolinguistic need.

As our study progressed, it became evident that transformation to a bilingual school system took place neither easily nor rapidly and that the change was facilitated or impeded by numerous forces. In some cases, unexpected or seemingly minor events played a significant role in the process of change. That is why it was necessary for us to uncover all the facts and to include many of them in our study. In compiling this historical account, a systematic effort was made to determine who did what and in what order.

This account is based on lengthy personal interviews, on-site visits, and an extensive analysis of all relevant documents, some of which had been reproduced or summarized in the press. We must therefore acknowledge a debt of thanks to all those who made it possible for us to gather this information—the Dade County school authorities, the school principals and teachers, those persons who submitted to the extensive interviews, those who spent their time with us in the schools, and those who supplied and classified the documents.

We reserve a special thanks for Pauline Rojas, Paul W. Bell, Ralph Robinett, Rosa Inclán, and Herminia Cantero who supplied so much valuable information. We also take pleasure in giving special thanks to Karin Dhatt for the efficient way in which she helped us collate the contents of many documents. Finally, we would like to acknowledge the consistent support of the International Center for Research on Bilingualism throughout the years we worked on this study, and we additionally thank the Secretariat of the Center for helping us prepare the manuscript.

INTRODUCTION

This is the story of mutual adaptation within one American community. It relates the accommodation of two cultures to a new situation of direct contact caused by a political emergency. It describes the adjustment of the two peoples, Anglo-Americans and Cubans, particularly in the domains of language and education. The most notable manifestations of this adjustment were the creation of bilingual schools for biethnic classes composed of both Cubans and Americans and the generalization of a degree of bilingualism throughout an entire system of public education.

The process of mutual adaptation occurred within a wide national context and against the changing background of language usage in American education. The background covers the quarter century following the Second World War during which period the status of second languages evolved from that of an optional or minor secondary school subject to that of an elementary school medium of instruction to that of equal status within bilingual public schools. This changing status was backed by the power and influence of the United States government in a continual flow of federal legislation spanning two decades. A series of federal laws evolved into a virtual language policy covering the educational rights of bilingual citizens. This policy influenced state and municipal policies and, in turn, was influenced by them. This cumulative influence at the local and national levels favored the survival of certain ethnic minorities whose economic fortunes had long depended on their complete assimilation into the mainstream of Anglo-American culture.

For many years the most established, most populous, and most wide-spread of these ethnic minorities in the United States was the Hispanic group, counting millions of Spanish-speakers in the American Southwest and in a few large urban centers like New York, Los Angeles, and Miami. These Spanish-speakers included the traditional Spanish-American families, the Mexi-can-American, the Puerto Ricans, and a minority of Cuban-Americans. It was the great and rapid increase of this latter group that caused the profound bicul-tural adaptation within the community described here. This sudden increase was really an accident of history caused by a class revolution in Cuba. The re-sulting exile of hundreds of thousands of Cuban nationals to the nearest major foreign city increased the population of the Miami area by a quarter of a million speakers of Spanish. It also placed an unexpected burden on the educational system serving this southern corner of the State of Florida, the Dade County Public Schools (see maps in Figure 1).

The influx continued for more than a decade, punctuated by periods of conflict and crisis. The Cubans' hopes of counter-revolution and repatriation gave way to the despondency of exile and isolation and to concern for the free-dom of compatriots. This concern, which generated the memorable Freedom Flights, caused a further increase in the Cuban population of the area. These newer arrivals also became resigned to the permanence of exile and to the shaping of a new homeland for themselves, maintaining their culture and lan-guage as best they could. The probability for cultural maintenance of the first generation of Cuban exiles depended on the grouping of a number of favorable demographic, economic, social, and cultural characteristics. This population of Cubans was large enough and concentrated enough to constitute a viable ur-ban community. Being largely skilled or well educated, it quickly achieved a high level of employment and income, assuring its economic independence. In general, it maintained favorable ethnic relations with other groups and had the political sympathy of those in power. In this way, the Cuban exiles were able to maintain their institutions and their language.

For the second generation, however, the probability of cultural mainte-nance depended largely on what was to happen in the schools. Although some Cubans took this responsibility into their own hands by creating their own pri-vate Cuban schools, more and more of their children began to enter the public schools of the area. The influx of thousands of unilingual Spanish-speaking children into unilingual English-speaking Miami classrooms created a massive problem with which the county's school system was ill prepared to cope. Like other American school systems, it had been organized on principles, not of eth-nic law, but of inter-ethnic integration providing education which was equal, if not identical, for all citizens. This had meant schooling for all in the common language of the nation. For immigrants unfamiliar with this language, the sys-tem sometimes provided special Americanization courses to assist their rapid assimilation into the English-speaking mainstream. It was natural, therefore, that the school system serving the Miami area should first opt for this solution by designing special English courses for Cuban children.

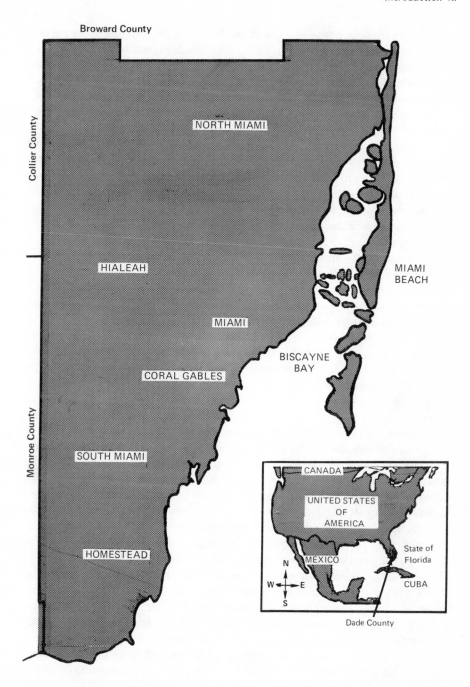

Figure 1   Dade County (Florida)

In this context, it was also understandable that the bilingual option of ethnic maintenance not provided for by the system would have to be initiated from the outside; and indeed it took the foresight of a few courageous outsiders and the backing of a private foundation to plant such an innovation within this essentially unilingual school system. The problem was to achieve cultural maintenance without ethnic segregation. This could not be done without the participation of English-speaking American children.

What was needed was a two-way bilingual school for both Cubans and Americans in which each would become integrated into the culture of the other while maintaining his own home language and cultural identity. In the context of American education, this was indeed a big order; it was asking of the system and its users much more than they had ever conceded. It was not surprising that the process of creating such an innovation turned out to be a long and painstaking task.

To begin with, an acceptable school in an appropriate community had to be found. The school authorities had to be cooperative. The people of the community had to become involved. Educators had to plan and develop a new program, recruit and train bilingual teachers, design a bilingual curriculum, and find or develop new teaching materials.

In order that this new type of school should not constitute an isolated curiosity or continue forever merely as an experiment, the model had to be evaluated, adjusted, and adapted to other schools. This involved an understanding of the differences between various school communities. It was on the basis of these differences and the cooperation of parents and teachers that the biethnic model was adapted and that the objectives, staffing, organization, curriculum, and resources of a number of appropriate programs were developed.

Proof of the adaptability of the biethnic model of bilingual education set the stage for its expansion and standardization. After a decade of caution, this type of bilingual schooling spread to other elementary schools in the area. The bilingual program also extended upward to the secondary school level. Meanwhile, other types of bilingualism entered the regular schools throughout the system. The formula of transitional bilingualism, involving English and the native languages of Cuban, Haitian, Vietnamese, and numerous other non-English-speaking students became widespread.

As bilingual education entered more schools and became part and parcel of the school system, there was a greater need for controls and the development of norms and standards. Educators and other community members wanted to take a closer look at existing programs of bilingual education. They demanded some comparative evaluations while remaining open to further experimentation. Meanwhile, the necessity of administering a type of schooling that was becoming more and more general obliged the educators to standardize bilingual education under two general types—maintenance and transitional.

All this would not have been possible without the necessary external and internal support. In a democratic society where school board members are elected officials, it was important to have the backing of public opinion. Local and national opinion in the United States was largely sympathetic to the plight of the Cuban refugees. Coupled with the rising status of ethnicity in the United States during the sixties, this created a climate favorable to the making of public policy promoting the support of ethnic minorities, particularly the Spanish-speaking groups. Several sources of public funds, applicable to different types of bilingual schooling were generated under a variety of legislative titles. Encouraged by the support of the public and the availability of funds, educators had become deeply involved in the elaboration of new programs, the training of bilingual teachers and development of appropriate teaching materials.

This phenomenal development of new types of bilingual schooling to support the educational needs of a community that had become bicultural did not take place, however, without a certain amount of struggle. There were, admittedly, a number of setbacks, disappointments, and difficulties due to a lack of understanding on the part of both the public and the educators. Some of the misunderstanding was purely a matter of semantics. People were using the same terms for such vaguely different and emotion-laden concepts as race, culture, and language. Cubans were sometimes categorized by race and blacks by culture.

It is therefore necessary for us in the following chapters to keep these basic concepts clear and distinct. Along with most modern anthropologists, we shall maintain the distinction between race and culture as one of heredity and environment, race being inherited and culture acquired. Racial differences are therefore biological differences; cultural differences are differences in what is learned as an individual or as a member of an ethnic group. It is the latter that includes such cultural traits as language, religion, custom, and social behavior. Since both race and culture are mutually exclusive, it is possible for blacks and whites to share the same culture; conversely, people of the same race may be separated by different cultures.

Since culture is not hereditary, children may belong to a culture different from that of their parents and may find that of their grandparents completely incomprehensible. That is why ethnic-origin is no guarantee of ethnicity, no more than is a person's surname. Unfortunately, these imprecise criteria of ethnicity have been used as a basis for some of the official statistics quoted in the following chapters; they should, therefore, be used with caution. Similarly, the student categories, based on language ability ("native Spanish-speaking" or "native English-speaking"), that appear in the text and in tables and figures as well as the terms "Spanish-speaking" and "English-speaking" really do not reveal anything about the degree of that language ability. In fact, each group may include individuals with skills ranging from an extremely limited home-based ability to express oneself in a language replete with dialectal and foreign elements to a fluent knowledge of the language comparable to that of the unilingual of the same age. Despite these limitations, we generally have preferred in this text to employ the terms "Spanish-speaking" and "English-speaking", which infer at least some language ability, over the terms "Spanish language origin" and "English language origin" which are even less functional for this purpose. One cannot reason that so many people of "Spanish language origin" are identical to the number of people who are culturally Spanish or who speak the Spanish language. Nor can one reason that they are therefore racially identical, since the group can include many of Amerindian or African origin whose ancestors had become assimilated into an Hispanic culture.

In our context, we have refused, therefore, to put the Cubans into a separate racial category. We have treated them as a cultural entity within the Hispanic world, and as an ethnic and cultural group within the United States.

The main determinant of cultural identity and the main criterion of cultural differentiation is the home language or language variety spoken by an ethnic group. If the ethnic group is bilingual, cultural identity may include the type, degree, and range of binguality. Cubans are identified by their use of Cuban Spanish which in its spoken form is audibly different from other varieties of Spanish spoken throughout the world. Spanish taught throughout the schools of the United States had rarely included these varieties. The teaching objective was mastery of a non-regional construct of a standard of Latin-American speech. Similar non-regional standards were used in the teaching of other languages.

These distinctions in language, race, and culture will be kept in mind as we begin our story with a description of the background against which it unfolds, that of the evolution of language education in the United States.

1

LANGUAGE EDUCATION IN THE AMERICAN CONTEXT

LANGUAGES IN AMERICAN SCHOOLING

All children in the United States of America are granted equal opportunities for public education by the nation's Constitution. The Constitution delegates the responsibility for the public education of the citizens to the government of each state. The state is responsible for educating all citizens, not only those whose mother tongue is English. In a land of immigrants, this responsibility inevitably has posed the problem of deciding the language of instruction, since schooling in an incomprehensible tongue could hardly be defined as equal education. The necessity for such decisions presupposed the existence of a degree of bilingualism in the schools, a practice which indeed goes back to the very beginnings of education in the United States and a long and honorable tradition within the context of both tolerance-oriented and promotion-oriented language policies.[1]

A well-established nation can afford to tolerate and even encourage diversity among its populace. Citizens in a newly-emerging nation, however, may tend to standardize their behavior in order to establish a national identity. The United States has indeed been a nation of immigrants. With the exception of the indigenous Indians, the early residents were immigrants from several different countries, primarily England. During the 19th Century and the first years of the 20th, a few public schools in German-American communities (Ohio, Minnesota, Maryland), French-American communities (Louisiana), and Spanish-

American communities (New Mexico) allowed instruction for non-English-speaking students to be presented in the students' home language.

As nationalism and the ideal of national unity became fashionable in Europe, the United States mosaic began to be regarded as the American Melting Pot. The dominant image of "America" became that of a nation in which all of the inherent differences were blended supposedly into a good mixture, no single ingredient being discernible. As the idea of an "American culture" emerged, English was established as *the* American language. Eventually, this language began to be considered as *the only* American language. The more the citizen of the United States was locked into the American culture and the American way of pronouncing the English language, the more he or she was perceived as truly "American". As long as the United States was prosperous and independent, there was no economic need and no political necessity to modify this American image. The great majority of the citizens of the United States were confined to this American culture and bound to the English language.[2]

Within this climate of nationalism in the United States, it was very unlikely that bilingual education (in this case, the use of English and another language as mediums of instruction) would be introduced into the public schools.[3] As in Europe, classical languages continued to be studied in the United States as basic subjects in educational programs. The inclusion of modern languages, however, depended upon their political popularity at the time. They were alternately added and withdrawn from the curricular offerings in public schools. The increase in nationalism generated by the First World War reduced the popularity of the teaching of modern languages and the use of any language other than English as a medium of instruction in American public schools. And the isolationism which followed the war discouraged foreign language learning to such an extent that, on entering the Second World War, the United States found itself totally unprepared to communicate with the inhabitants of the many areas of the globe in which its military forces had to operate.

To make up for this weakness in language competence, a number of specialized language-training schools were created throughout the United States under the Army Specialized Training Program (ASTP). The intensive courses, lasting several months, produced results which convinced the postwar academic community that it was possible for Americans to become fluent speakers of foreign languages through classroom training. During the postwar period, the need for Americans to know foreign languages was demonstrated by events which showed that even academics were unaware of scientific activities in other countries because of an inability to read any language other than English. The most dramatic event was the appearance in the skies of the first spacial satellite -- the Sputnik from the Soviet Union, a country that had long been considered as being technologically backward.

The postwar rivalry with the Soviet Union encouraged reassessment and comparison, and it came to be felt that there might be a superiority in the Soviet Union's level of school attainment in the sciences, in mathematics, and in foreign languages which could threaten the United States' defense operations. To redress the balance, the American Government initiated a program of massive federal support to these three fields through the National Defense Education Act (NDEA). This provided, among other things, for the elaboration of new methods and materials for foreign language learning and for the training of foreign language teachers. Foreign language learning had become a national priority.

It was pointed out, however, that in the case of foreign language learning, age was a crucial factor and that by secondary school, which had traditionally been the period at which a foreign language could be studied, the child had already passed the optimum age for language acquisition. School systems, therefore, were urged to make provisions for the teaching of Foreign Languages in Elementary Schools (FLES) and the new departure became known as the FLES movement. The foreign language was to be learned essentially as a skill at an age when skills are most easily acquired. Unlike the other skills, however, the foreign language skill became an end in itself. And, because it was not used for anything in particular, there was no motivation to develop and maintain the skill.

To make up for this deficiency, it was suggested that certain school subjects be taught in the foreign language even though knowledge of that language was limited. Such a program had been reported to be feasible, provided special materials and techniques were developed.[4] The preparation of such programs became the object of the Foreign Language Innovative Curriculum Studies (FLICS) as a complement to the FLES movement.[5] By agreeing to teach school subjects in a foreign language, educators had now accepted what could be described as a certain type of bilingual schooling even though they did not name it as such.

In sum, this chain of events and subsequent policy decisions, beginning with the Second World War to which the foregoing alludes, led up to the creation of a climate in which the existence of bilingual education within certain school systems could be accepted as a possibility.

THE RETURN TO THE IDEA OF BILINGUAL EDUCATION

Underlying this gradual acceptance of the possibility of bilingual education was a growing reaction against the melting-pot theory of nationalism. Some educators even began thinking in terms of language maintenance in place of language transfer and assimilation.

By 1970, "bilingual education" was a term that had become recognized by most educators and laymen throughout the United States. In almost all major cities and numerous small towns and rural areas, "bilingual programs" were accepted as a viable alternative to the traditional monolingual instructional programs. As in the past, however, these "bilingual programs" were generally perceived and designed as special education for the non-English-speaking students of Mexican origin, Portuguese origin, French-Canadian origin, German origin, and other non-British groups. These programs were seldom designed to involve and seldom did involve significant numbers of English-speaking students of Anglo origin. In fact, bilingual education in several states was defined as instruction in both English and Spanish (or other languages) so that the child's home language could be strengthened while he became familiar with English. But a broader goal had appeared. It was that of bilingual, bicultural education for all children, Anglo and non-Anglo, in any given school. This would mean, wrote Armando Rodriguez of the United States Office of Education, "that the school must put into proper forms the . . . contributions of these citizens whose language and cultural values and customs differ from the majority", enabling the minority child to feel that his ways are respected and bringing to the English-speaking youngster "sensitivity and comparison and understanding of the richness of difference". "Bilingualism" according to Rodriguez, "must come to be accepted as a blessing, not a problem".[6] If so, it was good for English-speaking children, and more of them seemed to favor the idea.

The blessing of bilingualism eventually became the concern of those whose task it was to teach English to speakers of other languages. In 1971, at the meeting of the Association of Teachers of English to Speakers of Other Languages (TESOL) during its Fifth Annual Convention in New Orleans, the Committee on Socio-political Concerns of Minority Groups presented a resolution stating the organization's position on bilingual education. After discussion by the members present and some changes in the original wording, the resolution was passed, as follows:

> Whereas we recognize that any human being's language constitutes his link with the real world, and
> Whereas we are collectively engaged in teaching another language to human beings who already possess a fully articulated and developed linguistic system,
> Therefore, be it resolved that TESOL affirms:
> 1. That bilingual education must be assumed to mean education in two languages;
> 2. That this, in turn, presupposes full recognition by every available means of the validity of the first language;
> 3. That such recognition includes positive attitudes of all teachers and administrators toward the student's language;
> 4. That the validity of that language not only as a communication system but as a viable vehicle for the transfer and reenforcement of any subject content in the classroom must be central in curricular policy; and
> 5. That, where numbers of individuals justify such concern, the student's own language must specifically constitute a segment of the curriculum.[7]

By the mid-seventies, bilingual education was beginning to be regarded as a right rather than a privilege. In a 1975 report, the United States Civil Rights Commission endorsed bilingual education for non-English-speaking children, with courses taught in their native language. Except where "minority language" students make up less than 10 percent of the population, the Commission recommended that English be taught as a second language with basic reading and writing skills taught in the student's native tongue. Along with the right to bilingual education came the corresponding need for mutual understanding between ethnic groups. This need, dramatized by racial and ethnic revolts in the 1960's, was felt throughout the United States. [8]

Bilingual and multicultural education, however, was not without accompanying problems. One of the serious problems in bilingual education was the qualifications of teachers. It was unlikely that bilingual programs would have much success in finding enough Anglo teachers who were fluent in Spanish. The National Education Association had warned of a "very real teacher shortage" for bilingual education programs throughout the country. In New York City, for example, some 25,000 to 65,000 new pupils were to be directly involved in a bilingual program agreed to by the Board of Education in order to improve the level of education of Spanish-speaking pupils. To implement the program, which called for bilingual instruction in science, mathematics, and social studies, the New York City school system needed to recruit, in mid-1975, some 3,500 bilingual teachers. [9] As a result, monolingual teachers found that the employment situation was exacerbated by the sudden demand for qualified bilinguals.

The demand succeeded in giving increased status to bilingual teachers. By the mid-seventies, bilingual education had become a profession with its own professional body, the National Association for Bilingual Education (NABE). The NABE was founded to promote bilingual education as the continuous use of two languages, one of which was English, as a means of instruction. Concepts and information were to be introduced in the dominant language of the student and reinforced in the second language. Cultural differences and similarities would be recognized in the teaching process. The NABE considered bilingual education as (Article 1): "The continuous use and preservation of two languages and their corresponding cultures." Membership in the NABE was available to all persons interested in bilingual education in the professional and para-professional categories (Article 3). According to Article 5, each state or territory chapter chose its representative to NABE's Delegate Assembly. The Board of Directors of NABE was to meet at least once annually (Article 8).

In summary, it is no exaggeration to speak of a bilingual education movement which began in the United States in the second half of the 20th century.

EVOLUTION OF FEDERAL POLICY ON BILINGUAL EDUCATION

Over a period of 15 years, there evolved a federal policy on bilingual education as a result of years of public discussions going back to the late 1940's. It emerged during the enactment by the United States Congress of a series of equity-oriented laws giving financial support to special educational programs for economically disadvantaged sections of the population. Between the mid-sixties and the mid-seventies, the policy evolved from one of language transfer to one of language maintenance. It was punctuated by public federal laws on Elementary and Secondary Education, Economic Opportunity, and Emergency School Aid, each comprising a number of "titles" launching elaborate programs, some of them also known under the name of legislative "acts". They included the Bilingual Education Act, the Indian Education Act, the Migrant Education Program, the Ethnic Heritage Program, the Head Start Program, and the Follow Through Program.

The initial pressure for federal legislation came from a belated realization that poverty existed among certain minorities whose economic and social disadvantages were being perpetuated through their inability to profit from public education. The large majority of the non-English-speaking students enrolled in public schools in the United States were of Spanish language origin. For example, according to the Superintendent of Schools in New York City, more than 226,000 students in the city's schools were of Puerto Rican origin and approximately 100,000 were classified as non-English-speaking.[10]

In 1960, of all Puerto Ricans 25 years of age and older in the United States, 87 percent had dropped out without graduating from high school. The rate of dropout for 8th grade was 52.9 percent. In 1968-69, the dropout rate for Puerto Rican students by the 12th year of schooling was 80 percent compared to 46 percent for black students and 28.7 percent for Anglos. Hardly 5 percent of Puerto Rican college-age youth were moving to higher education. The rate for blacks was 15-20 percent and for the general population 45 percent. According to one report, the dropout rate for Puerto Ricans admitted to college was 60 percent.

The situation for *Chicano* (Mexican-American) students was quite similar to that for Puerto Ricans. In the southwestern section of the United States, the average Chicano child had only a seventh grade education. In the State of Texas, it was reported that the Chicano child usually repeated first grade three times and dropped out of school in fourth grade.[11] The dropout rate for Chicano children who continued into high school in that state was 89 percent. College enrollment for Chicanos was infinitesimal. In California, where 14 percent of public school students were Chicanos, less than ½ percent of college students at the seven University of California campuses were Chicanos.

In the late spring of 1967, extensive hearings began in both the United States Senate and in the House of Representatives concerning proposed legislation to support bilingual education. At that time, the estimated number of non-English-speaking school-age children was close to 6,000,000, and 5,000,000 of them were Spanish speakers. Apparently convinced that the best remedy for this situation would be the allocation of special funds to enable local school systems to develop and initiate demonstration projects that utilized for instruction both English and the native language of the non-English-speaking student, the United States Congress passed the Bilingual Education Act in December, 1967. Subsequently, $7,500,000 was appropriated for operations during the first year. Basically, these initial funds were to be allocated to public school systems for the organization and planning of bilingual programs to begin in September, 1969.

The legal foundation for this act can be traced to Public Law 89-10, which was a series of amendments to the Federally Impacted Areas Legislation of 1950 (Public Law 874). This earlier legislation provided federal financial relief to public schools that were "impacted" with students whose parents did not pay local property taxes to support the community's public schools because they lived or worked on property owned by the federal government. The Bilingual Education Act was simply one of a series of additional amendments to Public Law 874. It was included in the second package of extensive educational legislation in the mid-sixties that provided federal financial relief to schools in the United States with large enrollments of disadvantaged students. The first group of amendments became known as the Elementary and Secondary Education Act of 1965. The second group was identified collectively as the Elementary and Secondary Amendments of 1967, and the Bilingual Education Act was listed as Title VII (see Figure 2).

Although passage of the Bilingual Education Act established "bilingual education" as a nationally-acceptable feature of public school instruction, it should be noted that the Bilingual Education Act was not an affirmation of the educational *advantages* of bilingualism for citizens of the United States. Instead, as stated in the act, it was designed "to provide a solution to the problems of those children who are educationally *disadvantaged* because of their inability to speak English".[12]

Subsequently, in 1972, the Congress passed the Emergency School Aid Act. One of the purposes of this act was to facilitate desegregation in the schools. Under this act, bilingual projects were authorized for migrant education (Title I -- Migrant, ESEA) and Indian education (Indian Education Act of 1972), and other funds were made available through the Ethnic Heritage Program (Title IX). Additional federal legislation followed that supported bilingual education either directly or indirectly, and an office of bilingual education had been established in the United States Office of Education.

Projects were also funded to locate and to develop appropriate instructional materials for teaching in a language other than English within the United States. In addition, local school systems utilized other federal programs (Titles I, III, and IV of the Elementary and Secondary Education Act plus programs of the United States Office of Economic Opportunity) as well as state government programs to fund projects involving bilingual education for adults, migrant workers, and other students. The provision of federal funds for bilingual education and funding by the governments in certain states stimulated the establishment of numerous bilingual education projects across the nation (see Table 1).

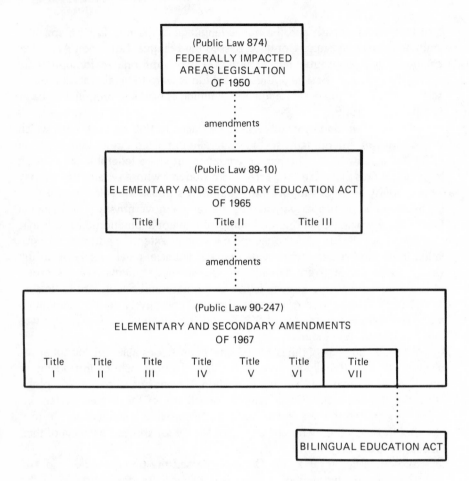

Figure 2   The Bilingual Education Act in the Federal Legislative Structure

Back in the mid-sixties, the mere possibility of federal funding had generated support for bilingual education in some school systems. By the 1967-68 and the 1968-69 school years, 56 bilingual programs already had been started. With few exceptions, these programs were functioning at the pre-primary or elementary grade levels and approximately one-third of the programs were located within the State of Texas.[13] The federal government's offer of planning grants stimulated even more interest in bilingual education programs throughout the country. By the Dec. 20, 1968, deadline (approximately one year after the Congressional adoption of the Bilingual Education Act), 312 educational agencies had submitted preliminary proposals to the United States Office of Education. Seventy-six proposals from 22 different states were selected for funding during the school year 1969-70. More than 70 percent of these programs were located in five southwestern states: California (26), Texas (19), New Mexico (5), Arizona (4), and Colorado (1). English was one of the lan-

Table 1
STATE AND FEDERAL BILINGUAL PROJECTS
(School Year: 1973-74)

State	State Funding	ESEA Title VII Projects	ESAA Projects	Languages [Cultures]
Alaska	$200,000	1		Yupik (Eskimo)
Arizona		9	1	Navajo, Spanish (MA)*
California	$4,000,000	61	3	Spanish (MA), Portuguese, Chinese, Pomo Indian, Tagalog (Philippine)
Colorado		7		Spanish (MA), Ute, Navajo
Connecticut		3	1	Spanish (PR)**
District of Columbia	$175,000(est.)		1	Spanish
Florida		3	2	Spanish, Eeleponkee (Miccosukee)
Idaho		1		Spanish (MA)
Illinois	$2,300,000	4		Spanish
Indiana		2		Spanish
Louisiana		4	4	French (Cajun), Spanish
Maine		3		Passamaquoddy (Algonquin) French
Massachusetts	$4,000,000	7		Spanish, Portuguese, Italian, Chinese, Greek, French (Haitian)
Michigan	$88,000	4		Spanish
Montana		3		Cheyenne, Crow, Cree (Chippewa)
New Hampshire		1		French
New Jersey		4		Spanish
New Mexico	$694,140	12	2	Spanish (MA), Navajo, Zuni, Keresan, Acoma
New York	$1,500,000	26	4	Chinese, Spanish, French (Haitian)
Ohio		1		Spanish
Oklahoma		3	1	Muskogean (Seminole), Choctaw, Cherokee
Oregon		1		Spanish (MA), Russian
Pennsylvania		2		Spanish (PR)
Rhode Island		2	1	Spanish, Portuguese
South Dakota		1		Dakota
Texas	$700,000	40	19	Spanish (MA)
Utah		1		Navajo
Washington	$500,000 (est.)	2	1	Spanish (MA), Chinese, Japanese
Wisconsin		1		Spanish
Guam		1		Chamorro
Mariana Islands		1		Palauan, Ponapaean
Puerto Rico		1		Spanish (PR)
Virgin Islands		1		Spanish (PR)
Total		213	40	

Note: States without bilingual projects for 1973-74 include Alabama, Arkansas, Georgia, Hawaii, Iowa, Kansas, Kentucky, Maryland, Minnesota, Mississippi, Missouri, Nebraska, Nevada, North Carolina, North Dakota, South Carolina, Tennessee, Vermont, Virginia, West Virginia, and Wyoming.

*MA — Mexican-American.
**PR — Puerto Rican

Source: Lawrence Wright, "The Bilingual Education Movement at the Crossroads," Phi Delta Kappan, Vol. LV, No. 3, Nov., 1973, p. 194.

guages utilized as a medium of instruction in all of the projects. Spanish was selected as the other language (or one of the two other languages in the three trilingual programs) in all but eight of the programs. American Indian languages, Portuguese, French, Chinese, and Japanese were the other languages involved.[14] By 1973, the United States Office of Education reported that there were 209 bilingual education programs functioning throughout the country, 85 percent of them for pupils having Spanish as a home language.[15]

In 1974, a major event occurred in the evolution of federal policy on bilingual education within the United States. The nation's Supreme Court decided in the case of *Lau v. Nichols* (No. 72-6520) that a city schools system in the State of California had denied approximately 1,800 students of Chinese ancestry, who did not speak English, a meaningful opportunity to participate in the public education program by failing to provide them with special instruction in the English language. The court interpreted this as a violation of these students' civil rights. That school system and any other public school system with significant numbers of non-English-speaking students which did not provide special English language classes were, therefore, ineligible for any form of federal financial assistance.

In sum, by the mid-seventies, the United States government was not only providing funds to local school systems to support bilingual education programs, but the country's highest court had prohibited that government from providing any financial assistance to local school systems which did not provide for the special English language needs of non-English-speaking students. In addition, federal legislation encouraged state and municipal governments to supply their share of support for bilingual schooling.

STATE AND MUNICIPAL POLICIES

After the passage of the federal Bilingual Education Act in the mid-sixties, more and more resolutions were proposed and adopted in state legislatures mandating bilingual education and urging that colleges and universities assume greater responsibilities in training bilingual teachers. Massachusetts, New Mexico, New York, Connecticut, Pennsylvania, Texas, and California all passed mandatory bilingual education legislation requiring public schools to offer instruction on a bilingual basis if a significant portion of their students were non-English speaking. One of the first new state laws governing bilingual education was the Massachusetts Transitional Bilingual Act of 1971; it was the only state at the time both mandating and funding bilingual instruction. Other states mandated bilingual education without providing necessary funds, as was the case in Pennsylvania. Some states provided funds without compelling implementation of bilingual instruction, as was the case in New Mexico, New York, and Washington. Texas passed legislation that established bilingual education as state policy for non-English-speaking students. In California, the law stipulated that at least one-third of the class be proficient in English in order to ensure that the class was actually bilingual. Louisiana embarked on an innovative program designed to preserve the French-speaking heritage of its Cajun ancestry. CODOFIL (Council for the Development of French in Louisiana) was created to restore the language and the culture of the French population after a century of neglect.[16]

In addition to the states, support came from the municipalities themselves, especially from those with large numbers of non-English-speaking children. The biggest of these was New York City, a great percentage of whose million-and-a-half pupils spoke Spanish at home, most of them children of parents who had immigrated from Puerto Rico. In this massive cosmopolitan metropolis, the idea of bilingual education rapidly evolved. By the mid-seventies, it had developed into a program of local support for ethnic language maintenance.

In 1975, some 30 New York City elementary and junior high schools and 10 high schools were pilot schools offering bilingual education. Subjects such as mathematics, social studies, and science were taught in Spanish. Intensive instruction in English was also given to Spanish-speaking pupils. The estimated number of participants was 100,000. New York City already had three completely bilingual schools in the Bronx with a total of about 1,800 pupils. There were about 30,000 pupils in bilingual classes in various schools throughout the city. These included pupils in the 37 federally-funded bilingual programs, the 10 state-funded programs, and the numerous city-funded programs.[17]

The increasing inclusion of bilingual curricula since 1970 marked a major step in the direction of cross-cultural understanding. Assimilation models in education, through which all children were expected to blend into the "mainstream", were beginning to be replaced by those which more nearly reflected the reality of a culturally pluralistic society.

THE SURVIVAL OF ETHNIC AMERICA

The evolution during the sixties and seventies of federal, state, and municipal policies favoring the survival of this culturally pluralistic society was in keeping with the tradition of American political pluralism. Outside the school system, the ethnic climate had evolved. It became known that millions of Americans, perhaps a third of the population, had, contrary to popular belief, quietly preserved their ethnicity and their languages.[18] The internationalism and egalitarian ideals of the postwar generation, stressing social and ethnic equality throughout the world, helped make ethnicity fashionable in the United States.

Among these millions of ethnic Americans, the Spanish-speaking group was considered the most important nationally in both size and ethnicity. Many in this group resided in five southwestern states (Texas, New Mexico, Arizona, Colorado, and California). In 1969, there were approximately 4,617,000 Americans with Spanish surnames in this area, ranging from 25 percent of the total population in New Mexico to 11 percent in California.[19]

In the seventies, the United States Bureau of the Census reported that about 5 percent or 9,200,000 Americans identified themselves as being of

Spanish origin. Of these, 55 percent were Mexican-Americans, 15.8 percent Puerto Ricans, and 6.1 percent Cubans. Further, 50 percent of these Spanish origin Americans spoke mainly Spanish at home and 20 percent spoke no English at all.

Both the concentration and the size of such an ethnic population were important in opting for a policy of language maintenance rather than one of language transfer, especially for Spanish language minorities in the United States. In this case, the home language, in addition to being that of large and territorially adjacent populations, was also one of world status representing considerable demographic, economic, cultural, and political force.[20] It was claimed that Spanish-speaking residents had made the United States the fifth largest Spanish-speaking nation in the world. The United States Bureau of the Census predicted that, because Spanish-speaking families were growing at twice the rate of English-speaking families, by the year 2000 more persons living in the Western Hemisphere would speak Spanish than English.[21]

Finally, there was the historical status of Spanish in North America. The Spaniards were the first of the European colonizers in the New World and for a long time the dominant ones both in number and in territorial expansion. As a North American colonial language, Spanish enjoyed a status equal to that of English and of French. Much of what is now the United States had historically been territorial possessions of Spain. One of the earliest was an area which was to become the State of Florida.

Notes

1. See the introduction to Heinz Kloss, *The American Bilingual Tradition*. Rowley: Newbury House, 1977.
2. Joshua Fishman, et al., *Language Loyalty in the United States*. The Hague: Mouton, 1966; Rene Cardenas and Lily Wong Fillmore, "Toward a Multicultural Society." *Today's Education*, Sept.-Oct., 1973, pp. 83-88.
3. Theodore Andersson and Mildred Boyer, *Bilingual Schooling in the United States*, Vol. 1. Washington: U.S. Government Printing Office, 1970, pp. 17-18.
4. William F. Mackey & J.A. Noonan, "An Experiment in Bilingual Education". *English Language Teaching*, 1952.
5. William F. Mackey & Theodore Andersson (eds.), *Bilingualism in Early Childhood*. Rowley: Newbury House, 1977. pear).
6. Alberta Eiseman, *Manana is Now: the Spanish-speaking in the United States*. New York: Atheneum, 1973, p. 169.
7. *TESOL Newsletter*. June, 1971, p. 8.
8. William F. Mackey, "Epilogue: Current Trends in Multinationalism" in W.F. Mackey & A. Verdoodt (eds.), *The Multinational Society*. Rowley: Newbury House, 1975.
9. *New York Times*. May 28, 1975, p.36-L.
10. United States Congress, House of Representatives, *Bilingual Education Programs*, Hearings before the General Subcommittee on Education of the Committee on Education and Labor, June 28 and 29, 1967, Washington, D.C.: U.S. Government Printing Office, 1967, p. 226.

11. United States Congress, Senate, *Bilingual Education*, Hearings before the Special Subcommittee on Bilingual Education of the Committee on Labor and Public Welfare, May 18, 19, 26, 29, 31; June 24; and July 21, 1967, Washington, D.C.: U.S. Government Printing Office, 1967, Part 1, p. 332.

12. United States Senate, *Elementary and Secondary Education Act Amendments of 1967, Report Together with Supplemental and Individual Views [to accompany HR 7819]*, Report No. 726. Washington, D.C.: U.S. Government Printing Office, 1967, p. 49.

13. Andersson and Boyer, *Bilingual Schooling in the United States*, Vol. 2, pp. 241-254.

14. *Ibid.*, pp. 256-290.

15. *Christian Science Monitor*, Oct. 6, 1973, p. 6.

16. Heinz Kloss, *Les droits linguistiques des Franco-Americains aux Etats-Unis.* (Publication A-2 of the International Center for Research on Bilingualism) Quebec: Laval University Press, 1971.

17. *New York Times*, Jan. 15, 1975, p. 64.

18. Supra Note 2

19. "The Little Strike that Grew to 'La Causa' ". *Time*, July 4, 1969, p. 17.

20. William F. Mackey, *Three Concepts for Geolinguistics.* (Publication B-42 of the International Center for Research on Bilingualism) Quebec: International Center for Research on Bilingualism, 1973. Reprinted in *Sprachen und Staaten.* II. Hamburg: Stiftung Europa Kolleg., 1976.

21. Stewart Dill McBride, "Bilingual Classes in the United States: the Debate Rages" *Christian Science Monitor.* Oct. 6, 1973, p. 6.

2

SPANISH IN FLORIDA AND THE CUBAN RESETTLEMENT

FLORIDA UNDER SPANISH RULE

The Spanish presence in Florida dates from the age of Columbus. As early as 1498, Juan Fernandez, pilot of explorer John Cabot, had traced a discovery route along the Florida West Coast. But it was not until 1513 that the area was formally claimed for Spain and named *Pascua Florida* (feast of flowers) by Conquistador Juan Ponce de Leon. He was not the first Spaniard in Florida. Upon arrival, he had met Indians who understood Spanish as a result of earlier contacts with some of Spain's explorers and adventurers like Pedro de Quexos who had roamed the region in search of Carib indians for slaves. These Caribs, known as *Ka lu lusa* or Caloosas, had inhabited the area for more than 2,000 years before the arrival of the first Europeans. Other Amerindian tribes had been in the area even longer. Archeological remains indicated that at least 10,000 Amerindians inhabited this southeastern corner of the North American continent.[1] While many of these had migrated from the north, some of the original settlers had sailed to the mainland in crude boats from nearby Cuba and the Bahama Islands.

A century after Spain had claimed Florida, Spanish forces subdued many of the original inhabitants in the northern and western sections of the peninsula, and a chain of missions was established. In 1763, however, the Florida area was given by Spain to England in exchange for Havana, Cuba. Twenty years later, England returned the area to Spain in exchange for the Bahamas and Gibraltar. The United States acquired the area in 1821 as repayment for $4,000,000 in American citizens' claims against Spain; and, in 1845, Florida became the 27th state of the Union.[2]

MIAMI AS A LATIN-AMERICAN MECCA

Although Florida had become a part of the United States and was consequently populated by more and more English-speaking settlers, its Spanish character did not fade. On the contrary, as certain areas became urbanized, they attracted larger and larger numbers of Latin-Americans who came either as workers, tourists, residents, immigrants, businessmen, or political refugees.

By 1900, there were approximately 500,000 inhabitants in Florida; at that time, 80 percent of these inhabitants lived and worked in rural areas. The population grew to 2,770,000 by 1950, but few of the many new residents settled in rural settings. Large urban areas emerged, the largest developing into the metropolis of Miami.[3]

In the 1920's, Miami (and Miami Beach) already had become renowned in the Western hemisphere as both a tourist mecca and a Latin-American trade center. By 1950, approximately 20 percent of the area's economy was based on tourism. Along with others, Spanish-speakers from Latin America visited Miami both for business negotiations and for vacations. In addition to this floating population, approximately 50,000 Spanish-speakers were year-around residents during the 1950's. Some of these full-time residents were political refugees from Panama, the Dominican Republic, and other countries in Latin America. Many of the Spanish-speaking residents, however, were seasonal or year-around laborers from Cuba, Puerto Rico, and Mexico.

Within this southern city, racial segregation was the practice until the 1960's. Mexican-Americans and many of the dark-complexioned Puerto Ricans and Cubans were generally involved in agricultural or migrant labor. The light-complexioned Cuban and Puerto Rican men usually worked as waiters and cooks in the hotels on Miami Beach, and the Cuban women worked in the garment factories in central Miami and in Hialeah in the northwestern section of town.

Many Spanish-speakers with African ancestry intentionally maintained a heavy accent when speaking English so that they would not be subjected to local segregation policies involving American blacks; however, there was little contact with any of the English-speaking residents. In fact, there was little interaction between the three Spanish-speaking groups in the Miami area. Many of the Cubans lived in a small section of downtown Miami or near the garment factories in Hialeah. The Mexican-Americans generally lived in the rural areas near the farms where they worked. Although they were a closely-knit group, many of these Mexican-American families were seasonal residents that followed the migrant stream to farming areas throughout the eastern United States. The Puerto Ricans who performed farm labor usually lodged near the fields where they worked, returning on the weekends to their families and permanent residences in a section of downtown Miami. They also banded together and many were dependent upon friends, relatives, or wealthier Puerto Ricans (padrinos) for their jobs. [5]

During this period, there was no significant involvement by any of the Spanish-speaking residents in the political processes within the continental United States. In the 1950's, the Cuban residents (Cubanos residentes) were still focusing their attention on the political situation in Cuba. They were, for the most part, opposed to the reigning dictator, Fulgencio Batista; yet they were divided among themselves. There were the supporters of former president Carlos Prio Socarras, whom Batista had ousted in 1952, and the proponents of a young revolutionary law graduate named Fidel Castro.

Other than assigning a few policemen who could speak some Spanish to the Miami Beach area as a courtesy to the wealthy Spanish-speaking tourists, community leaders in the Miami area (Dade County) had made no special adjustments for Spanish-speakers as of 1958. Although Spanish-speaking children had attended the public schools of the area for many years, they apparently had not created significant problems in the classrooms, and no special instructional programs had been designed for them. Yet suddenly, and unexpectedly, the situation changed.

SAGA OF THE CUBAN REFUGEES

Although there had long been small colonies of exiles in Miami from Latin American countries, as a result of the numerous revolutions which the politics of these countries had engendered, the Communist revolution in nearby Cuba was an entirely different phenomenon. It affected not only a few individuals or political cliques, but entire sections of the Cuban society, including whole classes of people comprising the complete social and economic strata of the population in Cuba.

The political activities within Cuba that began with Castro's rise to power in 1959 also had an immense impact upon all of the residents in the Miami area and their public school system. The events in Cuba from 1959 through 1973 and their effect upon the setting for bilingual education in Miami may be divided into three periods characterized by conflict and crisis, exile and isolation, and the Freedom Flights. The first revolutionary period, dating from Batista's downfall to the missile crisis, lasted from January, 1959, until October, 1962. The second period, dating from the Missile Crisis to Camarioca, extended from November, 1962, to November, 1965. The third period, that of the Freedom Flights, began in December, 1965, and lasted until April, 1973.

Conflict and Crisis

Castro's revolutionary activities began in the Sierra Maestra mountains in southern Cuba in the late 1950's. When, on Jan. 1, 1959, Batista departed Cuba and Castro ascended to power, military men, government officials, and wealthy businessmen associated with the dictator began to move with their families to Miami. By the end of June, 1960, some 7,500 Cuban refugees had entered the Miami area, and only about 500 moved to resettle in areas beyond.[6]

These early arrivals were referred to somewhat disdainfully as *Cubanos exilados* by the *Cubanos residentes* (the full-time Cuban residents in Miami). Many of the *Cubanos residentes* had fled from Cuba because of Batista's policies and had supported Castro at that time. The *Cubanos residentes* harassed the *Cubanos exilados* making it virtually impossible for them to acquire the traditional "Cuban jobs" in the hotels and garment factories. In the public schools, the children of the *Cubanos exilados* were jeered and called *Batistianos*, "murderers", and "butchers". The wealthy *Cubanos exilados*, therefore, stayed at home most of the time and enrolled their children in parochial schools. They lived with the money that they had brought with them from Cuba or that they had previously invested in American businesses or deposited in savings accounts in Miami. Those who were not wealthy, mostly military men, were left with no alternative other than to pick vegetables and fruit with the migrant workers in order to earn a living.

In the spring of 1960, the Castro government began its reform movements (confiscating private land, businesses, and industries) and, during the following summer, the first large influx of Cuban refugees entered Miami. At first, only those people personally displaced by the major reforms turned against the Castro government and decided to leave the country; they were the sugar mill owners, large landholders, cattle ranchers and other families of outstanding wealth, most of whom had previous contacts in the United States. Gradually others followed; journalists, professors, teachers, doctors, businessmen, clerks, and salesmen. Some families sent only their children to the United States, being themselves unwilling to leave their country.

During the following 12 months, some 47,500 Cubans decided to move to Miami as a temporary, self-imposed exile.[7] This sudden increase in the number of Cubans in the area permitted the *Cubanos exilados* to emerge from their social hibernation. The *Cubanos residentes*, on the other hand, either returned with their personal possessions to Cuba or began their conversion to anti-Castroism.

The refugees who arrived without financial resources, along with the significant number of unaccompanied women and children, received assistance from the wealthier refugees and also from the Catholic, Protestant, and Jewish welfare services in the area.[8] As had been the custom in Havana, the wealthier Cubans generally enrolled their children in private Catholic schools in Miami. It was difficult for these Cubans to believe that anything "public", whether it be a club, a beach, a park, or a school, could be truly worthwhile.

On Jan. 3, 1961, diplomatic relations between the United States and Cuba were severed. During these winter months, the Cuban refugees immigrating to Miami were primarily such professionals as judges, lawyers, doctors and their families. Although the early refugees continued to help their newly arriving friends and relatives, they eventually began to run out of money, and their hopes for an early return to Cuba began to wane. Some refugees decided to go into business for themselves and bought or started such modest enterprises as food stores, appliance stores, and small hotels. For many of the Cuban parents, it became an economic necessity to enroll their children in one of the area's (Dade County) public schools.

In February, 1961, the Cuban Refugee Program was established under the supervision of the United States Department of Health, Education, and Welfare. A Cuban Refugee Center was soon opened in downtown Miami. This center was to be the base for registration of incoming refugees, for program operations, and for the determination of the refugees' eligibility for federal support and services. Administrators of the program also were directed to coordinate the activities of all federal and private agencies providing assistance to Cuban refugees in the United States.

The Cuban Refugee Program provided six types of assistance:

1. Financial assistance, supplemented by surplus commodities, to provide food, clothing, and shelter to needy refugees registered at the Miami Cuban Refugee Center who lived in Florida or who resettled outside Florida with the help of voluntary agencies.
2. Financial assistance in relocating refugees to homes and jobs elsewhere in the United States.
3. Health services and long-term hospitalization.
4. Assistance to the public schools of Dade County, Fla., in providing instruction to the refugee children as well as English instruction and vocational training to adults.
5. Loans to refugee students in college and funds for English and refresher courses for lawyers, doctors, and other professional persons.
6. Care of children unaccompanied by relatives.[9]

During this period, the *Cubanos exilados* and the *Cubanos residentes* were merging into one large, "anti-Castro" group. Together, they focused their energies on an invasion of Cuba planned for that spring. On Apr. 17, 1961, a band of some 1,500 Cuban exiles (primarily businessmen, doctors, lawyers, and other professionals), that had been trained, supplied, and equipped, invaded the southern coast of Cuba at Bahia de Cochinos (the Bay of Pigs). Their fleet was comprised of four cargo ships and a dozen smaller landing craft. But only 72 hours after their landing, many of the participants had been captured by Castro's army or were dead.

The defeat was bitter and demoralizing for Cuban refugees. They focused once again upon the task of earning a living in the Miami area, and a new aura of permanence tainted their self-imposed exile. Some refugees continued their infiltration efforts and provided information that led to the United States Goverment's insistence in October, 1962, that all Russian missiles be removed from Cuban soil (the Missile Crisis). During the period following the Bay of Pigs invasion, from July, 1961 until June, 1962, approximately 77,000 Cuban refugees entered Miami;[10] and, by October, 1962, the Cuban Refugee Center had registered 153,534 refugees. Of those registering, 48,361 refugees were initially resettled outside of Dade County.[11]

During the first phase of the Cuban influx into the Miami area (January, 1959, to October, 1962), approximately one of every 35 residents of Cuba had fled to what they believed would be a temporary exile in the United States. The majority of the refugees arrived on commercial airline flights from Havana. Many represented the business and professional elite.[12] Whereas less than one-half of one percent of the citizens within Cuba in 1953 were lawyers and judges and approximately 4 percent were classified as professional and semi-professional, more than 3 percent of the incoming refugees during this first period were lawyers and judges and approximately 22 percent were identified as professionals and semi-professionals. On the other hand, while more than 40 percent of the inhabitants of Cuba had earned their living from fishing and farm work in 1953, less than 3 percent of the incoming refugees represented this occupational group. In 1953, less than one percent of Cubans had completed four or more years of college; but approximately 12 percent of the early Cuban refugees in Miami had achieved this level of formal education.[13] Some of the Cuban refugees had obtained portions of their formal education in private schools and colleges within the United States, and they were consequently well able to communicate in the English language.

During the latter part of this first period, however, the characteristics of the Cubans arriving by planes at Miami International Airport began to change. Since the beginning of 1961, each successive quarterly group of refugees had been younger and less well educated than the previous group.[14]

Exile and Isolation

Commercial airline flights between Havana and Miami ceased completely in January, 1961, when diplomatic relations between the United States and Cuba were terminated. The Bay of Pigs invasion and the Missile Crisis had widened the communication gap between the two countries, and there was a substantial decrease in the number of Cuban refugees fleeing to Miami. During this second period (from November, 1962, to November, 1965), the incoming refugees usually represented the middle-class in Cuba, including merchants, bank tellers, clerks, and white-collar workers. These refugees generally entered the United States in small boats or via a third country. They arrived with only small sums of money, and most reported to the Cuban Refugee Center. The Center registered only 29,962 arrivals during this three year period, less than one-half of the number of arrivals registered during the one-year period between July, 1961, and June, 1962.[15]

A somber lull fell over the Cuban community in Miami. The refugees were demoralized by the failure of the invasion at the Bay of Pigs and shocked by Castro's power in international politics, as had been demonstrated during the Missile Crisis. Dissension erupted among the Cuban refugees' community leaders. During 1963, a number of small insurgency groups emerged, including: *Movimiento Revolucionario del Pueblo* (MRP), *Segundo Frente Nacional del Escambray*, and *Alpha 66*.

Most of the refugees realized at this point that their self-imposed exile would last for two, three, even five years. They searched for permanent employment and stable business opportunities. Many started to work in the central business district of Miami. During this second period of the influx, the Cuban community acquired economic control of this downtown shopping area plus a firm foothold in the overall economy of Dade County.

The English-speaking residents of the area realized that the Cuban refugees were not merely temporary guests. Rather than resenting an "intrusion", many English-speakers found that the Cubans were industrious, capable, and affable. Although Cuban businessmen generally pursued trade with other Cubans, it became good business for English-speaking citizens to shop in Cuban stores and to employ Cubans. There was little resentment against "these hard workers who had sacrificed so much to escape from Communism". After all, in the beginning, most North Americans also had treated Castro as "a peasant's hero struggling against a dictator". Although there were many Spanish-speaking students in the public schools at that time, English-speaking students reported that "the Cuban kids kept to themselves pretty much". In addition, English-speaking citizens of Dade County were aware that special programs had been started for the Cuban students and that the United States government was paying most of the cost.

The Freedom Flights

The next large influx of Cuban refugees into Dade County began with the "Freedom Flights" that were initiated at the end of 1965. In early October of that year, Castro declared that any Cubans who wanted to leave the country would be permitted to do so. He designated the port of Camarioca as the "pick-up-station". Hundreds of Cuban exiles returned to Camarioca in all forms of ocean-going vessels in order to bring their relatives and friends back to Miami. Mass confusion ensued in the small harbor area, including serious traffic jams and sanitation difficulties. Communication with friends and relatives in mainland Cuba, travel to Camarioca by land, and finally, boarding the right boat at the correct time was a next-to-impossible undertaking. With the exception of male Cubans of military age (15 through 26 years old), citizens who chose to leave Cuba, however, were soon able to do so via an airlift to Miami.

The Freedom Flights, organized by a group of Cubans in the Miami area, began on Dec. 1, 1965, and every weekday during the following five-and-a-half years, two airlift planes arrived at a special unloading area at the rear of Miami International Airport.[16] In August, 1971, however, there began a series of progressively more frequent interruptions in this regular flight schedule, and on Apr. 6, 1973, the final Freedom Flight left Cuba for Miami.

By that date, 260,561 Cuban refugees had stepped off the 3,048 flights from Varadero Beach (Playa de Varadero), Cuba, and walked to a special immigration building to meet friends and relatives and to be legally admitted to the United States on "parolee" status.[17] Parolee status was an emergency category for immigrants introduced by the State Department under pressure from Cubans already established in the United States. (See Chapter 3, Naturalization). The majority of the Freedom Flight refugees were young (one to 18 years old) or middle-aged (30 to 49 years old). Statistics at the Cuban Refugee Center indicated that for every ten refugees arriving on the airlift during this period, seven refugees were resettled outside of Miami in more than 3,000 communities and in all 50 states.[18] (See Chapter 3, Distribution).

The parole program continued during 1974 and 1975. There were then some 35,000 Cubans awaiting entry into the United States via a third country (approximately one in every six was expected to settle in Miami), and the overall numbers reaching the United States increased from 600 to 1,800 a month. There had been hopes that the Cuban Refugee Program would last beyond its scheduled termination in 1977 and continue its services indefinitely.[19] In November, 1974, however, program personnel already had been cut by some 77 percent, that is, from 156 to 36 employees.[20]

As the years wore on, the initial plans to return to Cuba appeared to be less and less feasible. Many of the early arrivals, resigned to remaining in their new American homeland, labored to maintain a Cuban culture in a new Havana while adapting to the economic and linguistic demands of an English-speaking America.

Notes

1. Florence Fritz, Unknown Florida. Miami (Coral Gables): University of Miami Press, 1963, pp. 19-26.
2. Edwin Raisz and associates, Atlas of Florida. Gainesville: University of Florida Press, 1964, pp. 17-21; State of Florida Atlas. Charlotte, N.C.: Champion Map Corporation, 1969, p. 4; Al Volker, "Latin Connection in Florida as Old as the New World". The Miami Herald, June 30, 1972, p. 4-E.
3. Ibid.
4. Community Improvement Program, County Manager's Office, Dade County, Fla., "Family Income," Press Release, Apr. 28, 1972.
5. M. Estelle Smith, "The Spanish-Speaking Population of Florida," pp. 120-133, in June Helm, ed., Spanish-Speaking People in the United States. Seattle: University of Washington Press, 1968
6. Juanita Greene, "Cubans in Dade: 1 in 4 by 1975." The Miami Herald, June 18, 1971, p. 2-G.

7. Ibid.
8. This was accomplished under the directorship of Monseignor Bryan O. Walsh. See ... Children's Bureau, Social and Rehabilitation Service, United Stated Department of Health, Education, and Welfare, *Cuba's Children in Exile.* Washington, D.C.: U.S. Government Printing Office, 1967. Types of assistance: pp. 11-12.
9. Ibid.
10. Supra Note 6
11. Cuban Refugee Program, Social and Rehabilitation Service, United States Department of Health, Education, and Welfare, "Fact Sheet". Miami, Fla. Dec. 1, 1969.
12. The Research Institute for Cuba and the Caribbean, Center for Advanced International Studies, University of Miami, *The Cuban Immigration, 1959-1966: And Its Impact on Miami-Dade County, Florida.* Coral Gables: University of Miami Press, 1967, p. 15.
13. Richard R. Fagen and Richard A. Brody, "Cubans in Exile: a Demographic Analysis", *Social Problems,* II (1964), pp. 391-392, p. 398.
14. Ibid.
15. Supra Note 11
16. To commemorate the inauguration of the Freedom Flights, Cuban American Day was celebrated in Miami on the first of December each year.
17. Hilda Inclán. "End of Airlift Creates Despair". *The Miami News,* Apr. 7, 1973, p. 5-A.
18. Cuban Refugee Program, "Fact Sheet", Dec. 31, 1972; Cuban Refugee Program, "Geographic Distribution of Resettlements", January, 1961, through December, 1971.
19. *The Miami News.* July 10, 1974, p. 9-A.
20. *The Miami Herald.* Nov. 27, 1974, p. 1-A.

3

The Shaping of a Bilingual Homeland

The pattern of Cuban life in English-speaking America was determined by demographic characteristics of the resettlement and economic development of the refugees, their social adaptation, and the maintenance of their language and culture.

DEMOGRAPHIC CHARACTERISTICS

Ethnic survival of the Cubans during the first decade of their resettlement in the United States depended not only on their number but also the pattern of distribution and growth of this displaced population.

Number

The starting point for any demographic study of this population is Cuba itself. In little more than a decade, this island nation had lost almost 10 percent of its population to emigration, mostly as a result of post-revolutionary political exile. During this period, some 800,000 out of a total population of some 8,200,000 left Cuba to live elsewhere. Of these, about 650,000 entered the United States and some 150,000 settled in Europe, Latin America, Canada, and elsewhere. [1]

The overall effect on the ethnic character of the United States population of approximately 213,000,000 was an increase in the already important Span-

24

ish element to such an extent that, by the mid-seventies, persons of Cuban origin made up almost 10 percent of the 11,200,000 Americans whose ethnic origin was Spanish. [2]

Distribution

Had this population of more than half a million Cuban refugees been proportionately distributed from the beginning throughout the country's cities and states, its impact on a population almost 400 times its size would have been negligible. The policy of resettlement had indeed been to direct the Cubans to any part of the country in which jobs could be found, and it was reported that, in fact, Cubans settled in nearly all of the 50 states. [3] If we examine the figures more closely, however, we find that this nationwide distribution is neither equal nor is it proportional to the general population distribution in the United States. Most of the Cuban population was in fact concentrated in a few areas of the country, the most important being that of Miami, which in 1972 already harbored two-thirds of the total. The others were mostly distributed in any sizable number among about a dozen states (See Table 2). More than one-third of this non-Florida population, it will be noted, were concentrated in New Jersey, many in the area directly across the Hudson River from New York City.

In sum, most Cubans tended to concentrate in or around two great metropolitan areas on the country's eastern coast with historically or numerically important Spanish-speaking populations. This tendency increased during the decade and a half of resettlement, favoring a greater and greater concentration in the Miami area rather than the New York City — New Jersey region. In fact, a number of Cubans left the latter even though it had provided better economic advantages.

By the seventies, some 100,000 Cubans had settled in New Jersey, more than half of them in the twin cities of Union City and West New York, where they became the majority of the local population. In Union City, Cubans represented 65.3 percent of the population of 65,000. In West New York, they made up about 68 percent of the population of 48,000. The number of regis-

Table 2

U. S. CUBAN POPULATION OUTSIDE FLORIDA: 1972

New Jersey	108,791	Pennsylvania	3,863
New York	80,483	Connecticut	3,833
California	39,223	Michigan	2,801
Illinois	22,243	Georgia	2,366
Massachusetts	8,184	Virginia	2,097
Texas	5,353	Maryland	1,803

Source: U. S. Department of Health, Education and Welfare, Resultados finales: Programa para refugiados cubanos. Washington: Dec. 31, 1972.

tered Cuban voters increased; and, in Union City, Cubans owned 60 percent of the businesses. Other achievements of the Cubans in this city were noted:

- Two out of nine school board members were Cubans.
- At every city emergency number, there were Spanish-speaking bilingual operators on duty round-the-clock.
- A full page in Spanish appeared daily in the local *Dispatch* newspaper.
- A major bank was owned and operated by Cubans.
- The bilingual education program was led by a Cuban director. In addition, it was reported that during the 1974 municipal elections, 14 percent of the 17,975 voters had Spanish surnames.[4]

In spite of the achievements of these resettled Cubans in their new northern home, a number moved with their families from Union City to Miami. Many were willing to work in Miami for two or three thousand dollars a year less than what they had earned in the north. The attraction of Miami was not therefore economic; it was cultural, ethnic, and environmental. In a sense, a return to Miami had taken the place of the vanishing dream of a return to the Cuban homeland.

The tendency to return to Miami was also noted among Cubans who had settled in other parts of the United States. To the thousands of these refugees scattered throughout the states, *their* Cuba existed only in Miami.

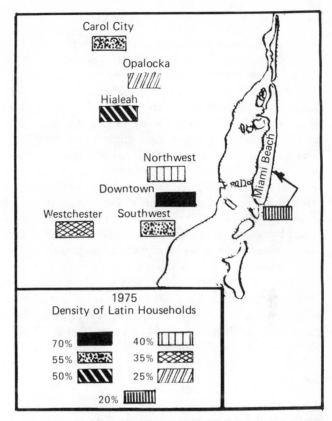

Approximate percentage of homes in each of eight areas

Source: Strategy Research Corporation, Human Communications 1975

Figure 3   Spanish-Speaking Homes (Distribution and Density: Dade County 1975)

In the early seventies, a research report verified what many Miami citizens had known for a number of years. Approximately one-third of the more than 350,000 Cuban refugees living in Dade County at that time initially had been resettled elsewhere.[5] In addition to the familiar life style, they wanted their children to profit from the language and the Cubanism which had taken root in the Miami environment. Although in the late sixties more mobile English-speaking Cubans began to move to various sections in the Miami area, distribution of the Cuban population was not uniform. Traditionally Cuban areas in the downtown, southwest, and Hialeah sections tended to become more Cuban, and the proportion of Cubans in these quarters grew to such an extent in the mid-seventies that it represented from half to almost three-quarters of the population (see Figure 3).[6]

Growth Rate

In 1959, a little less than 5 percent of the approximately 900,000 residents of Dade County were Spanish-speakers, and one-half of these were Cuban. In 1966, 15 percent of the residents were Spanish-speakers and approximately 13 of every 15 Spanish-speakers were of Cuban origin.[7] By 1970, the population in Dade County had grown to 1,267,792. Spanish-speakers represented 24 percent (319,000) of this total,[8] and a little more than 87 percent of the Spanish-speakers were of Cuban origin.[9] The growth continued. During the decade and a half of resettlement, the Cuban population in the Miami area had increased at an annual rate of more than 10 percent to comprise by the mid-seventies more than a third of the area's total of a million-and-a-half people. At that time, a study by Dade County's Metro Planning Department reported that, between 1970 and 1975, Latins had outnumbered other newcomers to the county by twenty-six to one. It was predicted that the Latin population (as they were sometimes classified locally) would surpass 46 percent by 1980 (See Table 3). It was predicted also that there would be a proportional decline in the percentage of non-black, unilingual Anglo-Americans (See Figure 4). One projection predicted that, if the trend continued, "Latins" would comprise the majority of the labor force of the area by 1980. Also, the largest single ethnic group in the public school would be Latins, that is, 37 percent compared to 35 percent Anglos and 28 percent black.[10] In sum, by the end of the decade, Dade County would become an equally balanced triethnic community with a large Latin population.[11]

Table 3
POPULATION BY ETHNIC BACKGROUND
(Dade County, Florida: 1950-80)

Year	Total Population	Hispanic Number	% Of Total	Blacks Number	% Of Total	All others Number	% Of Total
1950	495,084	20,000	4.0%	64,947	13.2%	410,137	82.8%
1960	935,047	50,000	5.3%	137,299	14.7%	747,748	80.0%
1970	1,267,792	299,217	23.6%	189,666	15.0%	778,909	61.4%
1975 (Est.)	1,487,800	488,500	32.8%	233,800	15.7%	765,500	51.5%
1980 (Est.)	1,662,800	683,900	41.1%	261,900	15.8%	717,000	43.1%

Source: Dade Latin Market - 1976. Strategy Research Corporation, Miami: SRC, 1976, p. 5.

ECONOMIC DEVELOPMENT

How did this growing population of Cubans fare in the Miami area? How did they make a living and what sort of a living did they make? What sort of employment did they find and what level of income did they reach?

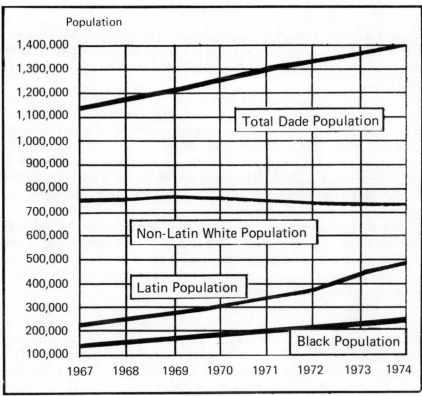

Source: Population Survey Report, *The Miami Herald,* Oct. 7, 1974, p. 1B.

Figure 4   Ethnic Population Trends
              Miami (Dade County): 1967-74

Employment

The employment pattern of the Cuban refugees was determined by what they brought with them to the United States in the form of marketable skills, education, experience, and enterprise. The socio-demographic character of the population was not that of so many previous immigration waves to American shores. On the contrary, their socio-demographic traits were rather more like those of previous post-revolutionary emigre populations as typified by the French and Russian revolutions which had disinherited entire classes of the population. The Cuban refugees did not come to a land of opportunity to supply a reservoir of unskilled labor; they came to a land of refuge from the wealthy, educated, or better trained classes of their country. The large majority did not become wards of the state, but succeeded in making their own living in jobs to which they could adapt. How they adapted depended to some extent on what they had been trained to do as businessmen, professionals, or skilled workers.

The Businessmen

Many of the Cubans belonging to the first waves of emigres went into business, either as bilingual employees or as small, self-employed entrepreneurs. Some who started as employees, in time, bought the firms for which they had worked.

As a group they fared well. By the mid-seventies, more than a third of the businesses in the Miami area — some 8,500 firms — were owned and operated by Cubans. Although most of these came under the category of small businesses, they represented all types of enterprises. For example, the presidents of five banks (out of a total of 70) were Cuban as were more than a dozen senior vice-presidents. Three-quarters of all the automobile service stations were owned or operated by Cubans. And the Cuban restaurants and night clubs numbered in the hundreds.[12]

Not all of these enterprises, however, were equally successful. Although most made a living for their owners and employees, the vast majority, some 7,000, eventually lacked capital for expansion since they were owned by one man and were initially under-capitalized. Many existed primarily, if not solely, for the convenience of Spanish-speaking customers.

According to Leonardo Rodriguez, professor of management at Florida International University, Cuban businesses would have to "break away" from simply trying to serve a Latin market. They would have to hire American workers, American consultants, and American expertise.[13] In the mid-seventies, it seemed that Cuban entrepreneurs might be forced to adopt American management techniques and compete for the non-Latin market in order to survive.

The Professionals

Many of the Cuban refugees were professionals: doctors, lawyers, dentists, accountants, teachers, and nurses. Although as a group they did not fare as well economically as did the businessmen, members of some professions were able to adapt more readily than others. This depended on the type of service offered, the population served, the difference in licensing requirements, and the length of the period of retraining. It also depended on the demand. Because of the growing number of Cuban children, there developed an increasing need for bilingual Spanish-speaking teachers and teaching assistants. On the other hand, professionals trained in pre-revolutionary Cuban law could find little demand for their special expertise. Consequently, it was not uncommon to find Cuban lawyers and other professionals working as taxi drivers, service station attendants, and waiters or doing other work in hotels, restaurants, and factories. It was estimated that even in the mid-seventies, some 3,000 Cuban were working below the level of their professional skills.

Secondly, there was the problem of obtaining a license to practice one's profession in the United States. Although some 1,500 Cuban medical doctors had been licensed by the mid-seventies and some two dozen out-patient clinics were being operated by Cuban medical directors, there were still hundreds of Cuban professionals who had not yet been licensed. These included some 500 nurses, 300 dentists, 200 physicians, 140 optometrists and 120 veterinarians. In addition to the language problem, some of the difficulties of obtaining a license included differences between Cuba and the United States in the type or level of the requirements. Some professionals needed further training or refresher courses in order to qualify for practice in the United States. Consequently, in 1974, a bill approved by the Florida House of Representatives required the State's 27 licensing boards to create year-long refresher courses and bilingual exams for foreign residents. The purpose of the bill was to make it easier for foreign physicians, dentists, nurses, accountants, and other professionals to practice in Florida.[14] Group organization also helped. In 1975, a Confederation of Cuban University Professionals in Exile, for example, succeeded in obtaining almost $400,000 from the Cuban Refugee Program to pay tuition costs of courses taken in Spanish at the University of Miami by professionals for purposes of obtaining licenses to practice.[15]

Thirdly, there were restrictions of citizenship. Jobs that could be filled only by American citizens were, of course, not available to the non-naturalized Cubans. These included many government jobs. It was pointed out that, even in the mid-seventies, although more than half of the residents within the city of Miami were of Spanish origin, they occupied little more than 10 percent of the jobs in that city's government.

The Skilled Workers

Many of the later arrivals — including the escapees — were neither businessmen nor professionals. A great number were young, blue-collar workers. In 1974, a study of 20,000 escapees made at the Miami-Dade Community College revealed that their average age was 26 and that the great majority were non-professional workers.[16] In the same year, 85 percent of Miami's garment industry's factory operations were performed by Cuban labor, and 65 percent of the construction workers were Spanish-speaking.

As the economic recession reached the United States, however, there were fewer jobs for everyone, including the Cubans. In keeping unemployment statistics, however agencies did not always distinguish between Cubans and other Latin-American ethnic groups. They preferred to place all "Latins" in the same category, all blacks in another and all Anglo-Europeans in a third, despite the fact that some Latins were "black" and some "Europeans" were not Anglos. Thus it was that in 1975, the unemployment figures supplied by the local Spanish American League against Discrimination (SALAD) for the month of February totaled 23,800 for the Latins, 14,500 for the blacks, and 19,500 for the Anglo-Europeans, noting that during the same month Latins made up 27.8 percent (183,000) of the labor force, blacks, 15.1 percent (99,600) and Anglo-Europeans 57 percent (375,000). Predictions for 1980 put the figure for employment of Latin-Americans in the Miami area at approximately 315,000. Employment, however, was not the only indicator of the economic development of the Cuban refugees in the United States. Income and purchasing power were equally significant.

Income

During the first decade of resettlement in Miami, the average income of Cuban refugees doubled. Between 1967 and 1973, when their unemployment rate was less than 2 percent and their gross business revenues had registered a 200 percent increase, their average family income rose from $5,000 to almost $10,000 a year.[17] By 1976, it had surpassed that of all the other groups (See Table 4).

Income varied, of course, by type of employment. Professionals in 1975 were earning more than double the average. Yet 20 percent of the Cubans employed were receiving more than $15,000, while 62 percent were over the $7,000 mark. By this time, almost 90 percent of the Cubans owned at least one car, 42 percent owned two, and 17 percent owned three or more.

The gross income of the Cuban refugees as a group rose from $613,000,000 in 1970, to more than a billion dollars in 1975. As Carlos Arboleya, a prominent Cuban banker in Miami, pointed out, this total represented a per capita income greater than that of many areas within the United States and almost three times greater than that of any Latin American country.

From the point of view of purchasing power, the Cuban group began to represent an important market to all types of businesses, which gradually looked upon this segment as an asset to the area's economy. This was not only because it represented purchasing power of more than a billion dollars a year but also because it attracted international trade and Latin American tourism.

A study undertaken at the School of Business and Organizational Sciences at Florida International University found that the economic effects of international transactions in the Miami area resulted in the creation of some 93,000 jobs — or 15 percent of the total employment. The study also found that income generated amounted to 17 percent of the area's total estimated income. The study pointed out that the fastest growth had taken place since 1971, resulting from commodity exports, international banking services, and tourism, mostly involving the Caribbean, Central, and South America.[18]

As for tourism, Spanish-speaking Miami soon became "the gateway from Latin America". Frequently, the Latin American tourist came first to Miami where he felt some kinship with the large Spanish-speaking population. Consequently, about 51.6 percent of all Miami tourists in 1974 (or 400,377 persons) came from Latin America.[19] This had an important impact on Miami's economy. According to statistics published by *Sales Management Magazine,* Latin tourism accounted for about one-seventh of Dade County's roughly $2,000,000,000 in annual sales in general merchandise.

It should be noted that the economic success of the Cuban refugee group during the late sixties and early seventies did cause some resentment among other, long-established minority groups in Dade County. The Mexican-Americans and Puerto Ricans were bitter that they had not received special federal aid as the Cubans had under the Cuban Refugee Program.[20] They were aware that the median income of Cuban families quickly surpassed their own. There was little question that the influx of Cuban refugees had been economically harmful to Dade County's native-born, black Americans, yet no one denied that the Cubans had created their own job opportunities with hard work and ingenuity. Some black Americans in Dade County, however felt that businessmen had favored the Cubans and had given them the jobs that were about to be filled by local blacks.[21] This resentment became one of the many problems in the social adaptation of the Cubans to their new environment.

Table 4
MONTHLY FAMILY INCOME BY ETHNIC GROUP
(Dade County, Florida: 1976)

	Spanish	Other
$700 or less	45.7%	47.4%
$701—$1,200	29.6	31.5
$1,201 and over	24.7	21.1
	100.0%	100.0%
Average (monthly)	$860	$844
Average (annual)	$10,320	$10,128

Source: *Dade Latin Market - 1976,* Strategy Research Corporation, Miami: SRC, 1976, p. 26.

SOCIAL ADAPTATION

The necessity of social adaptation within an environment which was becoming their new homeland presented the Cuban refugees with problems of political affiliations as well as ethnic relations.

Ethnic Relations

When the Cuban refugees settled in the Miami area, they came into contact with three large ethnic groups which had shared this large metropolis — black Americans, Latin-Americans and Anglo-Americans. Each of these groups were different from the Cubans to varying degrees. While the differences from the other Latin-American groups seemed minor with respect to culture and language, there were important social, educational and economic differences.

On the other hand, with Anglo-Americans these later differences were minimal; but there were important language and cultural differences. Finally, the black Americans differed linguistically, culturally, economically and, for the most part, racially. It is not surprising that the Cubans' relations with these three groups—blacks, Latins and Anglos— also differed.

Although the economic success of the Cuban refugees had caused some resentment on the part of black Americans, it was not based on a tradition of mutual prejudice. Racial relations in Cuba had been quite different from what they had been in the United States. Not only were there some black Spanish-speaking Cubans, but, according to a study, Cubans as a group had less fear of racial conflicts than had comparable ethnic groups.[22] There was also a willingness to help other underprivileged racial minorities, as demonstrated by the relation between the Cubans and the later-arriving Vietnamese refugees. In Miami, an International Refugee Committee was created to take care of the relocation of different groups of Vietnamese refugees; the operation was staffed almost entirely by Cubans.[23]

Strained relations with the other minority groups usually were based on socio-economic differences. While most Cubans had come to Miami for political or social reasons bringing with them the skills and training of their professional, business, or specialized group, most Puerto Ricans had come for purely economic reasons with few skills and little English. The Puerto Rican population, though much smaller than the Cuban one, also increased rapidly in the Miami area—from some 17,000 in 1970 to an estimated 35,000 in 1975— and it continued to increase.[24] But there seemed to be little communication between Cubans and Puerto Ricans. Puerto Ricans pointed out that favoritism of Cubans was exemplified in the school system's bilingual education program, which ignored the special needs of the Puerto Rican children. Puerto Ricans viewed themselves as an invisible minority, fighting with other minority groups for recognition and survival.[25]

There were even greater differences with the Mexican-Americans in Florida. Many of the urban and sophisticated Cubans could find little in common with these agricultural laborers who had come to Florida as unskilled migrant workers. Mexicans and Mexican-Americans of comparable socio-economic background and with business or professional training had not immigrated to Florida as a group.

Relations with the Anglo-American group were another matter. Upon arrival in the United States, the Cuban refugees realized that they had come as guests of a country which was largely English-speaking. They were well received and encouraged to find jobs and continue their life in their new country, maintaining their language and their culture.

In many ways, the preservation of Cuban identity was not only tolerated by citizens in Miami; it was actually promoted. In fact, early in 1973, Miami's Metropolitan Commission, recognizing that fully one-third of the residents of the Miami area spoke Spanish as their first language, declared Dade a bilingual and bicultural county with Spanish as the second official language (See Appendix C). In addition, the English language media put time and space at the disposal of the Cuban population in the form of television time and special Spanish sections in morning and afternoon dailies. The *Miami News* during the early seventies started to print one page in Spanish including local, national and international news. The reasons stated for publishing in Spanish were not only to meet the information requirements of the thousands of Spanish-speaking members of the community; but also to help create better understanding and communication between the English-speaking and Spanish-speaking cultures. For much the same reasons, the area's largest local newspaper, *The Miami Herald* (circulation 400,000) started publishing daily an entire section in Spanish in the spring of 1976.

Not all of Miami's citizens, however, remained favorable to the Cuban presence. Some thought it unfair that these new arrivals from a foreign country should obtain better jobs than some of the native American-born citizens. Others in positions of economic or political power began to view Cubans as potential rivals and decided to protect their positions through ethnic arguments. The Cubans, on their part, had no intention of abandoning their hard-earned gains and organized to defend their position.

By the mid-seventies, the anti-Cuban feeling in Dade County had reached a high. The reasons for this were believed to be the increased militancy that Cubans were assuming in local matters, a greater awareness that the Cubans' presence was no longer temporary, envy or resentment over their economic success, and fear of being displaced in jobs by bilingual personnel. Many eventually became jealous of the economic success of Dade County Cubans and seemed unable or unwilling to understand the Cubans' need to retain their own language and cultural heritage. The executive director of the Little Havana Activities Center noted that "the hostility grows in direct proportion with the success of the Cubans and is going to increase, because Cubans are now for the first time threatening people in a position of power".[26]

To counter this growing ethnic discrimination, some Cubans decided to cast their lot with the other more militant Spanish-speaking minorities. In March, 1972, an initial, yet futile, effort had been made to establish a unified coalition of Spanish-speaking residents in Dade County. "The coalition did not last long. The five Mexican-Americans, representing about 5,000 and the five Puerto Ricans, representing about 30,000, sided against the five Cubans who represented about 250,000.[27] But, as hostility increased, some Cubans joined a newly-formed Spanish-American League Against Discrimination (SALAD), a non-profit organization incorporated in the State of Florida. The objectives of the organization were to gather, analyze, and disseminate information dealing with discrimination in Dade County. Yet there were some who tried for a more powerful coalition. In the mid-seventies, leaders of Latin-American ethnic groups were working toward unity with the black American groups. Since more than half of the population of the city of Miami proper was Latin-American and about a quarter was black, an alliance could represent three-quarters of the city's population, eventually enabling both groups to achieve, through affiliation, political control of the area.

Political Affiliations

Although the Cubans came to be regarded as an important demographic and economic ethnic group, their political power was limited not only by a lack of concerted political organization but also by the tact that, not being American citizens, they had no votes to make them politically interesting. However, as more and more Cubans became American citizens, their political voice began to be heard at the local level, at the national level, and even at the international level of American politics.

Local Politics

Although Miami may have taken on much of the ambiance, color, and pace of "old Havana", it had not however become a Cuban city in politics or power structure. What did seem to be appearing was a new multi-ethnic mix that was bringing new problems and new possibilities. One of the problems was that ethnicity was becoming an important element in local politics.

It began to play a key role in the election of a local commissioner. There were a number of strong Spanish-American and black candidates in the 1973 election and for the first time there was a big push to get out the Latin vote. While there were about twice as many black voters in Miami, the Latin vote appeared to be higher in every election and its impact was felt more than ever before.

Latins began to have more and more success at the polls. Maurice Ferre, a Puerto Rican, had been elected mayor of Miami. He polled a large number of votes in heavily black precincts and across the city in precincts with Spanish or mixed voting groups. But once the ethnic factor became important in local politics, the underlying ethnic prejudice began to find public expression. It was noted, for example, that there were "bigoted anti-Cuban" sentiments unleashed during the 1974 campaign for the Dade County (Miami) School Board when the single Latin member was replaced by a North American.[28]

But even in the mid-seventies, Cubans had had little local ballot power. Although about 100,000 Cubans were United States citizens, less than half that number contributed the total of 55,370 Spanish-American registered voters, that is, less than 9 percent of all registered voters in the county.[29] It was not surprising, therefore, to find that figures forwarded to the Equal Employment Opportunity Commission in December 1974 showed "Latin" employment to be only 10 percent of the total 16,537 county employees.[30] To help resolve this situation, a Cuban, Anthony Ojeda, was appointed that year to be director of an Office of Bilingual Affairs and a special assistant to the Manager of Dade County.

Another problem was the emergence of many separate Cuban American organizations like the *Municipios,* making it impossible for any single one to speak for all the Cuban refugees. Yet as time went on, the advantages of coalition became evident. Soon, the Spanish-American Coalition became one of several active groups within Miami's municipalities and provided something of an established power base within the Cuban community. Cubans also began to realize that coalition could be an advantage in national politics.

National Politics

In October, 1971, the first national conference of Spanish-speaking Americans was called in Washington in order for the Hispanic citizens to discuss some of their common grievances and plan joint political action. Alternating Spanish and English, problems of mutual concern were discussed at the conference: inequality in law enforcement and employment, substandard housing and inadequate education. The federal government also recognized the need for considering the problems of the Hispanic groups as a whole. A Cabinet Committee had promoted federal action in placing Spanish-speaking Americans in responsible government positions, in the creation of minority businesses, in extending job opportunities, and in striking down existing discrimination. One important step aimed specifically at helping the Spanish-speaking population was the government's support of bilingual education projects.

Since the Spanish-speaking citizens had no political party of their own, they could exert political pressure at the national level only through such established parties as the Republicans and the Democrats. In the past, when Spanish-speaking citizens voted in Dade County, they generally voted Republican and conservative.[31] Although the potential existed in Dade County for the large number of Spanish-speakers to be a potent political force, both locally and nationally, it was not as yet fully realized or directed until the mid-seventies. At that time, attempts were made by the Democratic Party to attract Spanish-speaking voters, and local Spanish-speaking citizens joined the national Democratic Party at an ever-increasing rate. In fact, it was noted that Latins in the Miami area had been registering previously at the rate of four Republicans to each Democrat and that these proportions had been completely reversed in favor of the Democrats. This trend was apparently due to three factors:

1.   The rising cost of living, which the Cubans blamed on the Republican president's economic blunders.

2.   The "Watergate" scandal—and the feeling that Miami Cubans were used in the burglary under false pretenses.

3.   Disillusionment with the Republican president's stand regarding the Castro regime.

On this final aspect of international politics, the Cubans were understandably keen to have their voice heard.

International Politics

The aspect of American foreign policy in which the Cuban community of Miami had been most deeply interested had to do with the United States' relations with Cuba.

It was not until two years after the accession of Fidel Castro to power that diplomatic relations between the United States and Cuba were formally broken. This act of Jan. 3, 1961 was associated with a complete economic boycott on the part of the United States and the expropriation without compensation on Cuba's part of the extensive enterprises of American citizens on that island. As the Cuban Revolutionary Government continued to export its revolution throughout Latin America, actively fomenting uprising in some countries, the Organization of American States, which included most countries of the Western Hemisphere, also voted to apply economic sanctions on Cuba. The idea was to cut off Cuba from the outside supplies which it needed. In some countries, as in the United States, it became illegal to export or import goods of any kind to or from Cuba.

After a decade of sanctions, however, it became evident that the embargo did not stop other western nations from trading with Cuba and this island nation could be well supplied from Eastern Europe and the Soviet Union. Also, the growing rapprochement between the West and the East, as exemplified by the policy of "detente" between the Soviet Union and the United States, had created a climate which favored conciliation.

In this context some members of the United States' Senate Foreign Relations Committee visited Havana in September, 1974, to discuss with the Cuban government the improvement of relations in such humanitarian fields as freedom of travel and status of political prisoners and in certain areas directly affecting American citizens, such as the expropriation of their property in Cuba. There was no question, however, on either side, of a change in principles. The United States' officials made it clear that in no way did they approve the policies of the regime in Cuba. The Cuban government stated that it had no intention of changing its policies. It furthermore rejected any reconciliation with Cubans outside the revolution, including the Cuban communities in the United States.[32] On this basis, the Cuban government was ready to improve its relations with the United States, but only if, as a precondition, the United States were to discontinue the economic boycott.

A year later, Secretary of State Henry Kissinger expressed the new attitude of the American government in a public statement, pointing out that the administration now saw "no virtue in perpetual antagonism between the United States and Cuba".[33] Although resolutions had been proposed by senators and a bill to end the embargo against Cuba had been introduced by Senator Edward Kennedy, the United States was committed to the embargo as a signer of the declaration of the Organization of American States (OAS) which was still in effect. However, within the year, the OAS suggested the lifting of sanctions, and the United States voted with the majority for the resumption of trade and diplomatic relations with Cuba.

Members of the Cuban community in Miami did not all react in the same way to the changing relations between the United States and Cuba. Opinions ranged all the way from increasing efforts to liberate the homeland to the complete abandonment of such efforts. The first extreme became the policy of the National Cuban Liberation Front (FLNC), a militant organization with military objectives committed to defying any laws blocking anti-Castro activities.[34] At the other end of the spectrum, was the group of Cuban Christians for Justice and Freedom calling for the normalization of diplomatic relations with Cuba, the lifting of the economic embargo, the elimination of all Soviet and U.S. bases in Cuba, and the return of the Cuban revolution to the democratic ideals of justice and freedom. Fifteen years after the revolution, many Cubans were expressing these opinions no longer as Cuban nationals, but as full-fledged naturalized American Citizens.

The Naturalization of the Cuban Community

During the fifteen-year period following the revolution, the Cuban population in Miami had slowly evolved from one of a group of refugees on temporary resident status to a community of American citizens of Cuban culture and tradition.

Upon their arrival in the United States, Cuban refugees were placed on "parolee" status. After two-and-one-half years, these refugees could apply for "legal resident" status. Five years of "legal resident" status were required for all immigrants, including Cuban refugees, before they could become "naturalized" citizens of the United States. On Nov. 3, 1966, however, the United States Congress decided that the period of time that was required for Cuban refugees to become eligible for citizenship was to be shortened from seven-and-a-half to five years (Public Law 89-732) by applying their two-and-one-half years as "parolees" toward their "legal resident" requirement. By the early seventies, approximately 10 percent of the Cuban refugees had completed the naturalization process and had become citizens of the United States.[35] But as more and more of the 400,000 Cuban refugees in the area began to accept the United States as their permanent home, the percentage sharply increased. By the mid-seventies, Cuban exiles were becoming United States citizens at the average rate of 1,000 a month.[36]

At the beginning of the Cuban influx in 1959, the majority of Cuban refugees had clearly stated that they had little desire to become assimilated into the North American mainstream. An early opinion survey a few years after arrival, revealed that almost 80 percent intended to return to Cuba. A later study in the mid-seventies by the Department of Sociology at Miami-Dade Community College — admittedly of a small sample — seemed to indicate that more of the Cubans intended to remain in the United States. The study based on interviews with 151 Cubans over the age of 55 indicated that fewer than half the number intended to return to Cuba.[37] The reason was that American citizenship was becoming more advantageous as Cubans began to take roots in American soil. They had become shareholders in the community and sought the right to participate in its affairs. They had invested heavily in time, effort, and money while establishing themselves in the United States. In fact, by the mid-seventies, they had as a group returned in taxes to the government more than five times the amount that they had received in public assistance payments. But in order to have a voice in the political decisions which affected them, including the way their taxes were spent, Cubans had to obtain the right to vote. This meant both citizenship and registration. In the Miami area, Cuban leaders pointed out that only by voting full strength could the Cuban population counter the growing bigotry and influence social and education programs.

In order to encourage minorities to vote, the Voting Rights Act of 1965 was extended in 1975 for an additional decade. According to one of the new provisions of this federal law: "Instructions, written or oral, relating to the electoral process, including ballots, must be in the language minority which encompasses more than 5 percent of voting-age citizens of any language minority". This required the cities of Coral Gables and Hialeah to follow the 1973 example of Dade County and the City of Miami proper in translating their ballots into Spanish and also to hire Spanish-speaking poll workers. By mid-1975, the number of Spanish-speaking registered voters was almost 5 percent superior to the national average of registered voters (44.7 percent), according to the United States Census Bureau.[38]

Neither the act of voting in American elections or becoming naturalized United States citizens was viewed by the Cubans as an abandonment of their cultural heritage. On the contrary, many saw the opportunity of using their political power to further cultural maintenance within the community.

CULTURAL MAINTENANCE

The Cuban community in the Miami area was more successful than most other immigrant groups in maintaining their institutions and their language. But as time went on, it became more and more difficult for the younger generation to resist the acculturation which contact with the North American majority eventually produced.

The Maintenance of Cuban Institutions

Although many adult Cuban refugees were successful in their business encounters with English-speakers, they had made little effort to enter into North American social life. Traditional values and customs were steadfastly maintained in the beginning and prevented many Cuban children, especially girls, from social interaction with non-Cubans. Although they spoke English and may even have been born within the United States, for example, many Cuban girls did not attend public school dances or date North American boys due to the customary requirements of a family chaperone.

Many Cuban refugees spent their leisure time with one another, participating in the same recreational activities that they had enjoyed while in Cuba. The upper society of bankers, industrialists, and professionals created their own social clubs, admitting only the well-to-do Cubans. The clubs retained much of the class consciousness of Havana. For example, in 1967, some former members of the five most exclusive private clubs in Havana established the "Big Five" club in the southwest section of Dade County for the benefit of other former members in exile plus the members' close friends and relatives. Other Cuban institutions were also recreated in Miami. For example, Cuban military academies and parochial schools were founded throughout Dade County. Many of the private schools already had a waiting list of applicants on opening day. In addition, many neighborhood clubs and other organizations were founded whose main purpose was cultural survival.

The Problems of Language Survival

The increasing contact with the North American community brought a corresponding increase in the role of English in the daily lives of the Cuban refugees and long-term problems of Spanish language maintenance.

One thing that helped restore the balance was the creation of Spanish language media. By the early seventies, three television stations were broadcasting in Spanish in the Miami area — one of them full time. There were four Spanish language radio stations. In addition to the Spanish sections of the big urban daily newspapers, there were some forty Spanish language periodicals including local magazines and newspapers. There were also some Spanish language theater associations and playhouses in addition to Spanish cinema.

Although Spanish was the language most frequently used in the majority of Cuban refugee homes, the maintenance of Spanish continued to be a problem. Since very few of the Anglo-Americans spoke Spanish, Cubans had to learn English and use it more and more. And the younger they were, the more bilingual or English-speaking they became. This was illustrated by the results of a study, the Belder survey, in the mid-seventies. It found that Dade County had 155,000 Latin-American adults who still spoke Spanish most of the time and that 44 percent of these adults read little or no English. The younger the person, however, the greater his ability to communicate in English. Many of the younger generation spoke English and Spanish, 75 percent expressing themselves aptly in both languages. [39]

Threats to the survival of Spanish were not due entirely to the lack of tolerance nor to the fact that English was the area's dominant language. Indeed, it would have been illegal for an employer to prohibit the use of Spanish by the Cubans, according to the 1964 federal Civil Rights Act. Rather, it was the enormous demographic and socio-economic pressures of English that were felt throughout the United States and even beyond its borders.[40] As a result, the longer the Cubans remained in the United States, the more difficulty they had in resisting the pressures of acculturation.

The Dilemma of Acculturation

While older and middle age Cubans had been able to maintain their cultural identity, it was difficult for them to deny their children contact with the North American culture with its economic and social advantages, as well as disadvantages. This dilemma widened the generation gap within the Cuban community. The neglect of many older Cubans became the subject of a major study conducted by two Miami-Dade Community College sociologists. They found that the problems that accompany old age were magnified by language and cultural differences and the trauma of exile. Older Cubans felt that the language barrier helped create a "constantly broadening cultural gap" between the generations. Among the elderly, 23.1 percent cited loneliness as the greatest problem. This loneliness was found to be the result, according to the study, of economic and cultural pressure. The study also found that the lack of English led the elderly to maintain their old lifestyles, beliefs, values, and attitudes, while their children and grandchildren became increasingly assimilated into American society. Cultural diffusion had led an increasing number of young Cuban families to adopt American values. This influenced them to opt for privacy and not to support their older relatives. The neglect contradicted a basic Cuban tradition that old people are always cared for by their children.[41]

With respect to marriage, the number of divorces among Spanish-surnamed people in Dade County increased to an average of 63 to 64 divorces per 100 marriages, almost equal to the American rate of 66 percent. This was stunning, since divorce had been such a serious matter in Cuba. According to Cubans, this was one result of the Americanization of the Cuban marriage. The fact, however, was that the Cuban character had already undergone some changes.

While the old and middle-aged Cubans still sought out Latin music and hourly newscasts in Spanish on Miami's Cuban radio stations such as La Fabulosa and La Cubanisima, younger Cubans listened more frequently to English language rock music stations. Behind the facades of nearly 100,000 Cuban homes, a new identity was emerging – that of the Cuban-American. Being a Cuban-American was like having two sets of values and living with them in different worlds. For example, many school children lived an American life at school; and, at home, it became a Cuban life.[42] In sum, the most powerful forces of acculturation were in the public schools which the Cuban children attended.

Notes

1. "Cuban Americans: Fifteen Years After". *Miami Herald Sunday Magazine,* Vol. 8, July 14, 1974, No. 28.
2. The others, according to the 1975 U.S. Census reports on ethnic origins of the Spanish population element, were: Mexican, 60 percent; Puerto Rican, 15 percent; Central or South Americans, 6 percent; Others, 9 percent.
3. Supra Note 1
4. *The Miami Herald,* Sept. 2, 1975, p. 1-A.
5. Roberto Fabricio, "New Wave of Cuban Refugees Arriving in Dade—from the North." *The Miami Herald,* Oct. 2, 1972, p. 1-B.
6. William W. Jenna, *Metropolitan Miami.* Miami: Hunter Moss and Co. 1967. William W. Jenna, *Metropolitan Miami, A Demographic Overview.* Coral Gables: University of Miami Press, 1972.
7. The Research Institute for Cuba and the Caribbean, *The Cuban Immigration....,* p. 8.
8. Len Adde, "Quality of Life Now 'Unacceptable' in Some Dade Areas, Computer Says." *The Miami Herald,* Jan. 19, 1973, p. 20-A.
9. Carlos Arboleya, "Banker Arboleya Looks at Community". *The Miami Herald,* June 30, 1972, p. 8-G.
10. Strategy Research Corporation, *Prospectus of Dade County Growth - 1980.* Miami: SRC, 1975.
11. *The Miami Herald,* Oct. 7, 1974, p. 1-B.
12. Carlos Arboleya, "You Can Be Born or Buried Cuban Style."*The Miami News,* Aug. 24, 1973, Special Advertising Section, p. 2.
13. *The Miami Herald,* June 29, 1975, p. 1.
14. *The Miami News,* May 31, 1974, p. 4-A.
15. *The Miami News,* July 7, 1975, p. 3-A.
16. *The Miami News,* Aug. 21, 1974, p. 5-A.
17. "How the Immigrants Made It in Miami." *Business Week,* reprint from issue of May 1, 1971; Carlos Arboleya "Banker Arboleya Looks at Community" *The Miami Herald,* June 30, 1972, p. 8-G; "Latin Income at $10,000." *The Miami News,* Aug. 24, 1973, Special Advertising Section. p. 8.
18. Study by Jan Laytjes reported in *The Miami News,* Sept. 7, 1975, p. 7-A.
19. *The Miami News,* July 7, 1975, p. 14-A.
20. Hilda Inclan, "Friction among Ethnic Groups Prevents Any Real Latin Clout." *The Miami News,* June 30, 1973, p. 4-E.
21. "How the Immigrants Made It in Miami," *Business Week* reprint from issue of May 1, 1971.
22. *The Miami Herald,* Feb. 8, 1974, p. 3-A.
23. *The Miami Herald,* Feb. 5, 1975, p. 5-A; May 5, 1975, p. 1-A.
24. Supra Note 22
25. Ibid.
26. *The Miami News,* Nov. 18, 1974, p. 6-A.
27. Supra Note 20
28. Supra Note 26
29. *The Miami Herald,* Apr. 2, 1975, p. 6-A.
30. *The Miami News,* Mar. 12, 1974, p. 1.
31. Louis Salome, "How Dade County Voters Measure Up." *The Miami News,* Jan. 13, 1973, p. 15-A.
32. *The Miami Herald,* Mar. 26, 1975, p. 1-A.
33. *The Miami Herald,* Sept. 3, 1975, p. 1-E.
34. *The Miami News,* Aug. 28, 1974, p. 6-A.
35. "How the Immigrants Made It in Miami," *Business Week,* reprint from issue of May 1, 1971;

"Flight from Cuba - Castro's Loss is U.S. Gain," *U.S. News and World Report,* May 31, 1971, pp. 74-77.

36. *The Miami News,* June 10, 1974, p. 3-A.
37. Ibid.
38. *The Miami News,* May 12, 1975, p. 6-A.
39. *The Miami Herald,* July 28, 1974, p. 13-G.
40. Costa Rica, in 1975, decided to counter this influence by legislation. The national language being Spanish, a bill in the unicameral legislative body required any business signs in any other language subject to a $233 tax. *The Miami Herald,* May 17, 1975, p. 6-A.
41. *The Miami News,* Mar. 14, 1975, p. 1-A.
42. Ibid.

4

Cuban Children in Miami Schools

Although the traditional culture of the Cubans undoubtedly was modified by their presence in American classrooms, the rapid growth of the Cuban school population also had its effect upon the adaptive capacity of the local educational system. The adjustment of the schools to this new ethnic phenomenon was partly determined by tradition, and partly by the options open to them within the system. The wide range of options, however, was not readily understood and the problem was first handled as one of English language learning. It took much time and effort before the need and possibility of bilingual education finally was realized.

THE GROWING CUBAN SCHOOL POPULATION

The cultural and social adaptation of the Cuban refugees during the first decade of the resettlement was reflected in the type of schooling they gave their children. Among the most important Cuban institutions created in the area were the private sectarian schools to which Cubans, who could afford it, were accustomed to sending their children. By the mid-seventies, there were still some 30 Cuban-operated private schools accounting for some 15,000 students. Initially, the teaching in some of these schools was entirely in Spanish, except for lessons in English as a foreign language. However, as more English was added, these schools became bilingual. A survey conducted in mid-1974 seemed to indicate that most of these private institutions were in fact bilingual schools (see Appendix D).

The public schools of Dade County served the City of Miami and surrounding areas within that county (see Figure 1). Before the Cuban influx of 1959, approximately 1 of every 20 students was a native Spanish-speaker. Some of these students were from Cuba, but many of the group were from Puerto Rico, Mexico, and Central and South America. The Mexican-Americans were usually involved with migrant work and only attended schools in the agricultural areas in the southern section of Dade County. With only 5 percent of the student population representing native Spanish-speakers, no significant adjustments were implemented in the countywide instructional program.[1] The student membership, however soon reflected the significant changes within the community's population.

In the beginning of the first period of the influx from Cuba, the enrollment of Cuban refugee students was not overwhelming because many of the children attended private schools. By the spring of 1961, only about 5,000 of these students were attending the county's public schools. Between the beginning of the school year in September, 1961, and the beginning of the school year in September, 1962, however, the number of Cuban refugee students increased by 109.7 percent from 8,708 to 18,260 pupils.[2]

During the second period of the Cuban influx (November, 1962, to November, 1965), the enrollment of Cuban refugee students in the Dade County Public Schools actually decreased from approximately 9.5 percent of the total student population to about 7.7 percent, that is from 18,000 to 15,500 students.[3] The decline during this three-year period was due to the fact that the Cuban Refugee Center was resettling refugee families in communities outside of Dade County and commercial airline flights were no longer transporting refugees from Cuba to the United States.

When the freedom flights between Cuba and Miami began in December, 1965, the enrollment figures for Cuban refugee students started to rise rapidly and steadily. As Figure 5 and Table 5 indicate, Cuban refugee membership grew by approximately 3,000 to 4,000 students each year during this third period of the Cuban refugee influx into Dade County.

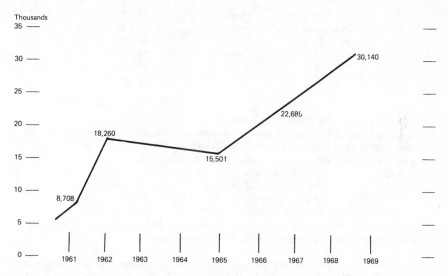

Source: Department of Administrative Research, *Cuban Refugee Report: Number Thirteen*, vol. XXII, no. 7, Dade County Public Schools, Miami, Florida, 1975, p. 19.

Figure 5   Cuban Enrollment in Dade County Schools (1961-1969)
(Cuban Refugee Children in Grades 1-12)

From 1971 to 1972, the Spanish-speaking student population in Dade County public schools increased from 55,303 to 60,283, despite the fact that the airlift was already ending. Of those figures, about 90 percent were believed to be Cubans, 8 percent Puerto Ricans and 2 percent from Latin American countries. By 1972, approximately 25 percent of the students in the county's schools were from Spanish-speaking backgrounds; and, for the first time, the "Anglos" (North American students who were not classified as either black or of Spanish language origin) no longer represented a majority of the student population[4] (see Figure 6). In other words, at the beginning of the 1972-73 school year, approximately one of every four children in the Dade County Public Schools was from a Spanish-speaking background and the numbers of

Table 5
NATIVE SPANISH-SPEAKING STUDENT POPULATION
(Dade County Public Schools: 1965-75)

Date of census	Pupil enrollment*	Cuban refugee enrollment	Spanish language origin enrollment**	Percent of total
1965	202,124	15,501	21,288	10.53%
1966	212,646	18,756	24,416	11.48%
1967	220,416	22,685	29,320	13.30%
1968	233,222	25,905	39,476	16.93%
1969	243,881	30,140	46,552	19.09%
1970***	240,258	——	49,379	20.55%
1971	245,025	——	55,303	22.57%
1972	241,797	——	60,283	24.93%
1973	244,351	——	66,439	27.19%
1974	246,534	——	72,773	29.52%
1975	244,221	——	74,128	30.35%

* Includes kindergarten and Head Start students.
** According to the Civil Rights Act: "Persons considered by themselves, by the school, or by the community to be of Mexican, Puerto Rican, Central-American, Cuban, Latin-American, or other Spanish-speaking origin." The definition is from "Individual School Campus Report: Form OS/CR 102-1," Fall, 1970, *Elementary and Secondary Civil Rights Survey*, required under Title VI of the Civil Rights Act of 1964, U.S. Department of Health, Education, and Welfare, Office of Civil Rights, Washington, D.C. In 1975, the title of the enrollment category was changed to "Hispanic." (See new definition in Chapter 7; see also the Glossary)
*** The Attendance Office in the Dade County Public Schools ceased to tabulate total Cuban refugee membership data at the end of the 1969-70 school year.

Source: Department of Administrative Reasearch, *Cuban Refugee Report: Number Thirteen, vol. XXII, no. 7*, Dade County Public Schools, Miami, Fla., 1975, p. 18; Planning and Evaluation Department, *Desegregation: September, 1975*, Dade County Public Schools, Miami, Fla., 1975, p.31.

these students had tripled in less than eight years (see Figure 7). Although these students represented more than a quarter of the school population, the number of native Spanish-speaking educators comprised only 7 percent of the teaching staff and 3 percent of the administrative positions (see Figures 8 and 9). Some Cubans considered this insufficient. It was believed that some 400 Cubans who were certified to teach could not get jobs. Demands were made to the Dade County School Board to hire Spanish-speaking teachers, counselors, and other staff members proportionate to the Spanish-speaking student enrollment. The board was also asked to expand its bilingual programs to prevent Cuban students from becoming retarded in major subject areas, because language problems had caused significant numbers of Cuban children to "cop out" by vegetating in the classroom and eventually "drop out" of school.

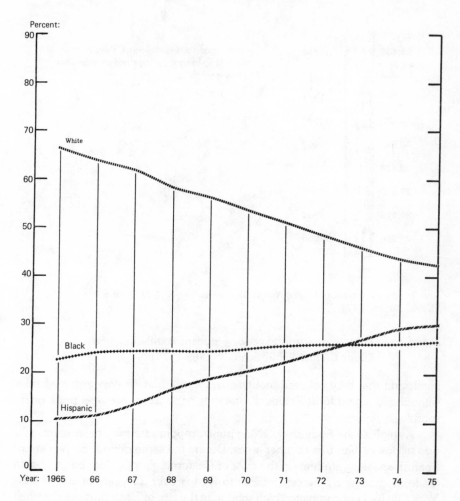

Source: *Desegregation: September 1975,* Dade County Public Schools, Miami, Florida 1975, p. 39.

Figure 6   Racial/Ethnic Student Population Trends
(Dade County Public Schools: 1965-1975)

A 1968 report by public school officials estimated that the dropout rate among Cuban and Puerto Rican students in the Dade County Public Schools was apparently 13 percent higher than the 27.3 percent rate for Dade County students as a whole. English deficiency was repeatedly asserted as a main cause for the eventual dropout of the native Spanish-speaking students. Some of these students claimed that they had actually been *forced* out of school. They reported that they were treated like very young children in school; that they saw no connection between their program of studies and future employ-

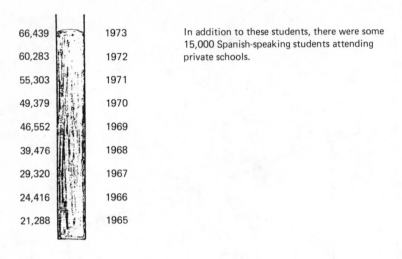

66,439	1973
60,283	1972
55,303	1971
49,379	1970
46,552	1969
39,476	1968
29,320	1967
24,416	1966
21,288	1965

In addition to these students, there were some 15,000 Spanish-speaking students attending private schools.

Source: Spanish American League Against Discrimination, *SALAD Report,* No. 1, Miami, Florida, August, 1974.

Figure 7   Growth of Spanish-Speaking Student Population
(Dade County Public Schools: 1965-1973)

ment; and that they believed that teachers and administrators enforced rules without any regard for the student's maturity or sense of personal pride or responsibility.

As high as the Spanish-speaking pupil dropout rate may have seemed, it was still lower than that of other areas. During the same period, 55 percent of Spanish-speaking students in the state of California dropped out by the eighth grade, and some 87 percent of Puerto Ricans over 25 years of age in New York City had not completed high school. In the city of Boston, more than half of the 10,000 Spanish-speaking students were not in school, and in the city of Chicago, the dropout rate for this group was more than 60 percent.

Due primarily to the influx of Cuban students and the migration of North American families from the northern to the southern sections of the United States, the Dade County Public Schools had grown to become the country's sixth largest school system. Only the cities of New York, Los Angeles, Chicago, Detroit, and Philadelphia had more students enrolled at the beginning of the 1975-76 school year. At that time, 244,221 students were attending Dade County's public schools, and a little more than 30 percent of these students were native Spanish-speakers, primarily Cuban refugees. In addition, 43,218 students were enrolled in 211 local private schools. Several of these schools were operated for and by Cubans as an alternative to a public school system whose characteristics had seemed unsuitable for maintenance of Cuban culture.

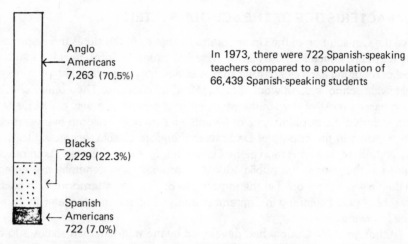

In 1973, there were 722 Spanish-speaking teachers compared to a population of 66,439 Spanish-speaking students

Source: Spanish American League Against Discrimination, *SALAD Report,* No. 1, Miami, Florida, August, 1974.

Figure 8   Proportion of Teachers by Ethnic Group (Dade County Public Schools: 1973)

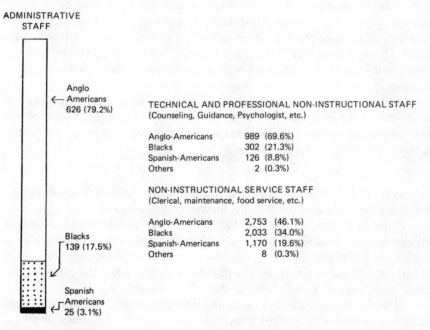

TECHNICAL AND PROFESSIONAL NON-INSTRUCTIONAL STAFF (Counseling, Guidance, Psychologist, etc.)

Anglo-Americans	989	(69.6%)
Blacks	302	(21.3%)
Spanish-Americans	126	(8.8%)
Others	2	(0.3%)

NON-INSTRUCTIONAL SERVICE STAFF (Clerical, maintenance, food service, etc.)

Anglo-Americans	2,753	(46.1%)
Blacks	2,033	(34.0%)
Spanish-Americans	1,170	(19.6%)
Others	8	(0.3%)

Source: Spanish American League Against Discrimination, *SALAD Report,* No. 1, Miami, Florida, August, 1974.

Figure 9   Administrative and Non-Instructional Staff by Ethnic Group (Dade County Public Schools: 1973)

CHARACTERISTICS OF THE SCHOOL SYSTEM

Since the Constitution of the United States delegates to the states the responsibility for public education, the Florida state legislature, in 1869, decided that instead of requiring each city or township to establish its own school organization, a statewide school system would be organized by counties. The county which encompassed most of the southeastern tip of the peninsula was called Dade, and it included the populous city of Miami. All American children five years or older residing in the county of Dade were therefore eligible, according to the Constitution, to free education in the Dade County Public Schools. As in other sections of the nation, the public education program was generally presented five days a week from 8:30 in the morning to 3:00 in the afternoon, with each new school year beginning in September and ending ten months later in June of the following year.

Although Dade County had developed by the mid-nineteen sixties into a network of 27 municipalities plus some unincorporated districts, these had no direct control over education since " . . . management of the schools is totally independent of metropolitan and city governments, subject only to the state statutes. The metropolitan government collects the school tax for a fee but exercises no control over its use".[5] Locally-elected members of the Dade County School Board were responsible for school policy. Administration of all public schools, classes, and courses of instruction and all services and activities directly related to public education were directed by a county superintendent and his staff.[6] Under these officials, the Dade County Public Schools system was decentralized into six districts, each with a district superintendent (see map in Chapter 7).

Legally, the Dade County School Board had the authority to make adjustments in the instructional program in order to meet the needs of the ever-increasing numbers of Spanish-speaking students. Within federal constitutional restrictions in the United States:

1) the state legislature had delegated to itself the "express" power to prescribe and proscribe courses of study, textbooks, and content;

2) the local board of education had the "implied" power to add, delete, or change courses of study, textbooks, and instructional materials which were supplementary to and did not violate the state requirements, to finance these programs with public funds, and to dismiss personnel when the primary purpose was to improve the efficiency of that school system;

3) the local school administrators and teachers had the "professional" right to determine the methodology for mediation of content in all courses; and

4) the students' parents had the "constitutional" right to exclude their children from participation in courses which were not essential to citizenship and the general welfare of the state.

If they selected to use it, then, the professional employees of any local school system in the United States and the local board of education had considerable power to invent and to implement changes in the local school system's instructional program. The historical, philosophical, and legal rationale for this principle of common law has been stated thus;

> Since the local board of education is the legal body most closely connected with what is taught boys and girls, operationally it has vast powers for determining a curriculum. The history of innovations in the curriculum of public schools in the United States is largely a history of local actions. That is to say, a curricular change conceived and initiated by a local board of education which proves successful is copied in other districts and gradually finds its way into general acceptance. Such development may be fostered by a permissive or a mandatory state law. In many instances, however, there is no firm legislative basis for performing a particular curricular activity which has become generally accepted. Among the offerings of most public schools today which originated in the aforementioned way are many athletic activities, kindergartens, dramatics, music and domestic science, as well as the high school as an outgrowth of the 'common school'. Analysis of court holdings leads to the generalization that in modern times so long as local boards of education do not go exceedingly far, the addition of courses or activities will be upheld by courts. Indeed, innovations are being less frequently challenged as time passes.[7]

Although the legal framework for the introduction of innovations (including bilingual education) into the instructional programs in local public school systems was consistent throughout the United States, a review of the historical, political, social, and economic setting within Dade County in the early sixties helps to explain why the movement for bilingual education involving native English-speaking as well as non-English-speaking students began in this school system rather than elsewhere in the United States.

Historically, the Dade County Public Schools, as opposed to some other school systems within the United States, had not enrolled large numbers of non-English-speaking students until the early sixties. Suddenly, the numbers of Spanish-speaking students soared. It was impossible for local community and school leaders not to recognize the sudden change in the characteristics of the overall student population caused by the rapid influx of Cuban refugees.

County school and community leaders, of course, could have prevented any adjustment in the public school programs; however, there was no apparent reason for them to do so at that time. The Cuban refugees had created little animosity or resentment among the established residents of Dade County. The majority of the refugees, especially during the early sixties, were well-educated, industrious Caucasians who spoke some English. They were polite in their encounters with the English-speaking population, yet they made no attempt to force their way into local social or political activities. Community leaders discovered that the Cubans were excellent credit risks, that very few requested public assistance, and that a strikingly small percentage were associated with any criminal activities.[8] Consequently, local receptivity to the concept of biculturalism began to improve immediately after the first large influx of Cuban refugees in the summer of 1960. During the early sixties, the majority of Cuban refugees in Miami were mainly professionals and successful businessmen, and the new Cuban regime had confirmed that nearby Cuba would become a communist nation. As the Superintendent of the Dade County Public Schools noted at that time: "Leaders of the community and of the school system, as well as the teachers, were sympathetic towards these homeless persons and were determined to demonstrate to them in a practical way that a democratic society could adjust to the problem."[9] Yet the adjustments, made as they were in good faith, were first conceived within a uniform and unilingual system which had already absorbed and assimilated ethnic minorities and had little room for options favoring the education of guest populations in their own language.

OPTIONS WITHIN AND BEYOND THE SYSTEM

In the past, any adjustment to the needs of non-English-speaking children in the United States had been in the form of courses, which effected a transfer of the dominant language from that of the mother tongue to that of the school. Using the home language as a starting point, the school language was used increasingly in order to achieve, through the educational system, the cultural assimilation of the ethnic minorities into the larger North American mainstream, thus providing the equal opportunity required by the Constitution.

Most of the nation's bilingual schools had likewise been of the transfer type, the objective being to change the dominant learning-language of the child from that of the home to that of the nation.[10] The extra burden of operating temporarily in two languages had to be born by the ethnic minorities going through a necessary period of transitional bilingualism in the process of integration from immigrant to citizen. This had been the fate of all non-English-speaking immigrant families electing to become Americans.

The case of non-immigrants and temporary residents, however, was somewhat different. The State had no constitutional obligation to educate them as individuals; but it was free to assume a moral obligation to accept them as a group and provide all or some of the rights they had enjoyed in their home countries, including education in the mother tongue. It was within this category of temporary non-immigrant residents that the Cuban refugees had placed themselves as guests of the United States.

The sudden arrival of half a million Spanish-speaking guests, many of whom had intended to return to Cuba the moment changes in the regime permitted, raised many problems for the education of their children. An educational policy designed to integrate them into a unilingual, English-speaking community would have been both unrealistic and unfair. But so would a unilingual education in Spanish, since no one knew how long these children would have to remain in the United States or whether they would not eventually have to find jobs in a new English-speaking homeland. A possible solution to the problem was bilingual schooling, not of the immigrant-oriented transfer variety but rather of the maintenance type, the purpose being to preserve a comparable degree of literacy in the home language.[11] But this was only one of the problems.

The second problem was that of school organization. In order to practice this maintenance type of bilingual education, should the Spanish-speaking guests be supplied with their own uniethnic schools? This option would have meant segregating the Cuban children at a time when the federal government was taking strong legal action against states practicing ethnic or racial segregation in public schools, since it seemed to violate the principle of equal educational opportunity. Yet integration into an all-English-speaking school system was hardly compatible with the maintenance of Spanish at a level of literacy appropriate to the age of the child, even if Spanish as a mother tongue were taught as a subject. It guaranteed the dominance of English and placed the burden of bilingualism entirely on the shoulders of a population already struggling to maintain its home language under less than ideal conditions. In order to place both English and Spanish on an equal educational footing, it would be necessary for the dominant group to assume some of the responsibility for becoming bilingual. This responsibility could have been met by making Spanish the language of instruction in uniethnic schools for English home-language students, that is, the immersion variety (see Glossary) such as was becoming popular in Canada at the time.[12] But this also would seem to promote a type of uniethnic segregation, because native English-speaking and native Spanish-speaking students would have been separated while in the process of becoming bilingual.

A second option was the organization of biethnic and bilingual schools, the purpose being mutual cultural integration and maintenance of both languages on an equal footing. Such a formula would have seemed preferable to some Cubans and their American hosts, even though it would have constituted a considerable innovation. This is the sort of consideration that one might have expected in the context of the American bilingual tradition. But the initial reaction of Dade County's school administrators was merely to provide special instruction in English as a Second Language.

ENGLISH COURSES FOR CUBAN PUPILS

Since Cuban children could not take advantage of the free education offered by the public school system at that time without a mastery of English, the teaching of this language developed into a top priority. Little assistance was available for Dade County's educators in identifying the linguistic and other educational problems of these Spanish-speaking students in local schools where instruction was presented solely in the English language. At that time, most school systems in the United States had neither identified nor confronted these problems. The initial decision of the Superintendent of the Dade County Public Schools and two of his assistants, therefore, was to place Cuban refugee students in "regular classes where they associate with English-speaking pupils, rather than . . . placing them in isolated classes or separate schools. This was the general pattern followed".[13]

As more and more Cuban refugee students entered the public schools and attended regular classes, their educational problems within the traditional program's structure became more and more apparent. Local school leaders apparently wanted to help but they did not know how to pinpoint or to resolve the specific problems that they believed were related to instruction of English as a Second Language. It became necessary, therefore, to obtain the assistance of an educator from outside the local school system who had expertise in the specialized field. That person was Pauline Rojas.[14] Soon after her arrival, she acquired the assistance of Paul W. Bell, a local teacher.[15]

Rojas' and Bell's principal duties during the school year 1961-62 were to visit classrooms within the Dade County Public Schools and to provide workshops for teachers who were presenting English-language instruction for Spanish-speaking students. Most teachers were using the *Fries American English Series* as the basic texts in their English as a Second Language programs. Rojas had directed the materials-development project in Puerto Rico which produced these texts that were designed to provide language-arts instruction in English for students who already could read in Spanish. Although the inherent audio-lingual techniques were helpful in the primary grades, the reading sections and exercises could not be effectively utilized by teachers for beginning-reading instruction for students who did not know how to read in any language. This lack of appropriate materials for teaching English Language Arts to Spanish-speaking students in the first two grades was identified as the pivotal problem at that school level.

During numerous early-morning conferences with administrators of the Dade County Public Schools in the spring of 1962, Rojas explained the need to develop materials for beginning-reading instruction in the English language designed for Spanish-speaking students. She convinced a number of the school administrators of the need, but she did not feel that the local school system could provide the special funds required for a materials-development project.

The Ford Foundation, however, had expressed interest;[16] and the possibility of special funding generated an increase in support among administrative leaders of the Dade County Public Schools.[17] A number of materials-development projects were outlined in a preliminary proposal, however only three such projects were included in the revised form which was funded by the Ford

MIAMI LINGUISTIC READERS

BIG BOOK I

Accompanies READINESS UNIT *through* LEVEL ONE-B

Ralph F. Robinett
Paul W. Bell
Pauline M. Rojas

Foundation. The grant became effective in January of 1963. On Jan. 24, the Superintendent of the Dade County Public Schools presented the proposal and the information concerning the grant to the Dade County School Board. Upon the recommendation of the superintendent, the members of the Dade County School Board unanimously approved funding and implementation of the Project in Bilingual Education of Cuban Refugee Pupils—Ford Foundation Grant.[18] Rojas was appointed to direct the project which included four objectives:

1.   The preparation of language and reading materials for non-English-speaking pupils entering first grade.

2.   The revision or adaptation of the books of the *Fries American English Series* for non-English-speaking bilingual pupils who can read and write their vernacular.[19]

3.   The preparation of guides and audio-visual materials for teachers of bilingual pupils.[20]

4.   The establishment of a bilingual school.[21]

It was this last part of the project that developed into the most important and innovative, since it had to do not so much with the teaching of English but with a whole new concept of bilingual education.

TOWARD A CONCEPT OF BILINGUAL EDUCATION

What evolved out of this last part of the project was a biethnic concept of bilingual education—for both Cuban and American children.

The planners had come to realize the need for this type of bilingual education by comparing the widespread unilingualism of Americans with the widespread bilingualism of educated people in other countries. In addition, the Spanish-speaking students attending all-English-speaking schools in the United States apparently were not receiving a proper education.

Rojas had been aware of the overall problem of Spanish-speaking students in other sections of the country at that time and had pointed out that all too often these students were dropping out or graduating from public schools as virtual "non-linguals". They had been discouraged from developing their linguistic ability and literacy in Spanish and they had never mastered the English language. She also had realized that most of the native English-speaking students in public schools in the United States were not learning to communicate fluently in any language other than English.

Both Rojas and Bell had decided that the setting in Dade County at that time provided an excellent opportunity to involve both native Spanish-speaking *and* native English-speaking students in bilingual schooling. Both had experienced the feasibility of bilingual schooling in their work in American binational schools abroad.[22] Both, therefore, had recognized the opportunity to introduce bilingual schooling within the Dade County Public Schools. Under Rojas' leadership, the initial process of promoting this type of instructional program for both Cuban refugee and North American students had required approximately 12 months. By the fall of 1962, she had gained financial support from a private foundation and administrative support from local school officials for a special project that included the establishment of a bilingual school.

The task of promoting bilingual schooling, however, was far from complete. Three of the four projects had been designed to improve the instructional programs in English Language Arts for Cuban refugee pupils, and few local residents realized that the fourth project, the establishment of a bilingual school, was designed to involve English-speaking, North American students. The project's leaders were confronted with the task of implementing this two-way model for bilingual schooling in an existing school and promoting this innovative concept within that school's surrounding community. But which school would be willing to take the risk of being the first?

Notes

1. Department of Administrative Research, *The Cuban Refugee: First Report, Early 1960 to December, 1961.* pp. 1-2.

2. Department of Administrative Research and Statistics, *The Cuban Refugee: Fifth Report, February, 1965, to October, 1965.* Dade County Public Schools, Miami, Fla., 1965, p. 4.

3. Department of Administrative Research, *Cuban Refugee Report: Number Ten,* Vol. XIX, no. 6. Dade County Public Schools, Miami, Fla., 1972, p. 24.

4. Tom Morgenthau, "Anglos a Minority in Public Schools". *The Miami Herald,* Oct. 25, 1972, p. 1-B.

5. Department of Administrative Research, *Statistical Highlights, 1970-1971.* Dade County Public Schools, Miami, Fla. 1971.

6. *Florida Statutes Annotated,* 230.02, Vol. 11, p. 175.

7. E. Edmund Reutter, Jr., *Schools and the Law.* Dobbs Ferry: Oceana Publications, 1964, p. 40.

8. "Flight from Cuba - Castro's Loss Is U.S. Gain." *U.S. News and World Report,* May 31, 1971, pp. 74-75; "How the Immigrants Made It in Miami." *Business Week,* reprint from issue of May 1, 1971.

9. Department of Administrative Research and Statistics; *The Cuban Refugee in the Public Schools of Dade County, Florida.* Dade County Public Schools, Miami, Fla. 1965, p. iii.

10. William F. Mackey, "A Typology of Bilingual Education" in Vol. 2 of Theodore Andersson & Mildred Boyer, *Bilingual Schooling in the United States,* Washington: U.S. Government Printing Office, 1970, pp. 63-81.

11. Ibid.

12. Wallace E. Lambert & Richard Tucker, *The Bilingual Education of Children.* Rowley: Newbury House, p. 197.

13. Ed Hurst, Interview with Ed Hurst, Assistant Superintendent for Support Services, Dade County Public Schools, Miami, Fla., Sept. 4, 1969.

14. Pauline Rojas, whose maiden name was Pauline Martz, was raised in the northern portion of the United States. In the early 1920's, she completed her college degree at the University of Puerto Rico, began to learn the Spanish language, and married Antonio Rojas, a native Puerto Rican.

Pauline M. Rojas' extensive experience with the teaching of English as a Second Language started in 1925 while she was teaching in an elementary school in Puerto Rico. At that time, the English language was employed for instructional purposes with the Spanish-speaking residents of this Caribbean island that was a possession of the United States. Subsequently, Rojas earned a master's degree in the teaching of English and a doctorate degree in the teaching of English as a Second Language at universities in the United States.

After completing her studies, Rojas' direct involvement in the area of teaching English as a Second Language continued. In the southwestern United States she helped direct a materials-development project for English as a Second Language. She returned to Puerto Rico and taught English in public secondary schools and at the University of Puerto Rico and directed the English section of the Department of Education of Puerto Rico. While in Puerto Rico, she also organized the project that produced the *Fries American English Series* (Charles C. Fries, et al., *Fries American English Series*. Boston: D.C. Heath and Company, 1953) which was subsequently utilized for instruction in English as a Second Language in elementary and secondary schools throughout the world. She was an Adjunct-Assistant Professor of English and the Teaching of English to Spanish-speaking children at New York University from 1957 until 1959. After resigning from the staff at New York University, Rojas was sent on a tour of Latin America by the United States Center of Applied Linguistics to gather first-hand information on the teaching of English as a Second Language. This trip provided Rojas with her first opportunity to visit some of the bilingual schools in those countries, and, in 1960, she accepted a one-year position as a Fulbright Professor of English in Bogota, Colombia.

Following her involvement with the bilingual education programs in the Dade County Public Schools (1961-66), Rojas resumed her travels and consultant work around the world. In the early 1970's, she returned to the Miami area.

15. Paul W. Bell, born in 1933, was raised and educated in the United States. In 1956, after completing his formal preparation for a career as a teacher, Bell travelled to Guatemala to manage a coffee plantation. While residing in this Central American country, Bell learned the Spanish language and secured a position as a teacher in a bilingual American school in the country's capital, Guatemala City. Upon his return to the United States in 1959, Bell accepted a teaching position at a public elementary school in downtown Miami and organized that school's first English as a Second Language program. After Pauline Rojas selected him as her Demonstration Teacher in 1961 to present the workshops for new teachers of English as a Second Language, Bell was appointed Coordinator of Special English, a newly-created position in the Dade County Public Schools. In 1963, he was selected also to serve simultaneously as Coordinator of the Ford Foundation Projects in Bilingual Education. As this special project drew to a close during the 1965-66 school year, the Dade County Public Schools promoted Bell and changed his title to Supervisor of Bilingual Education. Subsequently, Bell was promoted to the positions of Executive Director of the Division of Elementary and Secondary Education and Assistant Superintendent for Instructional Services. In these posts, Bell continued, along with his other administrative responsibilities, to oversee the development of bilingual education programs within the local school system.

16. During the summer of 1962, Rojas called a personal acquaintance at the United States Office of Education and inquired about possible sources of funding for a special project in Dade County. She was referred to Edward J. Meade, an official of the private Ford Foundation. Rojas called Meade and travelled to New York City to meet with him. They discussed the need for instructional materials for English as a Second Language instruction in Dade County and the opportunity for bilingual schooling that would include North American students. Encouraged by Meade's reaction yet realizing that she did not have the authority to submit a proposal in the name of the Dade County Public Schools, Rojas sent some sketchy notes to a local school official. This official, in turn, sent the notes to Meade at the Ford Foundation offices in New York City.

17. Rojas, Bell, and a local school administrator completed a proposal entitled Project in the Bilingual Education of Cuban Refugee Pupils. On Sept. 24, 1962, the Superintendent of the Dade County Public Schools officially submitted the proposal to the Ford Foundation.

18. The Board of Public Instruction of Dade County, Fla., Minutes of the Jan. 24, 1963 Meeting of the Board, pp. 2-3. The Project in the Bilingual Education of Cuban Refugee Pupils was susbequently retitled Ford Foundation Projects in Bilingual Education. It consisted of a three-year grant beginning in January, 1963, to the Dade County Public Schools from the private Ford Foundation for $278,000. In addition, a local contribution of $190,600 was allocated to the project by the Dade County Public Schools. This special project did not actually terminate until the end of the school year in June, 1966.

19. This part of the project was initiated but later abandoned due to lack of time and trained personnel.

20. This part of the project was never initiated.

21. Division of Instruction, Dade County Public Schools, "Project in the Bilingual Education of Cuban Refugee Pupils", Miami, Fla. September, 1962; Pauline M. Rojas, "Final Report, Ford Foundation Projects in Bilingual Education", Miami, Fla., Aug. 31, 1966, p. 1.

22. During her tour of Latin America in 1960, Rojas had visited a number of American Schools attended by North American students and native Latin American students. She was especially impressed by one school in Guayaquil, Ecuador, where instruction was presented in both English and Spanish to native English-speaking as well as native Spanish-speaking students. Bell had taught in an "American School" in Guatemala.

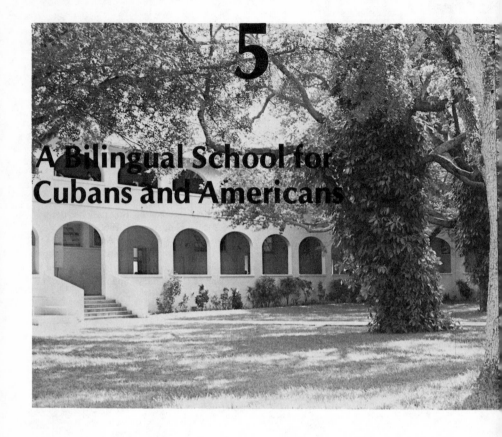

5

A Bilingual School for Cubans and Americans

In the early sixties it seemed unlikely that any of the administrators of the 150 public elementary schools in the Miami area would volunteer one of these institutions to become the bilingual school in the county. In the first place, most of them were not aware of the details of the recently-funded project which had stressed the preparation of materials in English as a Second Language. Even fewer were concerned with the sort of bilingual schooling included as one of the components of the project.

The first problem, therefore, was to select an appropriate elementary school located within one of the many biethnic neighborhoods that had emerged in Dade County as a result of the influx of Cuban refugees to the area. Secondly, local school personnel had to become directly involved in the process of developing the instructional program, selling the concept of bilingualism in the local community, and implementing the program within that particular school. As the characteristics of the student population changed over the years and curricular and organizational problems arose, modifications in the original program design also had to be developed.

PICKING THE COMMUNITY

Local school officials recommended, early in the spring of 1963, that Coral Way Elementary be the site for the experimental, bilingual school program. They based their selection on a number of criteria, including the linguistic and socio-economic characteristics of the school's community. Approximately 50 percent of the area's residents were from Spanish-speaking backgrounds and many had been successful businessmen and professionals in Cuba. Most had already achieved middle-income status in the United States and spoke some English. The other half of the area's residents were English-speaking citizens whose socio-economic status ranged from the lower to the upper strata. In addition, there were no impoverished sections in the area and it was considered to be a stable, middle-class community.

Initial inquiries revealed that the school's principal [1] was interested in the idea of providing bilingual schooling for children at Coral Way Elementary. For the experiment to succeed, it was imperative that the principal of the school favor the idea and give it his active support.

The physical surroundings were also favorable. The school building was a large one, its classrooms enclosing three sides of a tree-shaded patio. At that time, the facilities were more than adequate for the number of students enrolled.

As for the school population, it was determined that the English-speaking students enrolled in the school were representative of the average student in Dade County in terms of academic achievement, performance on standardized tests, and linguistic backgrounds. There was neither screening of pupils nor entrance requirements for enrollment.

GETTING PEOPLE INVOLVED

After the selection of Coral Way Elementary had been confirmed, the project entered an important research and planning phase in which various types of existing bilingual school programs in Latin America, Canada, and Europe were studied and compared. These efforts were led by Pauline Rojas, Paul Bell and Ralph Robinett. The latter had joined the project as a specialist in second language curriculum development. [2] During these research and planning sessions, school administrators informally agreed to provide special administrative considerations to Coral Way Elementary; for example, it was decided that there would always be one or more teachers allocated for every 30 students enrolled. That spring, however, the county school system was decentralized into six administrative "sub-districts", each with a district superintendent. Coral Way Elementary was located in the South Central District (see map in Chapter 7). Later in the spring of 1963, the newly-appointed Superintendent of the South Central District informed the school's principal that it was important that Coral Way Elementary be treated like any other elementary school in Dade County and that administrative policies, including the teacher-student ratio, should conform to the school system's countywide standards.

A third important step consisted in informing and involving the local community. At the regular monthly meetings of the school's Parents and Teachers Organization that spring, the principal briefly discussed the plans for a bilingual school program at the primary level (grades one, two, and three). In addition, a school bulletin was sent to the parents of all children who would be entering these three grade levels. In the bulletin, the school principal explained that participation in the bilingual school program would be voluntary. At any time during the upcoming school year, parents could either enroll their children in the experimental program or withdraw them from the program. Children that were withdrawn at their parents' request would be reassigned immediately to the regular instructional program. The bulletin stated, however, that all parents who planned to have their children participate in the bilingual school program would be required to attend four orientation meetings at the school that spring. During these meetings, Bell and Robinett explained the goals of the bilingual school program and discussed some of the technical aspects of organization and curriculum. "It was carefully explained that the program was not only for the gifted or academically talented. The staff was equally careful to explain that it was expected that pupils' progress would be comparable to that of pupils in a traditional program. That is to say, there would be 'A' students and 'F' students." [3]

Most of the work involved in convincing the students' parents of the merits of the bilingual school program fell upon the shoulders of the school's principal whose job it became to share his personal opinions in laymen's language with the parents. In doing so, he explained his feelings of inadequacy while travelling in foreign countries and not being able to speak the language of those countries when the foreigners could communicate with him in English. He also explained to the parents that the United States was spending more money per child in public schools than any other country and that the schools should certainly be able to provide North American children with the opportunity to become functional bilinguals.

Almost unanimously, the Spanish-speaking parents agreed with the concept of bilingual schooling. They explained that they wanted their children to learn the English language and the cultural background of North Americans; but they insisted that, at the same time, they did not want their children to lose their ability to communicate in the Spanish language or to forget their own cultural heritage. Although a few North American parents and one or two Cuban parents believed that it would be difficult for their children (who at that time were having problems learning to read and study in the English language) to receive instruction in the Spanish language during the regular school day, the American parents, as a group, generally concurred with the school's principal and supported his decision. If the principal believed that the bilingual school program would be a valuable supplement to the regular instructional program, these English-speaking parents were willing to take his word for it. If the school principal believed that all of the children would sharpen their general ability to think by working in two languages and not become confused, these parents were confident that this would prove to be true. Although the parents understood that their young children would be required to move to a number of different classrooms during the school day like older students in junior and senior high schools, they also knew that their children would have the opportunity to learn from "the cream of the crop" of Cuban refugee teachers. For these reasons, the great majority of the parents of prospective first, second, and third grade students selected to enroll their children in the experimental bilingual school program.

The school's principal believed that he and the other school officials were successful in obtaining community support for this innovative program for three reasons:

1) they had a worthwhile program to offer,
2) they themselves believed in the value of the program, and
3) they did not try to force the program on the community.

The school's principal admitted, however, that it was much more difficult to gain support for the innovation among the school's faculty. And this fourth step was indispensable in preparing for bilingual schooling.

Although three Cuban aides, funded by the Cuban Refugee Program, had been assigned to Coral Way Elementary to work with the large number of Cuban refugee students enrolling during the 1962-63 school year, there were no native Spanish-speaking teachers or teachers who were bilingual in the English and Spanish languages on the school's regular staff that year. And it was probable that all of the first, second, and third grade teachers would be directly involved in the bilingual instructional program during the upcoming school year. During the planning stages in the spring of 1963, a few of these teachers and a few teachers at other grade levels expressed their opposition to the bilingual school program to other staff members and to some of their students' parents. Although the school principal needed to acquire Spanish-speaking teachers in order to present the experimental program, school officials would not allow him to transfer teachers that opposed the bilingual program to another school unless the teachers requested that transfer. Prior to June of that year, only four of the 12 English language origin teachers in grades one, two, and three requested transfers to neighboring schools for the upcoming school year. The problem of creating two more staff vacancies to enable the principal to hire six teachers that were able to present instruction in the Spanish language portion of the bilingual program became critical. A six-week bilingual education workshop, planned for the summer of 1963 at Coral Way Elementary, helped to ease the solution of this staffing problem. Attendance at the workshop was mandatory for all first, second, and third grade teachers from the school. Two of the eight remaining teachers at these three grade levels were unable to attend. Their transfers to other elementary schools were authorized and arranged by the county's school administrators. At that point, six of the 12 teaching positions in grades one, two, and three were available for Spanish-speaking instructors.

A number of Cuban aides, including some of those working at Coral Way Elementary, were participating at the time in the Cuban Teacher Retraining Program (funded by the Cuban Refugee Program) at the University of Miami in nearby Coral Gables. This program, initiated in February, 1963, was established to prepare Cuban refugees, who had been teachers in Cuba but were still not American citizens, for certification and teaching positions in public schools within the United States. Cuban refugee teachers who worked as Cuban aides in Dade County Public Schools, acquired 12 graduate credits in specified education courses at the University of Miami, and performed successfully on the National Teachers Examination and the Graduate Record Exam became eligible for "temporary" teacher certificates in the State of Florida. It therefore became probable that a number of Cuban aides in this program would qualify for temporary teacher certification before the end of the summer in 1963.

At the beginning of the summer, the principal of Coral Way Elementary selected six of these Cuban aides to fill the six vacant teaching positions at the school. Adjustments were made in grade-level assignments among the school's staff so that the six selected Cuban aides and the six American teachers chosen to participate in the summer bilingual education workshop would be assigned to grades one, two, and three in September.

The six-week summer workshop, also funded by the Cuban Refugee Program, was one of a series of workshops in the county for teachers that would be instructing Cuban refugee students. In the mornings, the six selected Cuban aides reported to the schools where they had been assigned during the previous school year. In these schools, they assisted English as a Second Language teachers working with Cuban refugee students. Meanwhile, the six American teachers attended a morning workshop at a nearby high school, directed by the planning staff with the assistance of an experienced Cuban educator, Rosa Inclan. [4] During the afternoons, the six American teachers and the six Cuban aides gathered at Coral Way Elementary to consider classroom procedures for bilingual education and to analyze available curriculum and adapt it for bilingual instruction in the English and Spanish languages.

Robinett directed this afternoon portion of the six-week workshop with the assistance of three Cuban refugee educators who previously had acquired considerable experience in English as a Second Language instruction and bilingual schooling while working in Cuba. [5] While Robinett and his assistants met with the six North American teachers and six Cuban aides, Bell worked with the principal of Coral Way Elementary in the school's office developing a master schedule that would facilitate implementation of the model for bilingual schooling at the first three grade levels and Rojas managed the overall administrative tasks involved in initiating the innovative program.

By September, plans for the bilingual school program had been completed. In sum, students were to receive instruction in their first language in the mornings and in their second language in the afternoons. With the exception of the few students whose parents had selected the regular instructional program, all students in grades one, two, and three were categorized (by their former classroom teachers) as either Spanish-speaking or English-speaking and assigned to classes accordingly. There were to be four classes at each of the three grade levels, two with only English-speaking students and two with only Spanish-speaking students. Registration for the regular (non-bilingual) instructional program was so limited that only two classes were formed, a combined first and second grade plus one third grade. [6]

On Sept. 3, 1963, elementary and secondary schools throughout Dade County opened their doors to thousands of students for the beginning of a new school year. At Coral Way Elementary, approximately 350 first, second, and third graders became the first group in the United States to participate in a bilingual school program specifically designed for both native Spanish-speaking and native English-speaking students.

DEVELOPING A PROGRAM

In designing the bilingual instructional program for Coral Way Elementary, the planners were convinced that students could be provided with a comprehensive elementary school curriculum, including reading, mathematics, science, social studies, art and music, in spite of the fact that one-half of the instruction would be presented in the child's second language. The rationale for this conviction, based upon research in America and abroad, was that children can naturally transfer skills from one language to another.[7] The students participating in the bilingual school program, therefore, would acquire all of the concepts and skills that their peers were acquiring in traditional (unilingual) school programs. The students in the bilingual school program would, in addition, acquire second-language skills that were not being taught in the traditional programs.

The planners also believed in the mother-tongue sequence of language learning, that is, listening, speaking, reading, and writing.[8] An audio-lingual approach, therefore, was chosen as part of the basic method employed for both first and second-language instruction within the bilingual school program.

Defining the Aims

Back in the spring of 1963, Rojas developed seven instructional objectives for the experimental program at Coral Way Elementary. They were based on assumptions that had been developed through research and personal experiences. The goals were these:

1. The participating pupil will have achieved as much in the way of skills, abilities, and understandings as he would have had he attended a monolingual school and in addition will have derived benefits which he could not have attained in a traditional school.

2. He will be approximately as proficient in his second language as he is in his first. If he is a skilled reader in his first language, he will be a skilled reader in his second language. If he has mastered the fundamental processes and concepts in arithmetic in one language, he will handle them equally well in the other language. If he can express himself clearly and adequately in his first language, he will be able to do likewise in the other language.

3. He will be able to operate in either culture easily and comfortably.

4. He will have acquired consciously or unconsciously an understanding of the symbolic nature of language and as a result will be able to achieve greater objectivity in his thinking processes.

5. In general terms, he will be more acceptive of strange people and cultures and will thus increase the range of his job opportunities.

6. He will have skills, abilities, and understandings which will greatly extend his vocational potential and thus increase his usefulness to himself and the world in which he lives.

7. He will broaden his understanding of people and the world and be able to live a richer, fuller, and more satisfying personal life.[9]

No major alterations were made during the 1960's in the program's objectives for developing basic language skills or attitudes. Eight years of experience with bilingual education and increased sophistication of local educators in the statement of performance objectives, however, led to a restatement of these objectives in behavioral terms in 1971:

The effectiveness of a Bilingual School Organization can be assessed in relation to the achievement of these objectives:

a. Pupils demonstrate, in the English language, achievement in reading and mathematics skills equal to the achievement of comparable pupils who do not participate in the Bilingual School Organization.

b. English language origin pupils demonstrate language skills in Spanish which are superior to those demonstrated by non-participating English language origin students at the same age level who have had a comparable number of years of instruction in Spanish as a foreign language.

c. Spanish language origin pupils demonstrate language skills in Spanish which are superior to those demonstrated by non-participating Spanish language origin pupils at the same age level.

d. Pupils demonstrate a knowledge of Hispanic history and culture which is superior to the knowledge of non-participating pupils who have had a similar number of years of instruction in Spanish as a foreign language.

e. Within six years of continuous exposure to a Bilingual School Organization in which equal time is devoted to instruction in both languages, all pupils achieve objectives *a* through *d* and, in addition, achieve approximately as much proficiency in the second language as they do in their first language, as measured by an achievement instrument with parallel forms in English and in Spanish.[10]

Recruiting and Training Teachers

During the school years immediately preceding the introduction of the bilingual school program, the instructional staff at Coral Way Elementary was comprised of regular classroom teachers, Cuban aides, and supplementary personnel. In September, 1963, 25 classroom teachers had been assigned to the school. As noted above, six of these classroom teachers were Cuban refugees with "temporary" teacher certificates in the State of Florida after having successfully completed the Cuban Teacher Retraining Program. In subsequent years, some teachers at Coral Way Elementary reached retirement age and terminated their employment with the Dade County Public Schools. As the bilingual school program spread upward by one grade level each year, a few American teachers at the intermediate level (grades four, five, and six) requested transfers to other schools. These vacancies were filled with Cuban teachers so that the Spanish language portion of the instructional program could be presented at all grade levels.

Meanwhile, the student population at Coral Way Elementary had increased from 761 students in September, 1963, to 1,375 students in September, 1972. The fact that the number of students almost doubled during these nine years resulted in an annual increase in the percentage of teacher positions allocated by the school system to Coral Way Elementary. This enabled the school's principal to employ more teachers who were native Spanish-speakers. By 1972, 25 of the 45 classroom teachers at Coral Way Elementary were from Spanish-speaking backgrounds. Each of these 25 teachers was a functional bilingual, able to present instruction in either the Spanish or the English languages.

With the initial increase in Cuban refugee students at Coral Way Elementary during the 1962-63 school year, a total of four Cuban aides were assigned to the school the following September. As indicated in Figure 10, the increase in student enrollments each subsequent year was almost invariably the result of the influx of Cuban refugee families into the school's community; consequently, by 1972, the number of Cuban aide positions allocated to the school had increased from four to nine. These aides were responsible for the following:

1. Assisting in follow-up activities in English as a Second Language (ESL) classes.
2. Assisting in instruction in Spanish for Spanish-speakers (Spanish-S).
3. Assisting in communication between home and school, between pupil and school.
4. Assisting in instruction in Spanish as a Second Language (Spanish-SL) classes and in classes where curriculum is presented in the Spanish language (CCS).
5. Planning with other teachers for ESL, Spanish S, and Spanish-SL instruction.
6. Assisting in the library and/or the school office.[11]

Significant yearly increases in student membership and changes in the county school system's staffing policies resulted also in an increase in supplementary personnel. Allocations for teachers of music, art, and physical education at the school increased. A helping teacher, a visiting-teacher-counselor, a reading teacher, and a special education teacher were assigned to work at the school as was an additional librarian, a North American who was bilingual in English and Spanish. In addition to the English as a Second Language orientation teacher for newly arriving Spanish-speaking students, a Spanish as a Second Language orientation teacher was employed to prepare new English-speaking enrollees for instruction in the Spanish language..

Number of Children Enrolled	1963 - 1964	1967 - 1968	1970 - 1971

TOTAL ENROLLMENT: '63-'64 — 785

TOTAL ENROLLMENT: '67-'68 — 1009

TOTAL ENROLLMENT: '70-'71 — 1400

Native Spanish-speaking   Native English-speaking

Source: Adapted from "We Like Two . . . ¿y Tú?," Description of the Bilingual Program of Coral Way Elementary School, Dade County Public Schools, Miami, Florida, 1971, p. 3.

Figure 10   Enrollment at Coral Way Elementary School (1963-1971)

No exceptions to Dade County School Board policies were exercised in the employment of staff members for Coral Way Elementary. During the first years of the bilingual school program, however, a special hiring committee screened applicants very closely.[12] As the school's principal noted, "it readily became apparent that the unique needs of a bilingual school would require special personnel with special qualities. Some of the criteria the committee used to guide them in selecting teachers for the school were these:

1. Teachers, preferably perfectly bilingual, should teach in their native tongues.
2. They should themselves be bicultural as well as keenly interested in bilingual education.
3. They should have demonstrated an unusual competence in working with team members and aides in a climate of kindness, patience, and understanding.
4. They should have a linguistics and language structures background and be willing to undertake additional advanced training in this area.
5. They should be anxious to further the study of their second language.
6. They should be especially creative in designing and using a variety of visual aids.
7. They should possess proven power to maintain poise while being observed by frequent visitors and, furthermore, to communicate to them as well as to skeptical parents the philosophy of a bilingual school." [13]

Structuring the Bilingualism

The organization of the bilingual school was limited by some of the restraints which had gone into the choice of the type of school and its stated objectives.

In the first place, Coral Way was essentially a biethnic school. In the early sixties, models for such schools had to be sought abroad, either in some of the two hundred binational schools throughout the world or in the growing number of international schools. Secondly, the type and degree of bilinguality had to be determined. Would it be one of structured allocation or one of free alternation in the use of both languages? [14] Thirdly, there was the question of determining the bicultural or ethnic mix that would promote bilingual inter-pupil and teacher-pupil interaction, and which one of some four dozen ways of mixing students with languages would be included in the classroom structure (see Appendix B).

Important factors entering into the structure of bilingual schools had to be considered:

a) the *time factor* allowed for each of the languages;
b) the *treatment* and *use* of each language;
c) whether the language which is added to the previously existing system is the mother tongue or not.

One also had to determine whether individual instructors teach in one or both languages, whether one or two languages are employed within an individual class period, the relative socio-economic status of native speakers of each of the languages, and the relative prestige of each. [15]

The overall time-line for the bilingual school program began at the outset of the 1963-64 school year with implementation at the first three grade levels. By extending the bilingual school program to one new grade level each year, the students who participated initially in the primary grades would be able to continue to receive bilingual instruction throughout their years in elementary school. The overall plan was successful, and, by the 1966-67 school year, the instructional program for all students in grades one through six (plus the kindergarten) was presented in both the English and the Spanish languages (see Figure 11). Within the overall plan, however, the specific schedules for teachers and students were altered almost annually.

The bilingual school program progressed through three basic organizational phases. In the beginning, students were grouped within grade level according to their first language, Spanish or English. Each class of students received a full academic program in their first language in the mornings. At mid-day, all students at a particular grade level were brought together for art, music, physical education, and lunch. Teachers, Cuban aides, and students were free to

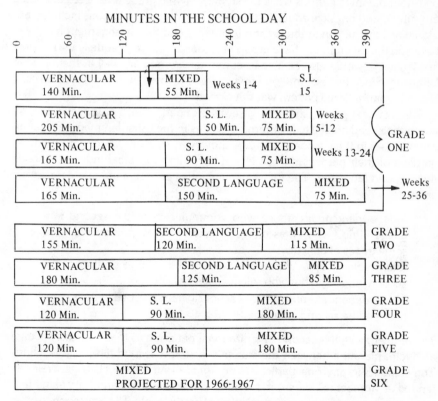

MINUTES IN THE SCHOOL DAY

| 0 | 60 | 120 | 180 | 240 | 300 | 360 | 390 |

VERNACULAR 140 Min.	MIXED 55 Min.	Weeks 1-4	S.L. 15	
VERNACULAR 205 Min.	S. L. 50 Min.	MIXED 75 Min.	Weeks 5-12	GRADE ONE
VERNACULAR 165 Min.	S. L. 90 Min.	MIXED 75 Min.	Weeks 13-24	
VERNACULAR 165 Min.	SECOND LANGUAGE 150 Min.	MIXED 75 Min.	Weeks 25-36	

VERNACULAR 155 Min.	SECOND LANGUAGE 120 Min.	MIXED 115 Min.	GRADE TWO
VERNACULAR 180 Min.	SECOND LANGUAGE 125 Min.	MIXED 85 Min.	GRADE THREE
VERNACULAR 120 Min.	S. L. 90 Min.	MIXED 180 Min.	GRADE FOUR
VERNACULAR 120 Min.	S. L. 90 Min.	MIXED 180 Min.	GRADE FIVE
MIXED PROJECTED FOR 1966-1967			GRADE SIX

Vernacular and *second language* (S. L.) mean the use of these as mediums of instruction. *Mixed* in grades 1-3 means physical education, art and music only. In grades 4-6 *mixed* also means combined classes of Anglos and Cubans alternating 3 weeks of each grading period working through English only, and 3 weeks working through Spanish only, in all subjects.

Source: Coral Way Elementary: Time Distribution Pattern. Miami, Florida, 1967.

Figure 11   Coral Way Time Distribution Pattern: 1967

use either language during these periods so that students would be able to hear and to use both their first and second languages in relaxed, non-classroom-type situations. In the afternoons, the class groups within each grade level exchanged rooms, and the students received instruction in their second language. The afternoon's instructional program was essentially a reinforcement, enrichment, and extension of the concepts developed in the students' first language during the morning sessions.

During this first organizational phase, students were grouped for instruction in the morning sessions by their ability to read in their first language. English-speaking teachers and Spanish-speaking teachers at each grade level were paired up in teams of two. Each teacher merely exchanged his or her class group with the other teacher's class group in the afternoon. This direct exchange enabled each pair of teachers to work together during their mutual, one-hour planning periods while the students at that grade level were attending art, music, and physical education classes. The afternoon sessions included audio-lingual instruction in the second language, and this arrangement had been based on the assumption that a group of students who read equally well in their first language would also be able to communicate equally well in their second language. Since this assumption proved to be incorrect in a number of cases, a second organizational pattern was developed.

In this next phase, students were still grouped at each grade level according to their reading ability for morning classes in their first language. For afternoon classes in their second language, however, students were regrouped, regardless of their particular grade levels, according to verbal independence in their second language. The following categories of verbal independence were created:

> *Independent pupils,* those who communicate in the second language almost as well as native speakers, although they still have some traces of difficulty.
> *Intermediate pupils,* those who understand a large portion of the second language, but who still need special attention.
> *Non-independent pupils,* those seriously handicapped in their command of the second language. [16]

The problem with this second organizational pattern was that it virtually eliminated joint planning between the students' first and second-language teachers. The students in any one particular, non-graded afternoon class generally attended a number of different morning classes with different first-language teachers representing a number of different grade levels. The afternoon teacher was not able to consult with all of the students' morning teachers, therefore, reinforcement and enrichment in the second language for each student in an afternoon group became impossible. In order to rectify this situation, the school's assistant principal developed a third framework for scheduling within the school.

In this final organizational phase, grouping for first-language classes in the mornings continued to be based upon students' abilities to read in their native language (high, average, or low). The viable features for second-language grouping that were established during the first and second organizational phases were combined. Students were still grouped in terms of their "verbal independence" in their second language but only within their own grade level. This procedure led to cross-exchanges of students within each grade level from the morning groups to the afternoon groups; however, during their common planning period, teachers were able to plan with all of the other teachers at their own particular grade level and to coordinate the morning and the afternoon's instructional programs. In 1970, the school's principal listed some of the activities at these grade level planning meetings:

1. Cultural differences are discussed.
2. Pedagogical ideas are exchanged and discussed.
3. Research is reviewed.
4. Methods and techniques are demonstrated.
5. Printed materials are evaluated.
6. Seatwork and other materials are constructed.
7. Follow-up work in the second language is planned.
8. Behavioral objectives are discussed and written.
9. New materials are reviewed.
10. Individual instruction of pupils is planned.
11. Placement of pupils is determined.
12. Informal meetings are held with subject-area and other consultants.
13. Language patterns are written and discussed.
14. A continuous awareness of the linguistic approach to teaching a second language is stressed.
15. Progress and needs of individual pupils are discussed by the team.
16. Personal problems of individual pupils are discussed by the team. [17]

To recapitulate, in the mornings, the students at Coral Way Elementary were grouped within grade levels with students who shared the same first language and demonstrated similar abilities to read in that first language (see Figure 12). In the afternoons, they were grouped within their particular grade level with students who demonstrated comparable abilities to speak and understand the second language. A North American teacher provided a full day's academic program in the morning to a group of students with English as their first language and similar abilities to read in English. In the afternoon, this teacher provided reinforcement, enrichment, and extension of the morning's program for a group of students who had demonstrated comparable abilities to speak and understand English as a second language. The bilingual Cuban teachers did the

CLASSES (student groups)	FIRST LANGUAGE INSTRUCTION (Mornings, one hour each)		SECOND LANGUAGE INSTRUCTION (Afternoons, one hour each)	
Native ENGLISH-SPEAKING	English Language Arts (ELA)	Curriculum Content in English (CCE-E)	Spanish as a Second Language (Spanish-SL)	Curriculum Content in Spanish (CCS-E)
Native SPANISH-SPEAKING	Spanish for Spanish-Speakers (Spanish-S)	Curriculum Content in Spanish (CCS-S)	English as a Second Language (ESL)	Curriculum Content in English (CCE-S)

NOTES
The shaded squares represent the additional components for bilingual education at Coral Way Elementary.

English as a Second Language (ESL) classes were presented by regular classroom teachers for the large majority of non-native English-speaking students. In addition, a special orientation program in English as a Second Language was provided for newly enrolled students. As soon as these students were able to perform effectively in the English language portion of the instructional program, they were transferred to an English as a Second Language class under a regular classroom teacher.

Figure 12   The First Model of Elementary Bilingual Schooling

Spanish counterpart by presenting instruction in the Spanish language to Spanish-speaking students in the mornings and to English-speaking students in the afternoons.

In sum, Coral Way Elementary became a school in which all pupils had the opportunity to become completely bilingual. It was thus the first public elementary school in the United States to offer such a program. It was a two-way bilingual school, each group learning through its own and the other's language.

Designing a Bilingual Curriculum

The curriculum comprised eight basic components, as shown in Figure 12. Four of these components were designed for the students with English as the home language. These included: English Language Arts (ELA), Curriculum Content in English (CCE-E), Spanish as a Second Language (Spanish-SL), and Curriculum Content in Spanish (CCS-E). The courses in English Language Arts (ELA) and Curriculum Content in English for students with English as a home language (CCE-E) were part of the regular instructional program for all elementary schools in Dade County. The courses in Spanish as a Second Language (Spanish-SL) and Curriculum Content in Spanish for students with English as the home language (CCS-E), at that time, were unique to the county's first bilingual school. The other four components, designed for students with Spanish as a home language, were: Spanish for Spanish-Speakers (Spanish-S), Curriculum Content in Spanish (CCS-S), English as a Second Language (ESL), and Curriculum Content in English (CCE-S). The instructional programs in Curriculum Content in English for the Spanish home-language group (CCE-S) and also the English as a Second Language (ESL) classes were adapted from the regular curricular program of the Dade County Public Schools.[18] The course in Spanish for Spanish-Speakers (Spanish-S) had been initiated two years earlier in a few schools, and the Curriculum Content in Spanish for the Spanish home-language group students (CCS-S) was a component developed especially for the bilingual school.

One of the main features of the bilingual curriculum, however, was the creation of a bilingual atmosphere within the school. A Spanish section was established in the library at Coral Way Elementary with more than 3,000 books and other resource materials in the Spanish language. Teachers, aides, office personnel, and students were permitted to use their first language (whether it was English or Spanish) and encouraged to use their second language in the halls, the school office, the cafeteria, and on the playground. Whenever necessary, conferences between Spanish-speaking parents or students and English-speaking school administrators or teachers were held in the Spanish language with the help of bilingual staff members. All printed messages to the students' homes were reproduced in both the English and the Spanish languages. Opening comments at meetings of the school's Parents and Teachers Organization were presented in both languages; and, upon request, bilingual staff members translated the remainder of the proceedings for groups of Spanish-speaking or English-speaking parents. In addition, special programs conducted in both languages were organized at the school to celebrate North American and Cuban holidays.

Finding Materials and Resources

All of the resources such as curriculum materials, instructional personnel, audio-visual equipment, and internal funds that were given to other public elementary schools in Dade County were also available to Coral Way Elementary before and after the initiation of the bilingual school program. Yet, no additional resources were allocated. During the first year of the experimental program, the three Cuban aides represented the only over-staffing of the school;[19] however, Cuban aides were assigned equally to all of the public schools in Dade County that enrolled a large number of Cuban refugee students. A few individuals, who did not receive their salaries from the regular budget of the Dade County Public Schools, however, acted as planners, organizers, and staff development leaders for the county's first bilingual school.[20]

Initially, publishing firms in Spain and Latin American countries were the major resources for curricular materials in the Spanish language. Local and national school supply companies began to specialize in the importation of these items in the late 1960's. The Cuban Refugee Program, as part of its general reimbursement to the Dade County Public Schools, provided funds for acquisition of instructional materials in the Spanish language and special equipment for bilingual education.[21]

Perhaps the key resource for bilingual schooling in Dade County was the availability of a large number of trained teachers from Spanish-speaking backgrounds that were able to present the Spanish language portion of the instructional program. In the continental United States, during the early sixties, this particular resource was unique to Dade County. Many of the former teachers and university professors from Cuba applied for positions as Cuban aides shortly after their arrival in the Miami area. If they were not already functional bilinguals, most of these refugees rapidly mastered communication skills in the English language. Many of the Cuban aides soon qualified for teacher certification in the State of Florida, and they were then hired as regular classroom teachers at Coral Way Elementary and other schools throughout the county.

SOLVING THE PROBLEMS

A number of problems related to the bilingual school program at Coral Way Elementary developed as time went on. Maintaining an equal numerical balance between English home-language and Spanish home-language children within the student population became one of the major problems. From the very beginning of the Cuban refugee influx into Dade County, the neighborhood surrounding Coral Way Elementary acquired a reputation as a popular area for Cuban refugees to buy or to rent houses. By 1963, the percentage of Spanish-speaking residents in the school's attendance area had risen to approximately 50 percent. This even division between native Spanish-speaking and English-speaking residents was one of the primary reasons why Coral Way Elementary had been selected to implement the Ford Foundation project in bilingual schooling. Rather than stabilizing at that point in time, however, the ethnic characteristics of the school's community continued to become more and more Cuban. As indicated in Figure 10, the overall student population had almost doubled between the 1963-64 and the 1970-71 school year, and the proportion of Spanish-speaking students in the school rose to more than 80 percent.[22]

Strict desegregation guidelines from the United States federal courts that were designed to establish equal educational opportunities for students of all races within the Dade County Public Schools, coupled with the local school board policies, prevented school officials from adjusting the attendance zone for Coral Way Elementary. It was impossible, therefore, to maintain or to regain the equal balance of Spanish and English-speaking children that had existed in 1963. With a larger percentage of Spanish-speaking students enrolling each year, modifications were required in grouping patterns, staffing, and program organization within the bilingual school. For example, each year more and more Spanish home-language students transferring to Coral Way Elementary from non-bilingual school programs were found to be more proficient in the English language than in the Spanish language. Instead of placing these students in the sequence of courses for the native Spanish-speakers, they were placed in the classes with native English-speakers.

The overall increase in student membership at Coral Way Elementary each year also enabled the school's staff to refine the class groupings even further. Special groups were formed at the upper grade levels where both Spanish and English could be employed as first languages for instructional purposes. A number of native Spanish-speaking students and a few native English-speaking students who had learned to function well in either language were assigned to these groups. Cuban teachers were also hired to fill most of the vacancies and new positions on the faculty each year so that the school's staff would be able to present most of the first-language classes in Spanish to the predominantly Spanish-speaking student body. These modifications, along with other organizational adjustments, compensated for the annual decrease in the percentage of students with English as a home language.

A second major problem that emerged was the failure to attain the goal of developing a high level of bilingualism among students whose only home-language was English. One of the seven original program objectives had been that the participating pupil "will be approximately as proficient in his second language as he is in his first. If he is a skilled reader in his first language, he will be a skilled reader in his second language . . ."[23] In 1966, students were tested in their first and second languages, and it was reported that they "were not as proficient in their second language as they were in their native language at the end of the third year of the bilingual program."[24] In 1970, another evaluation of students' abilities to read in English and Spanish was made in Coral Way Elementary, in two other elementary schools with bilingual school programs, and in three elementary schools without bilingual school programs. The results for Coral Way Elementary indicated that "Spanish language origin students had equal reading proficiency in Spanish and English in all grade levels tested", but "English language origin students read significantly better in their native language". These test results also indicated, on the other hand, that most students attending a bilingual school progressed as rapidly in the English language as their contemporaries in traditional school programs.[25]

The fact that most English-speaking students attending the bilingual school continued to maintain superior skills in English was not perceived as a program weakness but as a logical outcome of their living in an English-speaking environment. Along with the bicultural objectives of the program, however, as indicated by a statement of the overall goal for the bilingual school program in 1972, equal proficiency in both languages was maintained as the linguistic target:

"The ultimate goal of the program is to produce bilingual and bicultural individuals who can communicate orally and in writing in both languages with proficiency commensurate with their experiential and educational level, age, and interests, and who can interact with equal effectiveness with members of both cultures."[26]

The scheduling of all students in first through sixth grades for first-language instruction in the mornings and second-language instruction in the afternoons also created some problems. It was obviously more difficult for students to receive instruction in their second language. Teachers in grades one, two, and three found that the younger children were just too tired in the afternoons to perform adequately in their second language. In 1970, therefore, the schedule was reversed in the primary grade levels and these children received instruction in their second language in the mornings and in their first language in the afternoons.

Scheduling of team planning periods by grade levels, an integral feature in the presentation of each student's instructional program in two languages by two or more teachers, eventually presented problems at Coral Way Elementary. The increase in the number of students enrolling each year and the resultant increase in the number of classes at each grade level, however, provided some flexibility within the school's master schedule from year to year. By 1972, it was possible once again to release all teachers at a particular grade level from instructional responsibilities for a mutual, one-hour planning period (as originally intended) during each school day.

The difficulty of involving the Spanish-speaking parents in the school's Parents and Teachers Organization was a problem that Coral Way Elementary shared with other elementary schools in the county. Although the proportion of English-speaking students at Coral Way Elementary decreased each year, positions of leadership in the Parents and Teachers Organization almost always were occupied by mothers with English as a home language. It seemed that the mothers (and fathers) of Spanish-speaking students did not feel culturally comfortable attending the meetings of this type of organization. These parents frequently reported that they simply did not have the time nor the desire to leave their younger children at home in order to go to the school for meetings. The school's administration, on the other hand, realized that it needed to communicate with this ethnic group within the school's community. Meetings of the Parents and Teachers Organization were usually the main means of achieving this interaction. Beginning the meetings in both English and Spanish, appointing a Cuban refugee to the assistant principal's position, and providing bilingual translators at all meetings helped to solve this communication gap between the school's staff and the majority of the students' homes.

As one would expect, a number of other problems related to the introduction of a bilingual school program emerged at Coral Way Elementary, and alternative procedures and solutions were implemented on an on-going basis.

EVALUATING THE MODEL

By the late 1960's, there were several indications that the bilingual school program at Coral Way Elementary had been successful. One such indication was the determination by teachers at the upper grade levels that learning had become equally effective through either English or Spanish for a number of students. This discovery resulted in the introduction of bilingual classes where both languages were used interchangeably for instruction. Another indication was the result on successive administrations of the Cooperative Inter-American Tests. The students' performance on the equated forms in English and Spanish revealed that their learning curves were beginning to coincide in both languages.[27] In addition, Bell reported in 1969 that the students at Coral Way Elementary were learning to operate effectively in two languages and in two cultures. They were broadening their understanding of other people, and they were being prepared to live satisfying lives and to contribute to their bicultural community and their country.[28]

The ability of the staff at Coral Way Elementary to adjust to unforeseen complications, to modify program features as time went on, and to continue to present bilingual instruction for both ethnic groups provided considerable credibility, at both the local and national levels, to this innovative concept of bilingual schooling within the United States. After a series of visits to Coral Way Elementary in 1966, the principal of Central Beach Elementary School on Miami Beach asked the county's Coordinator of Bilingual Education to assist him in organizing a variation of the Coral Way model for bilingual schooling. His adaptation constituted a significant test of how generalized the model could become.

Notes

1. Joseph Lee Logan, principal of Coral Way Elementary from 1960 until 1972. Born and educated in the United States, Logan was a public school principal in the State of West Virginia before moving to Miami in 1945. When he retired from the Dade County Public Schools in 1972, Logan continued to reside in Miami and worked occasionally as an educational consultant.

2. Ralph F. Robinett, born in 1924 in the United States. After completing his formal education within the continental United States, Robinett moved to the island of Puerto Rico and began his career as a classroom teacher. Within a few years, he became a specialist in English as a Second Language for Puerto Rico's Department of Education. It was in this capacity, in 1949, that Robinett first met Pauline Rojas. She was the Director of the English Program in Puerto Rico, and, during the 1950's, Robinett worked on Rojas' staff producing the *Fries American English Series*.

    In 1963, Rojas asked Robinett, who had succeeded her as Director of the English Program in Puerto Rico, to come to Miami to direct the curriculum development segments of the Ford Foundation Projects in Bilingual Education. In fact, Rojas stated that she would not have committed herself to the Ford Foundation Projects in Bilingual Education if Robinett had not agreed to lead the curriculum development efforts that, by 1966, produced the *Miami Linguistic Readers*. This language program was used extensively within Dade County and other areas of the United States for initial reading instruction in the English language for native Spanish-speaking students at the primary grade levels.

    After the completion of the Ford Foundation Projects in Bilingual Education, Robinett moved to the northern United States to direct a special project that developed curriculum for the children of migrant laborers. In 1970, he returned to Miami as project manager of the Spanish Curricula Development Center, a federal program that created instructional materials in the Spanish language to support bilingual education programs in elementary schools throughout the United States. In addition to his responsibilities as manager of this national project, Robinett was appointed Director of Bilingual Programs for the Dade County Public Schools in 1974.

3. Paul W. Bell, "The Bilingual School," a paper presented at the annual meeting of the International Reading Association, Detroit, Mich., May 3-4, 1965, pp. 2-4.

4. Rosa G. Inclan, one of the leading educators among the Cuban refugees who settled in Dade County in the early 1960's. Born in Havana, Cuba, in 1921, Inclan had studied in the United States as well as Cuba. She was the director of the training program for teachers of English as a Second Language at the University of Havana before her departure for the United States in 1960. Following her initial involvement in bilingual education in Miami with the Ford Foundation Projects in Bilingual Education (1963-66), Inclan was employed by the Dade County Public Schools; and, in 1969, she was appointed to the position of Coordinator of Bilingual Education for the school system.

5. One of these three Cuban refugee educators was Rosa G. Inclan. The second one was Herminia Cantero. Born in Las Villas province in Cuba in 1915, Cantero was the supervisor of English as a Second Language instruction in elementary and secondary schools in Cuba before departing for the United States in 1961. In fact, Cantero had employed Pauline Rojas as a consultant for the English as a Second Language program in Cuba; and, soon after her arrival in Miami, Rojas hired Cantero to work with the Ford Foundation Projects in Bilingual Education. At the termination of this special project, Cantero was employed by the Dade County Public Schools and, in 1973, was appointed as one of the coordinators for the school system's bilingual instructional programs.

    The third Cuban refugee educator, Illuminada Valle, was born in Cuba in 1922. She was a teacher in a private bilingual school in Havana before leaving Cuba in 1961. Valle settled in the Miami area and worked as a Cuban aide and then as a second-language teacher in Dade County's first bilingual school (Coral Way Elementary). In 1974, Valle was appointed to be the assistant principal of that school.

6. Supra Note 3

7. "We like Two . . .y Tu?" Description of the Coral Way Elementary School, Dade County Public Schools, Miami, Fla., 1971, pp. 4, 11.

8. Ibid.

9. Supra Note 3

10. Division of Instruction, *Procedures Manual: Bilingual Education Program*, Bulletin 1-C. Dade County Public Schools, Miami Fla., 1971, pp. 53-54, 58-59,63.

11. Ibid.

12. The hiring committee was comprised of the school's principal and assistant principal plus Bell. Bell was included because, in addition to his coordinating responsibilities with the Ford Foundation Projects in Bilingual Education, he was the Coordinator of Special English (English as a Second Language) at that time for the Dade County Public Schools.

13. J. Lee Logan, "One Will Do But We Like Two". *The National Elementary Principal*, November, 1970, pp. 86-87.

14. William F. Mackey, *Bilingual Education in a Binational School*. Rowley: Newbury House, 1972.

15. A. Bruce Gaarder, "Organization of the Bilingual School", *The Journal of Social Issues*, Vol. XXIII No. 2 (Apr., 1967), pp. 110-111, 115; R. C. Gardner and W. E. Lambert, *Attitudes and Motivation in Second-Language Learning*. Rowley: Newbury House, 1972.

16. Supra Note 7

17. Supra Note 13

18. Special orientation classes in English as a Second Language were provided for non-English-speaking students until these students were able to function effectively in the English-language portion of the bilingual program.

19. Supra Note 3

20. During the initial stages and throughout the duration of the Ford Foundation Projects in Bilingual Education (January, 1963, through June, 1966), some of the employees of this private foundation's program in Dade County worked intermittently at Coral Way Elementary. Rojas provided her expertise in planning and administrative support. Robinett was the technical expert for Coral Way Elementary; and, prior to his total involvement in the materials development segments of the Ford Foundation Projects in Bilingual Education, Robinett led and directed the school's staff in their efforts to develop, adapt, organize, and present an appropriate instructional program in both the English and the Spanish languages. Bell was responsible for the overall organization of the bilingual program and all staff development activities.

21. Supra Note 10

22. Department of Administrative Research, *Desegregation: September, 1971,* vol. XIX, no. 2. Dade County Public Schools, Miami, Fla., 1971, p. 26.

23. Supra Note 3

24. Mabel W. Richardson, "An Evaluation of Certain Aspects of the Academic Achievement of Elementary Pupils in a Bilingual Program," unpublished doctoral dissertation, University of Miami, 1968, p. 63.

25. Department of Program Evaluation, *Evaluation of Programs for Spanish Language Origin Students, 1970-71,* Dade County Public Schools, Miami, Fla., 1972, pp. 55, 58-59.

26. Dade County Public Schools, *Program Budget for Fiscal Year 1972-73,* Miami, Fla., 1972, p. 35.

27. Supra Note 24

28. Paul Bell, "Bilingual Education in an Elementary American School" in H. H. Stern (ed.), *Languages and the Young School Child.* London: Oxford University Press, 1969, p. 118.

6

Adapting the
Biethnic Model

A second bilingual school program for native Spanish-speaking and native English-speaking students in Dade County began in September, 1966, at Central Beach Elementary. A number of the tested features of the county's first bilingual school program at Coral Way Elementary were adopted; however, the organizational framework and some of the instructional components in the second bilingual school program were new.

DIFFERENCES IN THE SCHOOL COMMUNITY

As the center of tourism in Dade County shifted from Miami to southern Miami Beach in the 1920's, Central Beach Elementary was constructed two blocks inland from the oceanfront (see map in Chapter 7).[1] The school's community was essentially comprised of upper income families, and the school's population rose to 1,200 students. Along with the junior and senior high school, Central Beach Elementary was considered to be part of an excellent school system not only for year-around residents of southern Miami Beach, but also for seasonal tourists.

As the years passed and the lucrative tourist industry moved further and further northward along Miami Beach, many senior citizens and some low income families began to move into the older section surrounding the school. There was a significant decrease in student enrollments; and, after the mid-sixties, less than 500 students enrolled at Central Beach Elementary each school year. The school's surrounding neighborhood had become one of low-cost residential hotels and apartment buildings. By 1973, the area was described as one of the 14 "poverty pockets" in Dade County: "The 41,657 residents, most of them elderly Jews who have retired from up north, have the lowest income ($4,605 a year) of any of the areas [in Dade County], and the highest percentage (79) paying more than they should for housing. The area has three times the population density of the county as a whole and nearly 30 percent of the units are overcrowded." [2]

When the Cuban refugees began to enter the Miami area in the early sixties, a number who worked in hotels, restaurants, and other tourist facilities settled in southern Miami Beach. Their children attended the public schools in the area. By 1966, the student population at Central Beach Elementary was equally divided between native English-speaking and Spanish-speaking children. This even balance remained fairly constant into the mid-1970's. [3] The presence of so many senior citizens in the school's attendance area and the refusal of some landlords to rent or to sell to families with young children prevented any significant increases in the number of students attending the school.

Although many of the children residing in the neighborhood of the school during the late sixties and the early seventies were Spanish-speaking, the school's attendance area also included three residential islands in nearby Biscayne Bay. Approximately 17 percent of the students had to travel to the school by bus from these islands. These children were almost invariably from English-speaking backgrounds. They represented middle and upper income families and generally achieved above average scores in standardized measurements of basic intelligence and performance. A number of these children's parents were influential members of the local community in the realms of business, politics, and the professions.

The principal of Central Beach Elementary [4] was the first school principal in Dade County to request a bilingual school program. When the student population at Central Beach Elementary became equally divided between native English-speaking and Spanish-speaking students in 1965, he became convinced that bilingualism would be a personal attribute for those residing in the area. [5] He therefore decided to extend the school's standard second-language program (English as a Second Language classes plus 30 minutes of daily instruction in oral Spanish) to a bilingual school program somewhat similar to the one at Coral Way Elementary. Both schools served communities that had become bilingual as a result of the influx of Cuban refugees, however, there was a significant difference between the linguistic characteristics of the two communities. Many of the Cuban students enrolling at Coral Way Elementary, when the county's first bilingual school program was introduced in 1963, were not able to communicate effectively in the English language. By 1966, many of the Spanish-speaking students residing in the attendance area of Central Beach Elementary were able to communicate in the English language and to participate effectively in the regular instructional program presented in the English language.

ORIENTING PARENTS AND TEACHERS

After the principal of Central Beach Elementary expressed his convictions to the county's Coordinator of Bilingual Education in January, 1966, an overall design was developed that would facilitate interaction between all children in the school by placing native English-speaking and Spanish-speaking students together in as many classes as possible during the school day. The principal's next step was to sell the idea to the students' parents. In late January, he requested a conference with the president of the school's Parents and Teachers Association, a mother of one of the students. The principal knew that the president, who lived on one of the residential islands in the school's attendance area, was influential locally and exceptionally energetic. If she believed in the merits of bilingual schooling, convincing other members of the community would be easier. After studying the local needs for bilingualism and biculturalism and the overall program design, she, in fact, did become convinced of the program's value. In turn, she approached other members of the Parents and Teachers Association to gain their support, and she and the principal brought up the plan at meetings of the association's executive board. Printed guidelines for implementing the bilingual school program, answers to general questions about bilingual education, and other informative documents were placed in the school office. The principal invited all parents to study these documents during the spring of 1966.

With very few exceptions, the Cuban parents did not have to be convinced of the merits of the idea. They had been accustomed to bilingual schooling in Cuba, and, from the very beginning, supported the plan. Some of the English-speaking parents, however, were reluctant to support the idea. Since 30 minutes of their children's school day had already been allocated to Spanish language instruction, they were opposed to any further reduction in the amount of time for instruction in the English language. Throughout February, March, and April, the school's principal and the president of the Parents and Teachers Association continued to discuss the plan individually with students' parents and community leaders and in small groups at the school. They assured the English-speaking parents that most of the school's instructional program would continue to be presented in the English language. They also explained that during the coming school year, the second-language program would be expanded to a bilingual school program only in the kindergarten, and the first, second, and third grades. In addition, parents were informed that participation by their children in the new program would be on a voluntary basis.

Although no formal assessment of the parents' opinions had been obtained and a few negative reactions were still being voiced, a memorandum was sent to the Superintendent of the Dade County Public Schools on Apr. 19, 1966, reporting general parent support. This memorandum also included a thorough explanation of the current instructional program at Central Beach Elementary, the proposal to extend the existent second-language program to a bilingual school program, and the adjustments that would be necessary.[6] Because there was indication of community support and evidence of thorough planning, administrative leaders of the Dade County Public Schools authorized the principal to implement the proposed bilingual school program.

During regularly scheduled faculty meetings that spring, the school principal informed his staff of the plans. With the assistance of the Coordinator of Bilingual Education, he explained that the program would be somewhat different from the county's first bilingual school program at Coral Way Elementary. Since additional Cuban aides would be appointed to the school for instruction in the Spanish language, there would be no need to replace monolingual teachers with bilingual teachers.

Most of the faculty was favorable to the overall concept of bilingual schooling. During the summer of 1966, the two Cuban aides assigned to the school during the previous year, the art teacher, and some of the regular classroom teachers participated voluntarily in a six-week summer workshop at Central Beach Elementary, funded by the Cuban Refugee Program. A bilingual teacher, who had taught in the bilingual school program at Coral Way Elementary since September, 1963, was assigned to direct this workshop and to act as coordinator of the bilingual school program at Central Beach Elementary during the first year. She trained the workshop participants in techniques of second-language instruction in English and Spanish and first-language instruction in Spanish. Under her guidance, appropriate instructional materials for the Spanish language portion of the program were either selected or prepared by the teachers.

By the end of August, the school principal and his staff were prepared to extend the school's standard second-language program in kindergarten, first, second, and third grades to a bilingual school program for native English and Spanish-speaking students. In a period of eight months, the program had been designed, the schedule established, the materials ordered or developed, the additional staff members employed, the faculty prepared, and support obtained from the school system's administrative leaders, the school staff, and the majority of the parents.

Initiating the second, rather than the first, bilingual school program in Dade County provided the principal of Central Beach Elementary with two distinct advantages: 1) previous acceptance within the county of the two-way biethnic type of bilingual instruction at the elementary school level, and 2) knowledgeable assistance of school personnel who had worked with the county's first bilingual school program. The school principal, however, was the one who had to accomplish most of the tasks required to initiate the second bilingual school program. He identified the need and originated the idea of expanding the second-language program at his school. He generated support among the parents, the local community, his staff, and his administrative superiors within the school system. With the assistance of the county's Coordinator of Bilingual Education, he developed the objectives and the basic design for the new bilingual school program, and, finally, he ensured that all of the preparations were completed by the end of the summer.

THE BILINGUAL INSTRUCTIONAL PROGRAM

A relatively standard introduction to communication skills in the Spanish language had been provided for English-speaking students at Central Beach Elementary, as well as other elementary schools in Dade County, since 1961. This program was based upon the Modern Language Association's Foreign Languages in the Elementary School (FLES) program which utilized brief radio and television broadcasts to schools as part of an audiolingual approach to foreign language instruction. Also, since the early sixties, special instruction in English as a Second Language had been provided at Central Beach Elementary for non-English-speaking students that had been categorized as "non-independent" or "intermediate" in their ability to communicate in the English language. In addition, during the 1965-66 school year, a Cuban aide had presented 30 minutes of daily instruction in Spanish for Spanish-Speakers (Spanish-S) at each grade level. This Spanish-S program, along with the English as a Second Language program, was part of a countywide program dating from the early sixties and funded by the local school system's Cuban Refugee Program (see chapter 8).

To expand the existent second-language program to a bilingual school program at the beginning of the 1966-67 school year, a new component, entitled Spanish CORE and Enrichment, was added to the instructional program at Central Beach Elementary. This new course was presented to mixed groups of native Spanish-speakers and English-speakers in kindergarten and grades one, two and three for 30 minutes each day. Spanish-S was still presented daily for 30 minutes to all the Spanish-speaking students. The curriculum of the Spanish FLES course, however, had been revised during the special workshop that summer, and the course was now called Spanish as a Second Language (Spanish-SL). English-speaking students at all grade levels, including intermediate grade levels (four-six), continued to participate in this revised second-language program for 30 minutes each day. Special classes in English as a Second Language were also continued for students whose oral proficiency in the English language impeded their progress in regular classrooms. Each year the Spanish CORE and Enrichment course was added to the instructional program at a higher grade level. By September, 1969, this course (along with Spanish-S and Spanish-SL) was being presented to all students in grades one through six at Central Beach Elementary.

Although 30 minutes of instructional time was allocated to language arts instruction in Spanish (Spanish-S or Spanish-SL) and 30 minutes provided for mediation of curricular content in the Spanish language (Spanish CORE and Enrichment), the majority of the instructional program at Central Beach Elementary continued to be presented in the English language for both ethnic groups. In 1970, the time allotment for each of the components presented in the Spanish language was increased to 45 minutes, thereby raising the total time for instruction in the Spanish language for both groups to 90 minutes a day. By comparison, at Coral Way Elementary, two hours of the school day (approximately one-half of the time provided for classroom instruction) had been allocated to instruction in the Spanish language. On the theoretical level, therefore, some educators debated whether Central Beach Elementary was a "bilingual school" or "an innovative, monolingual school with an expanded second language program."[7] Throughout the world, however, the designation "bilingual school" had been basically a question of local definition,[8] and Central Beach Elementary fulfilled all of the criteria established in 1971 for a Bilingual School Organization in the official procedures manual of the Dade County Public Schools. These were the following:

1. Spanish language origin and English language origin students are offered an organization of instruction which provides for: a) Second-language programs in Spanish and in English that enable the average student to attain an independent classification in oral proficiency in approximately three years; and b) Appropriate language arts programs in English and in Spanish (Spanish-S) which meet the county criteria.
2. Organization of instruction that provides for staged introduction of learning activities in Spanish in at least one subject in each of the two subject area groups below: a) Music, art, physical education, home economics, industrial arts, typing, shorthand. b) Social studies, science, mathematics.
3. Utilization of teachers and aides trained in teaching second-language and curriculum content in Spanish and in English.
4. Utilization of materials in English and in Spanish designed for native speakers of the language in their study of the various subject areas and of materials designed for second-language learners.[9]

Objectives

The bilingual school program at Central Beach Elementary was designed in the spring of 1966 in response to the emerging bilingual and bicultural characteristics of the school's community. The school's principal believed that it was the responsibility of the neighborhood school to promote mutual awareness and communication between the two ethnic groups attending the school and residing within the community.[10] Helping students to learn one another's native language and grouping them together for instruction in both languages was perceived as the most efficient way for the neighborhood school to initiate bicultural sensitivity, the primary objective of the bilingual school program at Central Beach Elementary.[11]

Staffing and Staff Development

One teacher specializing in English as a Second Language instruction and two Cuban aides had been assigned to Central Beach Elementary prior to the initiation of the bilingual school program. These three positions were funded by the Cuban Refugee Program and assigned by the county's Coordinator of Bilingual Education as a supplement to the regular number of classroom teachers allocated by the county's school system. This supplementary staffing procedure was extended in order to provide instructors for the Spanish language portion of the bilingual instructional program at the beginning of the 1966-67 school year. Under this policy, the principal would not be forced to replace monolingual, English-speaking teachers with bilingual, Spanish-speakers as had been the practice at Coral Way Elementary. Bilingual English-speaking teachers were almost impossible to find.

In September, 1966, four additional Cuban aides were assigned to Central Beach Elementary, raising the total number of these bilingual aides to six. Three of the aides worked as a team presenting the bilingual instructional program at the primary level (kindergarten plus grades one, two, and three). In grades four, five, and six, one of the newly-assigned Cuban aides taught the Spanish as a Second Language (Spanish-SL) classes for English-speakers while another Cuban aide presented the Spanish-S instruction to the native Spanish-speakers. The sixth Cuban aide was assigned to the school office to perform clerical work and to facilitate communication with Spanish-speaking students and parents. An experienced bilingual teacher from Coral Way Elementary joined the Central Beach Elementary staff to direct the bilingual instructional program during its first school year, 1966-67.[12]

As the bilingual school program was phased upward each school year to fourth, then fifth, and finally sixth grade, Central Beach Elementary became eligible for additional allocations of Cuban aides. During this three-year period, however, some of the Cuban aides who had been working at the school completed the Cuban Teacher Retraining Program at the University of Miami and obtained temporary teacher certification in the State of Florida. Rather than lose the services of the experienced Cuban aides who had achieved the status of teachers, some of these former Cuban aides were employed as "special Spanish teachers" at the school. For every two Cuban aides allocated to a school, county personnel policies permitted a school principal to employ one higher-salaried, special Spanish teacher. The number of Cuban aides and special Spanish teachers assigned to Central Beach Elementary, therefore, varied each school year.

During the 1972-73 school year, instruction in the Spanish language in all six grades plus kindergarten was presented by four special Spanish teachers and two Cuban aides. Also, one of the original two Cuban aides at Central Beach Elementary was promoted to Teacher on Special Assignment for Bilingual Education in the Northeast District of the Dade County Public Schools.[13] In addition to her responsibilities for coordinating instruction in the Spanish language and instruction in English as a Second Language in schools throughout the Northeast District, the Teacher on Special Assignment continued working at Central Beach Elementary presenting the Spanish language portion of the instructional program in grade one.

The student population at Central Beach Elementary declined from 481 pupils when the bilingual school program began in September, 1966,[14] to 416 pupils in September, 1972.[15] As a result, the allocation of regular classroom teachers and other personnel over the six-year period was reduced rather than increased. With few exceptions, the 13 regular classroom teachers in 1972 were monolingual in the English language. Along with the two special education teachers, the school secretary, and the school's cafeteria manager, however, most of the regular classroom teachers participated over the years in staff-development activities to enhance their bicultural sensitivity and their communication skills in the Spanish language. For example, during the 1966-67 school year, the entire instructional staff participated in a "self-study practicum" concerning three subject areas: 1) the bilingual program, 2) human relations, and 3) linguistics. [16]

Subsequently, a number of staff members enrolled in regular workshops for employees of the Dade County Public Schools, focusing upon instructional methodologies for second-language instruction in English or Spanish and first-language instruction in Spanish. These workshops, funded by the Cuban Refugee Program, were presented after school hours or during the summers. Also, during the 1970-71 school year, most of the teachers at Central Beach Elementary participated in a special year-long workshop at the school exploring the relationship between languages, social settings, and public education.[17] In addition, during the second half of the 1971-72 school year, Spanish-speaking teachers and Cuban aides attended a weekly workshop at the school to improve their pronunciation of the English language, while many of the English-speaking teachers attended a workshop in conversational Spanish in a nearby classroom. Besides improving the second-language skills of both groups of teachers, this simultaneous effort by the teachers (plus prior participation in staff-development activities) was one indication that the procedure for staffing at Central Beach Elementary was viable. If appropriate staff-development activities were provided, it appeared that Cuban aides and special Spanish teachers could be added to the staff of a new bilingual school rather than be employed as replacements for monolingual English-speaking classroom teachers.

Organization

During the six-year period from 1966 to 1972, under the leadership of four different school principals, the organizational structure for the bilingual school program at Central Beach Elementary remained virtually intact. The regular instructional program of the Dade County Public Schools was presented daily in the English language along with the original four components of the school's bilingual program:

1.   English as a Second Language (English-SL). Classes in American English Language and culture conducted mainly in English for pupils whose native language is not English.

2. Spanish for Spanish-Speakers (Spanish-S). Classes in Spanish language arts and culture for Spanish language origin students and bilingual English language origin students who are classified as independent in Spanish.
3. Spanish as a Second Language (Spanish-SL). Classes which provide instruction in Spanish to English language origin students who will ultimately study aspects of the regular curriculum in Spanish.
4. Curriculum Content in Spanish (CCS). Classes which provide instruction in Spanish dealing with the regular curriculum content which is normally taught in English in Dade County Schools.[18]

The title, not the content, of the fourth component was changed in 1971 from Spanish CORE and Enrichment to Curriculum Content in Spanish (CCS) in order to correspond to the terminology employed in the procedures manual for the overall bilingual education program in the Dade County Public Schools.

The organizational pattern of the bilingual school program at Central Beach Elementary differed from the pattern at Coral Way Elementary in two respects. First, 90 minutes rather than two hours were allocated for instruction in the Spanish language. Second, as indicated in Figure 13, students at Central Beach Elementary were scheduled for all instruction, except language arts, in biethnic classes in which both groups studied both Curriculum Content in English (CCE) and Curriculum Content in Spanish (CCS) together.

Students, regardless of their language background, were grouped for instruction in reading and mathematics in the English language in terms of their ability to perform these basic skills. The remainder of the daily curriculum in the English language, plus the Curriculum Content in Spanish (CCS) class, was presented to grade level groups representing both cultures and a wide range of academic abilities and interests. In the Curriculum Content in Spanish class (formerly called Spanish CORE and Enrichment), instruction was presented in the Spanish language by a special Spanish teacher or a Cuban aide. This class provided daily opportunities for Spanish-speaking students to help their English-speaking classmates. The special Spanish teacher or Cuban aide in this class generally assigned native Spanish-speakers and English-speakers to adjoining seats and used instructional activities that encouraged students to work in biethnic pairs or ethnically-mixed small groups.

In grades four, five, and six, students were grouped for instruction in Spanish-S and Spanish-SL on a non-graded basis. Spanish-speakers were grouped in Spanish-S classes with other fourth, fifth, and sixth grade students of comparable ability to understand, speak, read, and write Spanish. English-speakers received Spanish-SL instruction with other students from the three grade levels with comparable communication skills in their second language. In first, second, and third grades, however, students received instruction in Spanish-S or Spanish-SL in grade level groups. Similarly, English Language Arts

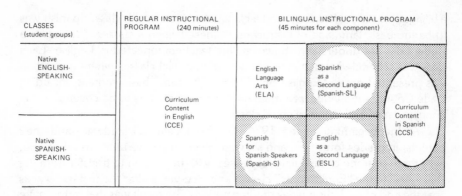

CLASSES (student groups)	REGULAR INSTRUCTIONAL PROGRAM (240 minutes)	BILINGUAL INSTRUCTIONAL PROGRAM (45 minutes for each component)		
Native ENGLISH-SPEAKING	Curriculum Content in English (CCE)	English Language Arts (ELA)	Spanish as a Second Language (Spanish-SL)	Curriculum Content in Spanish (CCS)
Native SPANISH-SPEAKING		Spanish for Spanish-Speakers (Spanish-S)	English as a Second Language (ESL)	

NOTES

The shaded squares represent the four additional components for bilingual education at Central Beach Elementary and South Beach Elementary.

English as a Second Language classes were presented by regular classroom teachers for the large majority of non-native English-speaking students. In addition, a special orientation program in English as a Second Language was provided for newly enrolled students. As soon as these students were able to perform effectively in the regular instructional program, they were transferred to an English as a Second Language class under a regular classroom teacher.

Figure 13   The Second Model of Elementary Bilingual Schooling

(ELA) and regular English as a Second Language classes (ESL) were presented to groups of students enrolled at the same grade level.

In summary, the instruction in the Spanish language at Central Beach Elementary was not presented as an isolated block during the school day. At any specific grade level, Spanish-speaking students received 45 minutes of instruction in Spanish-S while the English-speakers worked in English language Arts with the regular classroom teachers. Either the teachers or the students then exchanged classrooms, and the English-speaking students received 45 minutes of instruction in Spanish-SL while the Spanish-speakers worked in English as a Second Language with the regular classroom teachers. Immediately thereafter, or at some subsequent point during the school day, Spanish-speakers and English-speakers returned to their mixed grade level groups to receive 45 minutes of instruction in Curriculum Content in Spanish from one of the special Spanish teachers or Cuban aides. The curriculum content generally paralleled the topics taught in English including social studies, mathematics, science, and health. Art and music were employed during this instructional period to illustrate pertinent aspects of Latin-American culture.

During the 1973-74 school year, after some pilot testing, the Spanish language portion of the instructional program was reorganized in grades four, five, and six. The Spanish Language Arts component (Spanish-S or Spanish-SL) continued to be mandatory. The Spanish CORE (CCS) component was replaced at each of these three grade levels with a bilingual mathematics class, a bilingual social studies class, and a bilingual science-health class. Spanish was to be the basic language of instruction in these bilingual classes. Whenever a student did not understand, however, the teachers repeated in English. Each class was scheduled simultaneously with the parallel classes where instruction was presented on an "English only" basis. The same basic content, including Dade County's individualized mathematics program, was to be covered in the "English only" and in the bilingual classes.

At the beginning of the 1974-75 school year, all students (and their parents) in grades four, five, and six were given the opportunity to select one, two, three or none of the bilingual classes, with the option to transfer from the "bilingual" to the "English only" classes and vice-versa after the first two weeks or at the end of each nine-week grading period. The result was that most native Spanish-speakers and one-third of the native English-speaking students selected one or more bilingual alternative classes.

Curriculum

The English as a Second Language program at Central Beach Elementary was presented by regular classroom teachers, in addition to a specialist. The regular classroom teachers modified the county's English Language Arts program in order to present appropriate instruction for those Spanish-speaking students able to communicate relatively well in the English language. The specialist in the area of English as a Second Language worked with those non-English-speaking students who were unable to participate effectively in the regular instructional program due to their lack of mastery of the English language. The specialist utilized an audio-lingual approach in an effort to prepare these students as quickly as possible for the regular school program. The Cuban aides and special Spanish teachers also used audio-lingual techniques in their presentation of the Spanish-S and Spanish-SL programs.

The Curriculum Content in Spanish (CCS) program was a combination of the original "Spanish CORE" and "Enrichment" courses developed in 1966. Although, at that time, the curricular content for Spanish CORE differed from the content of the Enrichment portion, these two courses were frequently presented simultaneously or during the same time period on alternating days. As indicated in the original course descriptions, the Spanish CORE and Enrichment courses closely paralleled the reinforcement and enrichment classes presented during the afternoons at the county's first bilingual school, Coral Way Elementary. These course descriptions were:

> Spanish Core. The program groups both Spanish and English-speaking children for a period of 30 minutes daily. Once again there is a team-teaching approach used. Lessons which are planned by the English-speaking teacher in such subjects as science, health, social studies, and arithmetic are reinforced by the Spanish-speaking teacher.

Enrichment. The enrichment program provides a much needed opportunity for a reciprocal, cultural exchange between the native American and native Spanish children enabling each to derive basic cultural concepts from one another. Various informal activities such as songs, games, stories and listening experiences are the core of this 30 minute phase of the program. Both Spanish and English children are together so that they may have the opportunity to share each others' native expressions and pronunciations, along with the traditions that are unique to their respective lands. [19]

A bank of instructional materials for the Curriculum Content in Spanish (CCS) program was developed by the special Spanish teachers and Cuban aides teaching in these classes. Ever since the start of the bilingual school program in September, 1966, the special Spanish teachers and Cuban aides had planned the scope and sequence of the instructional program in mathematics, science, health, and social studies with the regular classroom teachers. In order to reinforce, enrich, and extend the curriculum presented in the English language, the special Spanish teachers and Cuban aides created appropriate audio-visual materials and activity sheets. In addition, relevant instructional materials produced in Spain and Latin America were purchased from local importers of educational materials.

Due to the primary objective of fostering bicultural understanding at Central Beach Elementary, a direct effort was made to establish a bicultural atmosphere within the school. At a national meeting of elementary school principals in the spring of 1972, the principal of Central Beach Elementary presented to his North American colleagues a list of suggestions that had helped establish this type of atmosphere within his school:

If students from two ethnic groups are to strive to learn one another's language and culture and to interact with one another comfortably, it is essential that the principal, teacher, and other staff members become living examples. Establishment of an atmosphere of mutual respect for both languages and cultures within the school can be initiated by the North American principal. With the assistance of native Spanish-speaking teachers, aides, students, or parents:

1. Morning announcements and school assemblies can be presented in both English and Spanish.
2. When appropriate, either the English or the Spanish language can be used in the principal's and teachers' conferences with students and parents.
3. All formal communication with the students' homes can be typed in English on one side of the paper and in Spanish on the reverse side.

4. All public relations activities can also utilize the local Spanish-speaking press, radio, and television stations.

5. Inservice-workshops can be organized that provide conversational Spanish instruction for native English-speaking school personnel and conversational English instruction for native Spanish-speaking employees.

6. Both native English-speaking and native Spanish-speaking teachers, aides, secretaries, clerks, and custodians can be encouraged to practice using their second language during the school day.

7. Books, magazines, newspapers, films, and filmstrips in the Spanish language can be purchased for the school's media center.

8. The school menu and bulletin boards in the hallways and classrooms can employ both languages.

9. Signs throughout the school can be reproduced in Spanish by students.

10. General meetings of the school's Parents and Teachers Association can be advertised and presented in both languages and at an hour and a location that is convenient for both cultural groups. If parents do not attend these meetings because they will not leave their children at home in the evenings, supervision for children can be provided during the meetings.

11. If the executive board of the Parents and Teachers Association (PTA) is comprised solely of native English-speaking parents, the principal can organize an ad-hoc Latin Advisory Board to assure communication with this segment of the school community. The long-range objective of the Latin Advisory Board would be its own demise. It would provide the means for some Latin parents to participate actively in PTA functions and demonstrate their support of school activities. Once these Latin parents become involved and are legitimately elected to executive positions in the school's PTA, the need for the Latin Advisory Board would dissipate.[20]

Resources

As at Coral Way Elementary, all of the resources that had been available to public elementary schools in Dade County were also available to Central Beach Elementary. Instead of supplementary allocations for the bilingual school program from the local school system, additional resources (instructional personnel from Spanish-speaking backgrounds, staff development activities, plus necessary instructional materials and equipment) were funded by the nation's Cuban Refugee Program.

PROBLEMS AND PROGRAM MODIFICATIONS

Although minor adjustments in scheduling and curriculum for the bilingual school program at Central Beach Elementary were made each year since 1966, no major program modifications were required. The student population continued to be small (400 to 500 students) and evenly divided between the two ethnic groups. Therefore, the original framework for the assignment of teachers and students proved to be viable. The presence of significant numbers of native English-speaking students each year, did create, on the other hand, a problem that was difficult to solve. The Spanish language portion of the bilingual instructional program had become mandatory and a number of students and parents at the intermediate grade levels had expressed their dissatisfaction. Some students wanted less instruction in the Spanish language each day and some wanted more.

As had been the case at Coral Way Elementary and throughout Dade County, Spanish-speaking parents at Central Beach Elementary generally supported bilingual education for both ethnic groups in all local public schools, but they seldom played an active role in the Parents and Teachers Association at the school. On the other hand, some English-speaking parents did not always agree that bilingualism and biculturalism were necessary attributes for their children in a country where English was the dominant language and Spanish was the language of a minority group. Most of these parents, however, did support the allocation of some regular school time to instruction in the Spanish language. Those who supported the bilingual program believed that their children would become bilingual in the English and Spanish languages by the age of 12 when they graduated from Central Beach Elementary. School officials had stated that the student who attended a bilingual school "will be approximately as proficient in his second language as he is in his first".[21] When this level of proficiency was not in fact attained, some English-speaking parents were disappointed.[22] Some of the older English-speaking students at the school also expressed dissatisfaction with the bilingual school program. It was difficult for them to participate actively for one-and-a-half hours a day in classes presented in the Spanish language, especially when they were competing with Spanish-speakers in Curriculum Content in Spanish (CCS) classes.

Each year, therefore, it was necessary for the school principal to convince a few English-speaking parents and older students of the value of the bilingual instructional program. With the assistance of some staff members, the principal explained to these dissatisfied students and parents that no school program, regardless of the amount of time allocated to second-language instruction, could force children to become equally proficient in two languages. It was explained, on the other hand, that bilingualism and biculturalism significantly increased career opportunities for students in the local area and that the bilingual instructional program enhanced all communication skills in the two languages and facilitated bicultural understanding.

In an attempt to solve the problem of discontent on the part of some of the students and parents, residents in the attendance area of Central Beach Elementary were permitted to enroll their children in nearby elementary schools that did not present a bilingual instructional program. Very few parents, in fact, did transfer their children. On the other hand, parents residing in the attendance areas of nearby elementary schools were allowed to enroll their children at Central Beach Elementary in order that their children could participate in the bilingual program, and, each school year, a few parents took advantage of this option.

According to the school's principal in 1972, the best solution was to offer bilingual instruction as an alternative rather than a requirement within the overall curricular program. If possible, the parents of both ethnic groups should be able to select an instructional program each year that included either a full half-day of instruction in the Spanish language, one-and-a-half hours of instruction in the Spanish language (the bilingual program as it existed in 1972), or a minimum of 45 minutes of instruction in Spanish Language Arts. Yet, since the school was small, establishing various second-language sequences was difficult to schedule. During the 1972-73 school year, however, the principal experimented with the concept of alternative second-language programs. All sixth grade students were required to participate daily in a Spanish Language Arts class, either Spanish for Spanish-Speakers (Spanish-S) or Spanish as a Second Language (Spanish-SL). The Curriculum Content in Spanish (CCS) class, however, was offered on a voluntary basis at that grade level. Approximately 70 percent of the native Spanish-speaking students and 50 percent of the native English-speakers in sixth grade selected, with their parents' consent, to participate in the Curriculum Content in Spanish class. During the 1973-74 school year, the single Curriculum Content in Spanish course was no longer offered for students in grades four, five, and six. Instead, they had the opportunity to participate, if they chose to do so, in a bilingual mathematics course and/or a bilingual social studies course and/or a bilingual science-health course. In this way, students and their parents could select how much of the school day would consist of instruction in the Spanish language.

In general, Dade County's second bilingual school program functioned smoothly at Central Beach Elementary since its inception in September, 1966. The organizational framework for the bilingual instructional program had not required major changes in the scheduling or presentation of the regular instructional program in the English language. Most parents supported this adaptation of the county's first model for bilingual schooling, and the majority of students participated actively in classes presented in either English or Spanish. The successful introduction of these first two models for bilingual schooling soon led to the initiation of additional adaptations at other local elementary, as well as secondary, schools and eventually to countywide standards for bilingual education.

Notes

1. Across the street from the original Miami Beach Junior-Senior High School.
2. "Metro Study Pinpoints 14 Blighted Dade Areas." *The Miami Herald,* Jan. 21, 1973, p. 2-B.
3. Department of Administrative Research, *Desegregation: September, 1970,* vol. XVII, no. 4. Dade County Public Schools, Miami, Fla., 1970, p. 6; Department of Planning and Evaluation, *Desegretion, September, 1975.* Dade County Public Schools, Miami, Fla., 1975, p. 8.
4. Leroy D. Fienberg, born in the United States in 1919, moved to the Miami area in the early 1950's. When he was assigned to be principal of Central Beach Elementary in 1962, he was already an experienced elementary school administrator. Following his death in the middle of the 1966-67 school year, the name of the school was changed to Leroy D. Fienberg Elementary in his honor. (To avoid confusion, the school is referred to as Central Beach Elementary throughout this text.)
5. "A Bilingual School in Dade County," Description of the Project at Leroy D. Fienberg Elementary. Dade County Public Schools, Miami Beach, Fla., 1966, pp. 2-5.
6. Richard O. Roberts, District Superintendent, Northeast District, Dade County Public Schools, Memorandum to Dr. Joe Hall, Superintendent, Dade County Public Schools, "Proposed Establishment of Bilingual School at Central Beach Elementary," Apr. 19, 1966.
7. Von N. Beebe, "A Process Description and Evaluation of the Program for Bilingual Education within Three Bilingual Elementary Schools in Dade County Public Schools, Florida," Miami, Fla., 1970, p. 88.
8. William F. Mackey, "A Typology of Bilingual Education." *Foreign Language Annals,* III, 1970, p. 597.
9. Division of Instruction, *Procedures Manual: Bilingual Education Program,* Bulletin 1-C.Dade County Public Schools, Miami, Fla. 1971, pp. 52-53.
10. "A Bilingual School Organization - Una Escuela de Estructura Bilingue." Leroy D. Fienberg Elementary School, Dade County Public Schools, Miami Beach, Fla., 1972.
11. Supra Note 5.
12 "Spanish-speaking Pupil Survey." Leroy D. Fienberg Elementary, Dade County Public Schools, Miami, Fla., Sept. 21, 1966.
13. Among other administrative and instructional positions in the Dade County Public Schools that were funded by the Cuban Refugee Program at that time, one Teacher on Special Assignment for Bilingual Education was allocated to each of the six administrative subdistricts to coordinate bilingual instructional programs in schools throughout that district.
14. Supra Note 12.
15. Department of Administrative Research, *Desegregation: September, 1972,* p. 10.
16. "Self-Study Practicum, 1966-1967." Leroy D. Fienberg Elementary School, Dade County Public Schools, Miami Beach, Fla.,
17. Lorraine E. Miller, Principal, Leroy D. Fienberg Elementary, Memorandum to Dr. Terrence O'Connor, Staff Development Center, Dade County Public Schools, "In-Service Course to be Held at Leroy D. Fienberg Elementary School 1970-71," Oct. 20, 1970.
18. Supra Note 10.
19. Supra Note 5.
20. Von N. Beebe, "Bilingual Education and the North American Principal," a paper presented at the annual meeting of the National Association of Elementary School Principals, Miami Beach, Florida, Apr. 10, 1972, pp. 13-15.
21. Paul W. Bell, "The Bilingual School," a paper presented at the annual meeting of the International Reading Association, Detroit, Mich., May 3-4, 1965, p. 3.
22. "Bi-Lingual Learning Questioned." *The Beach Sun,* July 20, 1971, pp. 1, 7.

7

Expansion and Standardization

The example set by the two pioneer bilingual school programs produced some far-ranging and long-term effects. In the first place, a number of other elementary schools in Dade County installed their own adaptations of these first two models for bilingual schooling. Secondly, there was a demand to continue bilingual instruction beyond the elementary level, resulting in the creation of bilingual programs in junior and senior high schools. Thirdly, the generalization of the demand produced a need for evaluation and the creation of standards for program organization and pupil achievement. The most remarkable of these effects, however, was the expansion of the program in the elementary schools.

THE OUTWARD SPREAD TO ELEMENTARY SCHOOLS
The demonstration that the biethnic model of bilingual education could be replicated in another school encouraged its expansion throughout the entire Miami area. In the space of a few years, seven new elementary bilingual schools were created.[1] Not all were equally successful, however, and a first reversal gave pause to the educational community when they began to realize the difficulties and possible complications of converting from unilingual to bilingual schooling.

The First Set-Back

In October, 1967, a third organizational model for bilingual schooling was introduced in grades one, two, and three at Mae Walters Elementary in the

Hialeah section of Dade County. School officials intended to expand this bilingual school program to one new grade level each school year so that, by 1970, Mae Walters Elementary would become another complete bilingual school organization within the Dade County Public Schools.

Mae Walters Elementary was located near the famous Hialeah Race Track, ten miles northwest of downtown Miami. The City of Hialeah was the center of Dade County's garment industry; and, since the beginning of the influx of Cuban refugees to the Miami area in the early 1960's, many Cuban women and some Cuban men obtained their first jobs in these clothing factories. This new source of skilled labor served as a stimulus for the local garment industry, and more factories were established. Soon, some Cuban refugees began to rent or to purchase small houses near their places of employment. During the mid-1960's, more and more Cuban refugee families moved to the Hialeah area for employment purposes or to join their friends and relatives. Many of their children were enrolled in the local public schools, and, by October, 1965, one of every four students at Mae Walters Elementary was of Spanish-speaking background.[3] Cognizant of the fact that his school's community rapidly was becoming bilingual and bicultural, the principal began to discuss the situation with the principal of Coral Way Elementary, the county's first bilingual school organization.

When both the number and the percentage of Spanish-speaking students at Mae Walters Elementary continued to increase during the 1965-66 school year, some local educators encouraged the school's principal to implement another model for bilingual schooling. The principal, however, was cautious. During the spring of 1966, he consulted also with the principal of Central Beach Elementary and studied the plans for the county's second bilingual school program that was scheduled to begin the following September. In October of 1966, he decided to develop a tentative plan for a bilingual school program for both Spanish and English-speaking students.[4] Assured that his administrative superiors would support the idea, he planned to launch a bilingual school program on an experimental basis during the 1967-68 school year.

The principal of this school believed that, in order to generate support among the faculty, it was necessary to convince the teachers that the idea of starting a bilingual school program was their own idea. Experience had taught him that some teachers would resist any innovation if they sensed that it was being imposed by the school principal or by other administrators. It was necessary first, he felt, to "plant the seed". After discussing Coral Way Elementary's bilingual school program at regularly-scheduled faculty meetings during the fall of 1966, some teachers expressed an interest in the bilingual school program and asked if they could observe classes at Coral Way Elementary. These teachers' observations generated further discussions at subsequent faculty meetings; and, as the 1966-67 school year neared an end, some teachers at the primary grade levels asked that bilingual instruction be organized in their classes during the coming school year. At that point, the school's principal requested that the Superintendent of the Northwest District of the Dade County Public Schools accompany him on a visit to Coral Way Elementary. He and the District Superintendent observed the first and second-language programs and discussed scheduling problems with that school's principal. Later, the District Superintendent assured him that he would support efforts to implement a bilingual school program at Mae Walters Elementary. In addition, he told him that, if significant problems arose, he could reinstate the regular instructional program of the Dade County Public Schools.

During those spring months, the principal also discussed the county's bilingual school program with students' parents at a general meeting of the school's Parents and Teachers Association. In addition, he continued to confer with the county's Coordinator of Bilingual Education,[5] who had pledged his office's support for this new bilingual school program and had agreed to add a sufficient number of Cuban aides to the school's staff to provide all of the instruction needed in the Spanish language during the first year.

A new organizational model for the bilingual instructional progam at May Walters Elementary was designed. At the principal's request, this organizational model was not identical to either of the county's two existent models for bilingual schooling. English-speaking students, for example, were not to be separated from Spanish-speaking students for a half-day's instruction in their second language, as they had been at Coral Way Elementary; because, so many of the native Spanish-speaking students attending Mae Walters Elementary already were able to communicate in the English language well enough to participate effectively in the school's regular instructional program in English. As at Central Beach Elementary, these students would attend most classes along with their native English-speaking peers. As at Coral Way Elementary, however, as indicated in Figure 14, Spanish-speaking and English-speaking students were separated for all instruction that was presented in Spanish. This instruction for Spanish-speaking students was comprised of two components: Spanish for Spanish-Speakers (Spanish-S) and Curriculum Content in Spanish for Spanish-speaking students (CCS-S). Instruction in the Spanish language for English-speakers was given in two classes: Spanish as a Second Language (Spanish-SL) and Curriculum Content in Spanish for English-speakers (CCS-E). Rather than provide a half-day of instruction in the Spanish language at the lower grade levels, as at Coral Way Elementary, this instruction totaled only 60 minutes each day in grade one and 90 minutes each day in grades two and three. The time allotment was similar to the one established at Central Beach Elementary. The long-range plan, however, was to increase gradually the amout of time that both groups devoted to instruction in Spanish as they progressed to higher grade levels. It was estimated that all students would be able to receive 50 percent of their instruction in Spanish and 50 percent in English by the time that they reached the sixth grade.

Although the principal of Mae Walters Elementary had received the support of his faculty, of the county's Coordinator of Bilingual Education, and of

CLASSES (student groups)	REGULAR INSTRUCTIONAL PROGRAM (285 minutes)		BILINGUAL INSTRUCTIONAL PROGRAM (45 minutes for each component)	
Native ENGLISH-SPEAKING	Curriculum Content in English (CCE)	English Language Arts (ELA)	Spanish as a Second Language (Spanish-SL)	Curriculum Content in Spanish (CCS-E)
Native SPANISH-SPEAKING			Spanish for Spanish-Speakers (Spanish-S)	Curriculum Content in Spanish (CCS-S)

NOTES
The shaded squares represent the four additional components for bilingual education at Mae Walters Elementary.

The large majority of non-native English-speaking students participated in English language arts classes with native English-speaking students. A special orientation program in English as a Second Language was provided for newly-enrolled, non-native English-speaking students. As soon as these students were able to perform effectively in the regular instructional program, they were transferred to regular English language arts classes.

Figure 14   The Third Model of Elementary Bilingual Schooling

his administrative superiors before the end of the 1966-67 school year, he postponed making a final decision until the beginning of the following school year when the percentage of Spanish-speaking children in the school had increased to almost 50 percent.[6] He then decided to implement the new bilingual school program.

At the beginning of the following school year (1968-69), the bilingual school program was expanded, as planned, to grade four and further expanded to grade five at the beginning of the 1969-70 school year. A normal percentage of teacher retirements and transfers, coupled with the continual increase in student enrollments, enabled the principal to employ 14 bilingual classroom teachers over the period from 1967 until 1969. These bilingual teachers, assisted by seven Cuban aides, taught the Spanish language portion of the bilingual school program in grades one through five during the 1969-70 school year.[7] This arrangement, however, was not to last.

In the middle of the school year, a federal court order and resultant school board policy directed each public school principal in Dade County to establish among his teaching staff a racial balance comparable to that of the school system as a whole. In order to comply with the desegregation guidelines, school principals were required to transfer some of their newest teachers to other schools within the county and to accept the transfer of teachers from other schools.

At Mae Walters Elementary, the newest teachers were generally the re-cently-recruited, bilingual classroom teachers. The school's principal requested that an exception to the county policy be adopted to protect the school's bilin-gual instructional program. County school officials, however, decided that the need for racial integration among each school's instructional staff was para-mount. No exception was authorized, and the principal of Mae Walters Ele-mentary consequently was required to transfer nine classroom teachers to oth-er elementary schools. Six of these teachers were bilingual, representing a loss of at least one bilingual teacher for each grade level involved in the bilingual school program. Since none of the black teachers transferred into Mae Walters Elementary was bilingual, only eight of the 43 classroom teachers at the school were capable of presenting instruction in the Spanish language with the assis-tance of Cuban aides.[8]

At that point, the principal began to reduce the Spanish language portion of the bilingual school program at all grade levels and to prepare for a return to the school's normal second-language program that had been presented before October of 1967. At the beginning of the 1970-71 school year, all Spanish as a Second Language (Spanish-SL) classes for English-speaking students and all Curriculum Content in Spanish classes for both Spanish-speakers (CCS-S) and English-speakers (CCS-E) were discontinued. As at other elementary schools in Dade County with large enrollments of Spanish-speaking students, howev-er, funds from the school system's Cuban Refugee Program continued to pro-vide specially-trained teachers to present an orientation program in English as a Second Language for newly-enrolled Spanish-speaking students and to pro-vide Cuban aides for classes in Spanish for Spanish-Speakers (Spanish-S) at all grade levels.[9]

Cautious Renewals

Following the introduction of the bilingual school program at Mae Walters Ele-mentary in 1967 and its demise two-and-one-half years later as a result of a new countywide staffing policy, no other bilingual school programs were cre-ated in the county's public elementary schools until the early seventies. Ironi-cally, the renewed expansion of bilingual programs at the elementary school level occurred within the Northeast District of the county's school system, one of the administrative sub-districts least affected by the influx of Cuban refugee students.[10]

The Northeast District, as shown in Figure 16, included the area of Miami Beach and the northeastern corner of mainland Miami. Only the southern sec-tion of Miami Beach had attracted large numbers of Cuban refugee families during the sixties and early seventies. Two elementary schools and one junior high school were located within this section and served the surrounding com-munity. One of the elementary schools, Central Beach Elementary, had al-ready initiated a bilingual school program in the fall of 1966 and, by the

1969-70 school year, all students in kindergarten and grades one through six were receiving instruction in both the English and the Spanish languages during each school day.

At the beginning of the 1971-72 school year, the Superintendent of the Northeast District of the Dade County Public Schools asked the Director of Elementary Schools in the southern Miami Beach area to assess the feasibility of introducing a bilingual school program in the neighborhood's other elementary school, South Beach Elementary. In early September, the director discussed the school's instructional program and the characteristics of the student population with the principal of South Beach Elementary. The percentage of Spanish-speaking students had increased to more than 60 percent,[11] and special orientation classes in English as a second language were being offered for the first time.[12] There were no plans and no available personnel to give instruction in the Spanish language for students attending the school. Agreeing that the community had become bilingual and bicultural and that many similarities were shared with the community served by nearby Central Beach Elementary, the director and the principal of South Beach Elementary decided that there was an immediate need to offer more second-language instruction or even perhaps a bilingual school program.

During conferences between the school's principal, the Director of Elementary Schools in the Northeast District, the principal of Central Beach Elementary, and the Teacher on Special Assignment for Bilingual Education in the Northeast District during mid-September of that year, it was decided that a bilingual school program should be created at South Beach Elementary as soon as possible. It was determined that many of the native Spanish-speaking students attending South Beach Elementary at the time were able to communicate in the English language and that exactly the same organizational model employed at Central Beach Elementary (see Figure 13) was appropriate for South Beach Elementary. It was also decided that the bilingual school program should be introduced in kindergarten and grades one, two, and three during that school year and extended each subsequent year to the next higher grade level.

In late September and early October, therefore, the administrators and instructional staff of South Beach Elementary visited the bilingual school program at Central Beach Elementary and participated in intensive, full-day workshops on bilingual instruction and cultural differences. A revised master schedule, organizing a two-way, bilingual instructional program identical to the one at Central Beach Elementary was also established. The county's Coordinator of Bilingual Education[13] assigned four Cuban aides immediately to provide the Spanish language portion of the bilingual instructional program in the primary grades and additional Cuban aides each school year as the program expanded to the upper grade levels. There was, therefore, no immediate need to replace monolingual teachers with bilingual teachers.

In early November 1971, class schedules were consequently reorganized at South Beach Elementary, and the bilingual school program was introduced for English-speaking and Spanish-speaking students in kindergarten and grades one, two, and three. The new program functioned without major complications. The percentage of Spanish-speaking students attending the school continued to increase gradually during the 1971-72 school year, and, in the late spring of 1972, the principal decided that the bilingual school program had progressed so well that it would be expanded to grade levels four and five, rather than to just grade four, during the upcoming school year. At the beginning of the 1973-74 school year, the bilingual school program was expanded to the sixth grade level and South Beach Elementary became an additional, complete bilingual school organization within the Dade County Public Schools.[14]

In contrast to the Northeast District of the Dade County Public Schools, the South Central District had been the most affected since the early sixties by the influx of Cuban refugees. By 1965, more than one fourth of the 12,330 students enrolled in elementary and secondary schools within this district were of Spanish-speaking background. By September, 1972, almost 50 percent of the 29,994 students attending public schools in this district were in that category.[15] Certain areas within the South Central Distrist had become especially popular with the Cuban refugee families, and the student population of schools located there became predominantly Spanish-speaking. Coral Way Elementary, the county's first bilingual school organization, was one such school.

Southside Elementary, located in a low-income neighborhood within five miles of Coral Way Elementary (see Figure 16) was another one of the schools faced with a sudden change in the ethnic make-up of its student population. By October, 1965, three of every four students in the school were Spanish-speaking,[16] and the numbers of Cuban refugee children in the student population continued to increase. By the beginning of the 1971-72 school year, the percentage of Spanish-speaking students had risen to more than 90 percent.[17]

During the 1971-72 school year, many pupils of Spanish-speaking background attending Southside Elementary were able to communicate effectively in English, and the regular instructional program of the Dade County Public Schools was taught to them in that language as it had been in the past. Special English as a Second Language classes were offered for the few students who were unable to participate in the regular instructional program due to their lack of mastery of English. For Spanish-speakers, there were also daily classes in Spanish (Spanish-S), of 45 minutes duration, taught by two Cuban aides.

In the spring of 1972, some of the parents and teachers decided that more instruction in the Spanish language would be beneficial for both the 357 pupils of Spanish-speaking background and the school's 30 English-speaking students.[18] They were interested in a program similar to the one at nearby Coral Way Elementary, and asked that this possibility be seriously considered by their principal.

At the request of the principal, county specialists studied the three organizational models employed previously for bilingual schooling at the elementary school level in Dade County and combined aspects of each into a fourth model that would be appropriate for initiating bilingual schooling in grades one through four at that school. In addition to the fact that there was a native Spanish-speaking classroom teacher at each of these four grade levels who was bilingual and able to present instruction in either the English or the Spanish language, the specialists were aware that a large majority of the Spanish-speaking students already were able to participate in the regular instructional program given in English. The new organizational model, therefore, as indicated in Figure 15, maintained the procedure of placing both ethnic groups together for the regular instructional program in both Curriculum Content in English and in English Language Arts. [19]

The specialists also realized that both the English-speaking and the Spanish-speaking students needed more concentrated work in the Spanish language. In this organizational model and accompanying master schedule, therefore, 90 minutes were provided for instruction in Spanish Language Arts: classes in Spanish for Spanish-Speakers (Spanish-S) and classes in Spanish as a Second Language (Spanish-SL) for the English-speakers. The model also allocated 70 minutes daily to classes in Curriculum Content in Spanish (CCS) for mixed groups at each of the four grade levels. In this way, the two groups were separated only during Spanish Language Arts classes. [20] Both the Spanish-speaking group and the English-speaking group, therefore, received approximately one-half of their instruction in Spanish during the regular school day. [21]

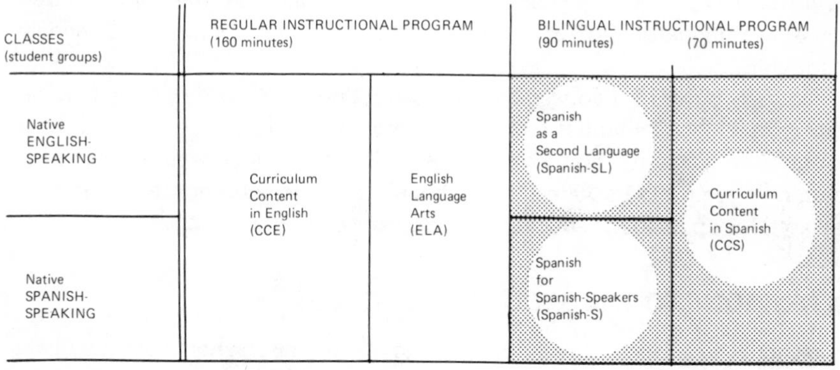

NOTES

The shaded squares represent the three additional components for bilingual education at Southside Elementary.

The large majority of non-native English-speaking students participated in English language arts classes with native English-speaking students. A special orientation program in English as a Second Language was provided for newly-enrolled, non-native English-speaking students. As soon as these students were able to perform effectively in the regular instructional program, they were transferred to regular English language arts classes.

Figure 15   The Fourth Model of Elementary Bilingual Schooling

Convinced of the parents' and staff's desire to initiate bilingual schooling at Southside Elementary and the appropriateness of the organizational model, school officials in the South Central District authorized the initiation of the bilingual school program, as designed, in September, 1972. On-going workshops on bilingual education were presented for the staff of 15 teachers throughout the 1972-73 school year. No major problems developed, and school officials extended the bilingual school program to grade five in 1973 and to grade six in 1974.

The successful implementation of two-way, bilingual education at South Beach and Southside elementary schools in the early seventies renewed interest in this type of programing among local school officials. At the beginning of the 1973-74 school year, therefore, a portion of the funds received by the Dade County Public Schools from the federal government's Emergency School Aid Act were utilized to initiate two-way, bilingual school programs at three more elementary schools: Miami Gardens, Rockway, and Springview. These schools were selected on the basis of their biethnic student enrollments and the interest in bilingual education expressed by their staff and community; however, at this point, county school officials added the additional selection criteria of geographic distribution. As indicated in Figure 16, each of the three selected schools was located in an administrative sub-district of the Dade County Public Schools that did not have any bilingual elementary school in operation at that time. The only administrative sub-district without a bilingual elementary school during the 1973-74 school year was the South District; and, the following September, a bilingual school program was initiated within that area at Caribbean Elementary.

In sum, by 1974, two-way bilingual school programs were successfully operating in eight elementary schools situated throughout the area of Dade County (see Table 6). Some were located in low-income sections within the downtown area, others were situated in suburban neighborhoods; some were designed for open-space education, others for self-contained classrooms.

EXTENSIONS TO THE SECONDARY LEVELS

As bilingual education spread outward to elementary schools in the Miami area, it also spread upward to higher levels of public education, first to junior high schools and later to senior high schools. As this type of education became more specialized at these levels, however, some adaptations were necessary.

Junior High Schools

While plans for the third bilingual elementary program were being developed, the pioneer class at Coral Way Elementary was completing sixth grade. Most of these students, along with sixth grade students from three other elementary schools, were to enter seventh grade at nearby Shenandoah Junior High School in September, 1967. Some local educators believed that these

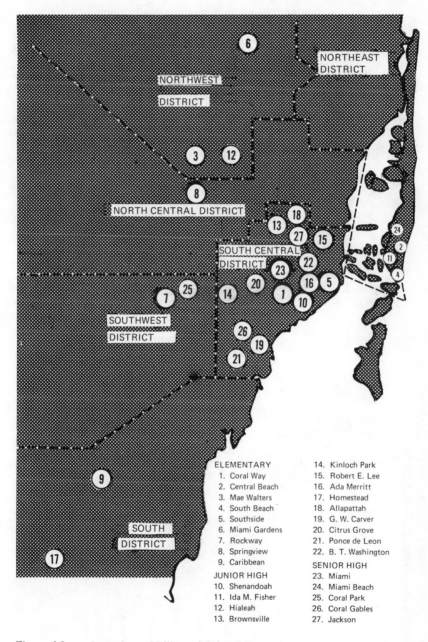

ELEMENTARY
1. Coral Way
2. Central Beach
3. Mae Walters
4. South Beach
5. Southside
6. Miami Gardens
7. Rockway
8. Springview
9. Caribbean

JUNIOR HIGH
10. Shenandoah
11. Ida M. Fisher
12. Hialeah
13. Brownsville

14. Kinloch Park
15. Robert E. Lee
16. Ada Merritt
17. Homestead
18. Allapattah
19. G. W. Carver
20. Citrus Grove
21. Ponce de Leon
22. B. T. Washington

SENIOR HIGH
23. Miami
24. Miami Beach
25. Coral Park
26. Coral Gables
27. Jackson

Figure 16   Location of Bilingual School Programs
(Dade County, Florida: 1975)

Table 6
SPREAD OF ELEMENTARY BILINGUAL SCHOOLING
(Dade County Public Schools: 1963-1975)

School Years and Grade Levels Involved [K = Kindergarten]

Schools	1963-1964	1964-1965	1965-1966	1966-1967	1967-1968	1968-1969	1969-1970	1970-1971	1971-1972	1972-1973	1973-1974	1974-1975	1975-1976
Coral Way Elementary	K-3	K-4	K-5	K-6	K-6	K-6	K-6	K-6	K-6	K-6	K-6	K-6	K-6
Central Beach Elementary				K-3	K-4	K-5	K-6	K-6	K-6	K-6	K-6	K-6	K-6
Mae Walters Elementary					1-3	1-4	1-5						
South Beach Elementary									K-3	K-5	K-6	K-6	K-6
Southside Elementary										1-4	1-5	K-6	K-6
Miami Gardens Elementary											K-2	K-3	K-4
Rockway Elementary											K-2	K-3	K-4
Springview Elementary											K-2	K-3	K-4
Caribbean Elementary												K-2	K-3

graduates of an elementary bilingual program should have the opportunity to continue their bilingual instruction in junior high school. After meetings with the principal of Shenandoah Junior High School and conferences with the Superintendent of the South Central District of the Dade County Public Schools, the decision was made to offer the graduates of Coral Way Elementary a bilingual sequence within the seventh grade instructional program at Shenandoah Junior High School during the 1967-68 school year.

English Language Arts, [22] science, mathematics, and social studies were required academic courses for students in junior high school (grades seven, eight, and nine) in the State of Florida. Students also were required to participate in physical education classes and to select one or two additional courses such as a foreign language, typing, band or orchestra. The plan at Shenandoah Junior High School was to encourage all graduates from Coral Way Elementary to take the course in Spanish for Spanish-Speakers (Spanish-S). For the first time, one or two classes in science and social studies at the seventh grade level would also be taught bilingually. Spanish-S classes were taught by Cuban refugee teachers who had by then obtained certificates as foreign language teachers in the State of Florida. The bilingual science and social studies classes were presented alternately in English and Spanish by bilingual instructors certified to teach these subjects in secondary schools. [23]

The scheduling pattern for the bilingual sequence (Spanish-S, Bilingual Science, and Bilingual Social Studies) proved feasible and was extended to the eighth grade and ninth grade levels over the next two school years. [24] At the beginning of the 1969-70 school year, therefore, Shenandoah Junior High School became the first complete bilingual school organization at the junior high school level in Dade County offering bilingual schooling at all three grade levels.

Experience at Shenandoah Junior High School revealed that students enrolled in Bilingual Science and Bilingual Social Studies classes needed simultaneous instruction in Spanish Language Arts; therefore, participation in either Spanish-S or Spanish-SL classes soon became a requirement rather than a recommendation for all students selecting the bilingual sequence of courses. [25] At the beginning of the 1971-72 school year, an additional modification was instituted in the school's bilingual program. For the first time, Spanish-speaking graduates from elementary schools other than Coral Way Elementary also were permitted to enroll in the bilingual courses at each grade level.

The other bilingual program at the junior high school level dates from the year 1970 when a seventh grade program was organized at the Ida M. Fisher Junior High School. It had been designed the previous spring by the school's principal and offered at the request of some of the parents of students who were completing sixth grade that year directly across the street at Central Beach Elementary. These sixth grade students had been receiving instruction in both the English and the Spanish languages over the previous four years and would be entering the seventh grade that fall.

In the regular instructional program at Ida M. Fisher Junior High School, the social studies course and the regular English Language Arts course were combined into a two hour CORE program in seventh grade. At the beginning of the 1970-71 school year, a bilingual CORE sequence was introduced. Instruction in social studies and English Language Arts was presented alternately in English and Spanish by a native Spanish-speaking teacher certified by the State of Florida to teach these subjects in secondary schools. The bilingual CORE sequence was offered to both the native English-speaking and Spanish-speaking graduates of Central Beach Elementary and Spanish-speaking graduates of other elementary schools. It was recommended that the Spanish-S course be taken by all Spanish-speakers in bilingual CORE classes; but, no Spanish-SL course had been offered at this junior high school. A Spanish-7 course had been one of the courses offered in seventh grade as preparation for the traditional Spanish as a Foreign Language program in grades eight and nine. One of these Spanish-7 classes was modified, therefore, during the 1970-71 school year and presented as an option for all English-speaking students in bilingual CORE classes.

Bilingual teaching of social studies and English Language Arts classes (the CORE program) did not prove to be feasible. English Language Arts classes, of course, had to be presented solely in the English language. In addition, enrollment in the social studies class within the bilingual CORE program had been limited basically to graduates of Central Beach Elementary, and the school's administrators and teachers believed that discussions in a social studies class should not be limited to the viewpoints of graduates from just one elementary school. Advisors pointed out to the principal that more curricular materials were available for teaching science in the Spanish language at the secondary level than for any of the other required subjects. During the 1971-72 school year, therefore, the principal recommended that the bilingual academic classes be switched from English Language Arts and social studies to science.

As at Shenandoah Junior High School, experience demonstrated that students needed to attend Spanish Language Arts classes in order to participate effectively in the bilingual science class. Spanish-S and Spanish-7, therefore, were required of these students during the 1972-73 school year.[26] For all other students in grades eight and nine, classes in Spanish-S and Spanish as a Foreign Language continued to be offered at Ida M. Fisher Junior High School as options. Special English as a Second Language classes, launched in 1969, were also offered to all those non-English-speaking students who had not achieved "verbal independence" in English. [27]

Although the original plan in 1970 had been to extend the bilingual sequence to the next higher grade level each subsequent school year, the bilingual science course was not offered at the eighth or ninth grade levels during the 1971-72 or the 1972-73 school years. It was, admittedly, a relatively small secondary school with only 715 students enrolled at the beginning of the 1972-73 school year.[28] With a limited number of staff members, it was difficult to offer alternatives, such as bilingual science, at all grade levels. Nor was there any significant demand expressed by students or parents for a continuation of the bilingual sequence into grades eight and nine. Although approximately 40 percent of the students were graduates of the bilingual school program at Central Beach Elementary, many of the native English-speaking students from that school had not selected the bilingual sequence in grade seven. Their motives were the same as those expressed at Shenandoah Junior High School; that is, the difficulty of continuing to study subject matter in the Spanish language, concern about evaluations on report cards, and the loss of opportunities to participate in optional courses other than Spanish. Although the majority of students attending Ida M. Fisher Junior High School during the 1972-73 school year were native English-speakers, only one of them, in contrast to 25 native Spanish-speakers, elected to take the bilingual science class in grade seven. During the second semester of that school year, therefore, one of the social studies courses was offered once again on a bilingual basis. This time, six of the 32 students enrolled were native English-speaking graduates of the bilingual school program at Central Beach Elementary. Additional bilingual classes were added the next year, and, by the 1974-75 school year, bilingual instruction in mathematics, science, social studies, and typing was available for students in grades seven, eight, and nine.

At this point, the opportunity to continue in a bilingual instructional program at the senior high school level became a concern for some graduates of Ida M. Fisher Junior High School as it had been previously for a number of graduates from Shenandoah Junior High School.

Senior High Schools

In the Spring of 1971, the fact that no bilingual sequence had been offered at Miami Senior High School during the 1970-71 school year for the initial group of graduates from the bilingual program at Shenandoah Junior High School was discussed at a meeting of the neighborhood's junior and senior high school principals and guidance counselors. The principal of Miami Senior High School decided that bilingual instruction in the English and the Spanish languages should be made available at his school for both graduates of the bilingual program at Shenandoah Junior High School and Spanish-speaking students from other junior high schools. He asked the county's Coordinator of Bilingual Education to help his staff design an appropriate program.

In reviewing the characteristics of the student population at Miami Senior High School at that time, the Coordinator of Bilingual Education noted that approximately 75 percent of the more than 3,500 students enrolled were of Spanish-speaking background.[29] For a number of years, classes in Spanish for Spanish-Speakers (Spanish-S) and special English as a Second Language classes had been offered for Spanish-speakers at Miami Senior High School. The Coordinator of Bilingual Education encouraged some of the teachers of Spanish-S classes and the leader of the foreign language department at the senior high school to visit bilingual classes at Shenandoah Junior High School.

The teachers determined that the native English-speaking students in bilingual courses at Shenandoah Junior High School would be able to participate effectively in the Spanish-S classes at Miami Senior High School. There was, therefore, no need to create a special Spanish as a Second Language (Spanish-SL) program. The problem, however, was to find a teacher at Miami Senior High School who was certified in an academic subject area and able to teach it in both the English and the Spanish languages at the tenth grade level. Although one of the biology teachers was of Cuban origin, she had lived in the United States all of her life. Yet the school's assistant principal for curriculum was able to convince her to teach two tenth grade biology classes bilingually beginning in September of the 1971-72 school year. A county specialist in bilingual education and the assistant principal for curriculum helped the biology teacher find and develop appropriate instructional materials. At the beginning of the 1971-72 school year, 47 tenth grade students enrolled in the bilingual biology classes;[30] each of these students was strongly encouraged to select Spanish-S as one of their optional courses.

During that same school year, a teacher of Cuban origin was also identified in the school's history department. In order to extend the bilingual sequence through the eleventh grade level during the 1972-73 school year, she was asked to teach two United States history classes on a bilingual basis. She agreed, and these two classes were added to the bilingual program for 1972-73 while the bilingual sequence for tenth grade students continued. At the beginning of the 1973-74 school year, a variety of courses was offered on a bilingual basis at all grade levels (ten, eleven, and twelve), making Miami Senior High School the county's first complete bilingual senior high school.[31]

During the mid-seventies, bilingual education programs spread rapidly to other junior and senior high schools, especially those in the heavily Spanish-speaking neighborhoods of the South Central District of the Dade County Public Schools (see Figure 16). At the same time, the traditional organization of the school year (two semesters plus summer school) was being converted at the secondary level to a sequence of five nine-week sessions (quinmesters) that would be presented year-around. As the regular curriculum in the English language was modified by local educators into nine-week courses, it was being similarly modified into Spanish to provide for bilingual instruction.[32]

In sum, as shown in Table 7, bilingual curriculum had spread to 18 secondary schools by the mid-seventies. In all, there were bilingual programs operating in 26 schools distributed throughout the county. In fact, by the mid-seventies, one could take the General Education Development Test (GED) entirely in Spanish and obtain high school credits towards graduation. It was even claimed at that time in Dade County that one could obtain a high school diploma without speaking English.[33]

Problems in Maintaining Biethnic Balance

The original objective for extending bilingual instructional programs to the secondary school level was to provide the opportunity for *both* native Spanish-

Table 7
SPREAD OF BILINGUAL TEACHING IN SECONDARY SCHOOLS
(Dade County Public Schools: 1967-1975)

Schools	School year in which Bilingual Curriculum Content was offered								
Junior High	1967-1968	1968-1969	1969-1970	1970-1971	1971-1972	1972-1973	1973-1974	1974-1975	1975-1976
Shenandoah	X	X	X	X	X	X	X	X	X
Ida M. Fisher				X	X	X	X	X	X
Hialeah								X	X
Brownsville								X	X
Kinloch Park								X	X
Robert E. Lee								X	X
Ada Merritt								X	X
Homestead								X	X
Allapattah									X
G.W. Carver									X
Citrus Grove									X
Ponce de Leon									X
B.T. Washington									X
Senior High									
Miami					X	X	X	X	X
Miami Beach								X	X
Coral Park								X	X
Coral Gables									X
Jackson									X

Curriculum content courses included social studies, science, mathematics, music, typing, and other subjects. These subjects were taught in English and Spanish through free bilingual alternation to all students regardless of their language background.

speaking *and* native English-speaking students to receive bilingual instruction throughout their enrollment in public schools in Dade County. The great majority of students taking advantage of this opportunity during the early and mid-seventies, however, were of Spanish-speaking background. One obvious reason was that there were more native Spanish-speaking students in attendance at the county's bilingual schools than there were native English-speakers.[34] Furthermore, some native English-speaking students had withdrawn from the bilingual sequences during their three years in the junior high school. Some of these, not having sufficiently mastered Spanish, found it more difficult to study facts and concepts in science and social studies in their second language.

Scores obtained in periodic tests on facts and concepts in bilingual science and social studies depended largely on the student's ability to communicate his or her thoughts in Spanish. Many of the native English-speaking students and their parents expressed concern that their relatively weaker communication skills in Spanish would result in lower overall scores reported on official school reports, thereby limiting their opportunities for admission at select colleges and universities. Also, the requirement that students participating in the bilingual science and social studies classes at the junior high school level select Spanish-SL or Spanish-S often made it impossible for these students to take other popular courses.

On the other hand, the bilingual courses were popular with students of Spanish-speaking background. For example, by October, 1972, at Shenandoah Junior High School, 227 seventh grade students, 176 eighth grade students, and 100 ninth grade students were enrolled in the bilingual sequence of courses at the school.[35] These students represented approximately one-third of the total student population.

Although participation was greater at the elementary than the secondary school level, significant numbers of native Spanish-speaking students as well as native English-speaking students in Dade County were involved in bilingual education programs at all levels by the mid-seventies (see Table 8). Local school officials, recognizing the need to establish additional norms and standards, analyzed the various programs within the county.

TOWARDS NORMS AND STANDARDS

Before any norms could be established, it was necessary to compare the characteristics of bilingual programs already in operation and to evaluate and experiment with a view to arriving at some sort of organizational standard.

General Characteristics of Existing Programs

It was immediately evident that, within little more than a decade, bilingual education had become generalized. As indicated in Tables 6 and 7, the opportunities for bilingual schooling for Spanish-speaking and English-speaking students over the 12 year period from 1963 until 1975 had expanded both horizontally at the elementary school level and vertically to the secondary school level. In the school year 1974-75, 3,683 pupils were participating in the bilingual elementary school programs alone. 2,608 of these students were from Spanish-speaking backgrounds and 1,075 were from non-Spanish-speaking backgrounds.

Participation in the bilingual school programs at the elementary level had generally been on a voluntary basis when the programs were initiated. The large majority of students usually participated at first, and, after a few years, the staffs at these schools frequently made participation in the bilingual program mandatory in order to facilitate the scheduling of classes. Students who did not choose to participate could transfer to a nearby school with a regular instructional program. Some community members stated that this was not an equitable policy for a public school; and, in 1974, county school officials declared that participation in any portion of the bilingual education program, except English as a Second Language classes, was to be solely on a voluntary basis at all schools in the county, including the elementary bilingual school organizations. The bilingual courses at the secondary school level had always been offered on an optional basis.

A number of different organizational models for bilingual schooling were employed at the elementary level. The amount of time allocated for instruction in the Spanish language ranged from one-quarter to one-half of the regular school day. The amount of time that students were separated for instruction in terms of their language background also varied from school to school. In each of these schools, English-speaking and Spanish-speaking students were separated for instruction in Spanish Language Arts: Spanish for Spanish-Speakers

Table 8
COUNTYWIDE BILINGUAL PROGRAM: ENROLLMENT AND COST
(Dade County Public Schools: 1975)

PROGRAM COMPONENTS	NUMBER OF STUDENTS	APPROXIMATE COST	DESCRIPTION
English as a Second Language	16,096	$1,812,249	Basic language and American culture course required of all non-English-speakers. 1-2 hours daily, K-12.
Spanish for Spanish-Speakers	41,850	$1,775,493	Optional language enrichment course for students who already speak Spanish. 30 minutes daily, K-12.
Spanish as a Foreign Language	40,763	$1,222,355	Optional language course for English-speakers. 30 minutes daily, K-12.
Bilingual Schools	5,620 (approximately)	$ 700,480	Eight elementary and some secondary schools offer the above 3 components plus some non-language courses in Spanish.

Source: The Miami Herald, Jan. 27, 1975, p. 8-A.

(Spanish-S) or Spanish as a Second Language (Spanish-SL). The extent to which the students were separated in terms of language background for the regular instructional program of Curriculum Content in English (CCE) or the Curriculum Content in Spanish (CCS) classes was determined by the linguistic characteristics of the student body and the objectives of the school's leaders at the time the program was designed.

Two basic staffing patterns were utilized. At some of these elementary schools, bilingual teachers of Spanish-speaking background, with the help of Cuban aides, were employed as regular classroom teachers to teach both in English and Spanish. In other elementary schools, only the Cuban aides and "special Spanish teachers" presented instruction in the Spanish language. These special Spanish teachers and Cuban aides were among the supplementary personnel assigned to schools with funds from the Cuban Refugee Program.

The amount of time allocated to instruction in the Spanish language at the secondary school level generally ranged from one-third (two of six classes) to one-half (three of six classes) of the instructional program for those students selecting the bilingual sequences. Some Spanish-speaking students and English-speaking students were separated for instruction in Spanish Language Arts during the bilingual sequences at the junior high schools. At the senior high schools, Spanish-speaking and English-speaking students participating in the bilingual sequence usually attended all classes presented in the Spanish language together, including the Spanish Language Arts class (Spanish-S).

At the secondary school level, instruction in Spanish Language Arts was presented by certified foreign language teachers and Cuban aides. The academic courses that were offered in the Spanish language as part of the bilingual sequences were always presented by bilingual teachers who were certified in these academic areas by the Department of Education of the State of Florida.

In addition to the elementary and secondary schools that offered bilingual school programs by the mid-seventies, most of the other elementary and secondary schools within the Dade County Public Schools presented English as a Second Language, Spanish for Spanish-Speakers, and Spanish as a Second or Foreign Language classes on a daily basis. In fact, two of these courses, English as a Second Language (ESL) and Spanish for Spanish-Speakers (Spanish-S), were established back in the early sixties as special language programs for students throughout the county who were from Spanish-speaking backgrounds.

In this context, it became evident that bilingual education in Dade County had developed to a point where some sort of evaluation was needed.

Evaluation and Experimentation

The generalization of bilingual education began to pose problems of policy, planning and organization. Bilingual education in Dade County had become a $7,500,000 operation, and every year the budget was steadily expanding. Bilingual programs had a combined enrollment of approximately 104,000, and the number of students in the county for whom Spanish was the first language was increasing faster than that of any other group — to 72,773 in 1974, almost 30 percent of the total 246,534 student population. The school system employed 719 educators in bilingual programs at that time, including 237 teachers, 435 aides and 47 support personnel, to meet the language needs of this growing population. The most frequent criticism from the community concerning the county's bilingual program was that some students were not mastering the English language, and school authorities identified the English as a Second Language (ESL) component as the program's top priority.

Once again, in the mid-seventies, school authorities insisted that only qualified instructors teach in English as a Second Language classes. They also demanded guarantees that instructional programs in Spanish be of high quality. According to the school board's experience, some school principals were not complying with these policies; some, in fact, even questioned their feasibility. Answers were sought to such questions as: who gets bilingual education and how much, how does a program assure equal competence in two languages, and do the existing programs achieve their goals? Policy makers demanded an evaluation.

Evaluation

Earlier evaluations of students' progress in the elementary bilingual school programs had revealed that many native Spanish-speaking students were approaching equal proficiency in the English and Spanish languages and performing as well on standardized tests in English as their counterparts in non-bilingual school programs. Native English-speaking students, on the other hand, continued to perform more proficiently in their native language, English. This was perceived as a logical outcome for members of a nation's majority language group, and indicated that one of the bilingual school program's objectives, that students achieve approximately equal proficiency in both languages, was unrealistic for these students. It was maintained as an "ideal" program objective, however, because these earlier assessments had also revealed that native English-speaking participants were more proficient in the Spanish language than their English-speaking contemporaries in nonbilingual schools. The results also indicated that participation in a bilingual school program had not hindered these students' performance on standardized tests in the English language. [36]

Since bilingual education, in the widest acceptance of the concept, affected the entire school system by the mid-seventies, there was a need for an overall evaluation of the bilingual program and its four components within the countywide curriculum: English as a Second Language classes, Spanish for Spanish-Speakers classes, Spanish as a Second Language classes and bilingual schooling.

Approximately 16,000 students were participating in the countywide English as a Second Language (ESL) program at the time. A sampling procedure was utilized for the evaluation of this extensive program, and the testing program was limited to an assessment of reading comprehension and vocabulary. It provided some unexpected results. While consistent growth in reading comprehension in the English language was associated with participation in the ESL program, there did not appear to be similar growth in the vocabulary scores. In addition, a subsequent cross-analysis of scores showed that reading comprehension in Spanish tended to decrease as students' participation in ESL classes increased.[37] Informal observations by teachers and other school personnel indicated that most students acquired sufficient oral proficiency within one, two, or three years of participation in the ESL program to be categorized as linguistically independent in the English language, however, no formal assessment of verbal communication skills was undertaken.

The extensive Spanish for Spanish-Speakers (Spanish-S) program involved approximately 42,000 students throughout Dade County's public schools in the mid-seventies. An assessment of the Spanish language reading skills of a sampling of the large number of participants in this program revealed that consistent gains and high levels of achievement were directly related to program participation. In addition, a cross-analysis of scores showed that students' English reading skills also improved as they participated in the Spanish-S program.[38] Oral communication skills in Spanish were not formally assessed in this countywide evaluation.

The Spanish as a Second Language (Spanish-SL) program in Dade County in the mid-seventies involved approximately 41,000 students, including those enrolled in the traditional Spanish foreign language classes offered for many years as part of the regular instructional program in junior and senior high schools. The countywide assessment of a sample of these students produced "a well-defined trend of improvement" in Spanish reading comprehension and vocabulary skills that was associated with the length of time that non-native Spanish-speakers participated in this program. Once again, as in the earlier evaluations of native English-speakers in the bilingual elementary school programs, a cross-analysis of test scores indicated that participation in the Spanish-SL program did not interfere with these student's acquisition of language skills in English. In fact, the results suggested the contrary, a positive relationship between participation in this second-language program and the development of reading skills in their native language. In addition, a curious result emerged from this assessment. Students participating in a Spanish-SL program in a non-bilingual school tended to read better in Spanish than their counterparts who were participating in a Spanish-SL program within a bilingual school.[39] Some school officials believed that this outcome was due to an emphasis on oral language skills within the bilingual school program, and no assessment of verbal communication skills was undertaken in this study.

The final phase of the evaluation concerned the bilingual school programs in the county that offered ESL, Spanish-S, and Spanish-SL courses in addition to the regular instructional program in English, plus curriculum content courses presented solely in the Spanish language or bilingually in the Spanish and

English languages. It was estimated that approximately 5,600 students were enrolled in bilingual school programs at the elementary and secondary school levels. No assessment results were reported for native Spanish-speaking participants, but the performance of a sampling of native English-speaking participants produced mixed results. Although these students' Spanish reading vocabulary improved with increased participation in the program, no general improvement in Spanish reading comprehension was demonstrated. There was no evaluation of the participants' oral communication skills in Spanish, but, again, cross-analyses of students with long-term participation in bilingual school programs revealed that there was no apparent interference with their development of English language skills. [40]

These evaluation results caused local educational policymakers to call a temporary halt to the expansion of bilingual school programs in 1975, especially at the elementary school level, pending additional investigations of this program's effectiveness. In addition, the evaluation results called for a more thorough analysis of the ESL [41] program. Any attempts to cut back the county's bilingual education programs, however, met vociferous and emotional objections from Spanish-speaking community members at public meetings of the Dade County School Board. They directly associated these programs with their right to remain bilingual, their right to preserve their cultural heritage, and the advantages of bilingualism and biculturalism for all community members in Dade County.

Although local evaluations raised serious questions concerning the efficiency of the local schools' programs for achieving their stated objectives, it was generally agreed that these objectives were more positive and more appropriate than those established for many bilingual education programs in other sections of the United States. For example, a general examination of the bilingual programs throughout the nation found that many of these programs had a number of characteristics in common, "they are for the most part remedial/compensatory in nature, i.e. they presume linguistic and/or cultural disadvantagedness or deficiency on the part of students with limited-English-speaking ability." [42]

Since its inception, a fundamental tenet of the bilingual education program in Dade County had been that proficiency in the Spanish language and a knowledge of the culture of Spanish-speaking people were advantages, skills worth maintaining and improving while the student learned the English language and the cultural heritage of the United States. As early as 1963, this philosophy was applied also in the public education program for native English-speaking students in the two-way, bilingual school program at Coral Way Elementary. Soon thereafter, the value of English-speaking students learning the Spanish language and the cultural heritage of its native speakers spread throughout the county in the form of additional two-way, bilingual school programs plus a countywide Spanish as a Second Language program. The underlying philosophical statement in Dade County was that knowledge of the Span-

ish languge and the culture of its speakers was so valuable for members of the community that it was important for non-Spanish-speakers to acquire it in the public schools. This concentration on the two-way philosophy of biethnic, bilingual education, however, may have received undue emphasis. As in many other public school systems in the United States, federal investigators determined in 1975 that many of the students with limited-English-speaking ability attending public schools in Dade County were not receiving an adequately bilingual instructional program.

The county school system's 1975 Bilingual Survey identified 16,406 students, 4,352 at the secondary school level and 12,054 at the elementary school level, as being either non-English-speaking or of limited-English-speaking ability (see Figure 17). In almost all cases, these students were provided with special English as a Second Language training, but, with the exception of those enrolled in the county's bilingual school programs, they did not receive bilingual instruction in curriculum content areas. Members of the United States Government's Civil Rights Task Force declared that, at the elementary school level alone, this constituted a violation of the constitutional right of 10,803 non-English-speaking and limited-English-speaking students to an equal educational opportunity.[43] If not corrected, this violation would probably result in the loss of all future federal funding to the Dade County Public Schools. This declaration by representatives of the federal government immediately led to the development of a countywide, standardized program that would comply with the guidelines of the Civil Rights Task Force. The program, developed by the county's Director of Bilingual Programs,[44] was designed for all non-English-speaking and limited-English-speaking students in the county's public schools, not just those with Spanish as a home language.[45]

Experimentation

As the deficiencies of various components of the county's bilingual program were discovered, school administrators began to experiment in a search for some solutions. One of these experiments was total immersion in a second language.

In the spring of 1975, a Spanish Total Immersion Laboratory was developed by the staff at one of the bilingual schools, Caribbean Elementary. The purpose was to find out how rapidly students could adapt to new circumstances, especially to a new language and culture, and how this would improve their language skills. A group of ten native English-speaking students, who had been attending 30 minute Spanish as a Second Language classes each day, were isolated during school hours for one week within a classroom that had been converted into a simulated Spanish-speaking island. Three bilingual teachers were assigned to play the roles of a Spanish-speaking mother, store keeper, and school teacher. Within this totally Latin American atmosphere, the English-speaking participants were forced to utilize Spanish for communication. They were assisted by two bilingual classmates. At the end of five school days, most of the participants had acquired "survival skills" in the Spanish language and had become relatively functional bilinguals. The initial success of this experiment led to more total immersion laboratories for larger groups of students during subsequent school years as well as a similar 10-day program for some native English-speaking teachers and administrators in the county. [46]

The idea actually originated out of the frustration of educators trying to make Spanish relevant to students who did not speak it except in their second-language classes. Through this experiment, it was hoped to awaken a deeper interest on the part of the English-speaking student in the language and culture of his Spanish-speaking classmate. It was inspired by an experiment in Culver City, Calif., where English-speaking students were given all of their instruction at school in Spanish. The Culver City Spanish Immersion Project was modeled after the St. Lambert Project in Montreal, 1965 to 1969. [47] In this experiment, the participating students (by the end of the fourth grade) had proven competence in both languages (English and French) with no symptoms of retardation or negative transfer and no signs of intellectual deficit. They had demonstrated less ethnocentricity and a high level of performance in non-language subjects. With the St. Lambert experiment serving as a model for a bilingual setting, English-speakers in Culver City were instructed entirely in Spanish. A new feature in the Culver City project (as compared to the St. Lambert Project) was the addition of six native Spanish-speakers to the original group during the second year of the project. It was found that, at the end of its second year, the English-speaking students had acquired competence in understanding, speaking, reading, and writing in Spanish while having maintained English language proficiency. [48]

Local innovations in Dade County such as the Spanish Total Immersion Laboratory at Caribbean Elementary and other individual school's experimental programs were not discouraged by county school officials, but the need for some basic standards for countywide programs was apparent.

Standardizing Bilingual Schooling

When the first bilingual school programs were initiated in the 1960's, school officials recognized the importance of designing programs that were appropriate for the unique characteristics of each school's community. As the number of bilingual school programs grew and the courses in English as a Second Language and Spanish for Spanish-Speakers spread to most elementary and secondary schools throughout the county, the variety of policies and procedures related to bilingual education at individual schools began to pose problems for the county's school administrators.

One of the first problems involved the seemingly simple procedure of accurately identifying Spanish-speaking students in the schools. Various descriptive terms had been employed during the sixties (native Spanish-speakers, Spanish-speaking students, Spanish-surnamed students, Cuban refugees, etc.)

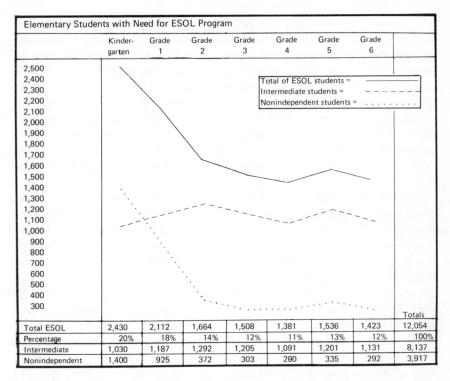

Elementary Students with Need for ESOL Program							
	Kinder- garten	Grade 1	Grade 2	Grade 3	Grade 4	Grade 5	Grade 6
							Totals
Total ESOL	2,430	2,112	1,664	1,508	1,381	1,536	1,423	12,054
Percentage	20%	18%	14%	12%	11%	13%	12%	100%
Intermediate	1,030	1,187	1,292	1,205	1,091	1,201	1,131	8,137
Nonindependent	1,400	925	372	303	290	335	292	3,917

Source: Division of Elementary and Secondary Education, "Plan for Meeting the Instructional Needs of Students of Limited-English-Speaking Ability: 1976-79," Dade County Public Schools, Miami, Florida, February 18, 1976, p. 3.

Figure 17   Elementary Students Needing English: 1975

causing confusion on the part of both county and school-level administrators when they were required to tabulate the number of students in this group or to perform comparative analyses.[49] In 1971, therefore, a standardized term, "Spanish language origin" students,[50] began to be employed throughout the county. It was clearly differentiated from the term "Cuban refugee", and its definition was drawn from the annual survey of students that was required by the Civil Rights Act of 1964: "persons considered by themselves, by the school, or by the community to be of Mexican, Puerto Rican, Central American, Cuban, Latin-American, or other Spanish-speaking origin". This standardized term alleviated many of the accounting and evaluation problems, but it was learned that some school administrators continued to confuse language origin and racial background when identifying students in reports. In 1975, therefore, county school officials directed school personnel to employ a new standardized term, "Hispanic", and provided the following definition: "a person of Mexican, Puerto Rican, Cuban, Central or South American, or other Spanish culture or origin, regardless of race." [51]

The number of schools, teachers, and students involved in bilingual education by the early 1970's prompted the compilation of a comprehensive procedures manual to provide overall standardization for all facets of the county's program. This manual,[52] published in 1971, included a general definition for the overall bilingual education program and each of its four components: English as a Second Language, Spanish for Spanish-Speakers, Spanish as a Second Language and the bilingual school organizations. For each component, there was a statement of rationale, criteria, goal, and objectives plus a section concerning placement of students, grading and promotion, instructional materials, and staffing. In addition, there was an extensive listing of program resources.

The continued expansion of Dade County's bilingual programs in the early seventies and the emerging intricacies of program implementation dictated a revision of the procedures manual in 1975. The standards and guidelines in the new manual[53] were more specific and comprehensive. For example, the categories for students participating in the English as a Second Language program were expanded from three to five.

Since the inception of the English as a Second Language program in the early 1960's, students were categorized in terms of their linguistic independence in the English language as either "non-independent", "intermediate", or "independent"; the latter group requiring little, if any, special second-language instruction in English. The instructional program and resources for students differed from one category to the next; however, during the 1960's, identification and placement of students in each of the three categories had often varied from school to school. The 1971 procedures manual had provided a standardized list of the linguistic characteristics for students that should be assigned to each level. By the mid-seventies, it became apparent that three categories were not sufficient, and the 1975 revision of the precedures manual provided guidelines for five levels of English as a Second Language instruction that included the following list of linguistic characteristics for student identification:

Nonindependent [non-communicating in English]   *[0%-20% proficiency]*

Understand only very limited if any conversation, approximately less than 10 percent of the time

Make constant errors in using the most frequent and useful significant grammatical structures, approximately 80-100 percent of the time

Speak with constant significant distortions of words and intonation, approximately 80-100 percent of the time

Use extremely limited vocabulary, approximately 80-100 percent of the time

Low Intermediate   *[20%-50% proficiency]*

Understand limited everyday speech, approximately less than 20 percent of the time, when English-speakers choose words carefully or restate ideas

Make frequent significant grammatical errors of interference, approximately 50-80 percent of the time

Speak with frequent significant distortions of words and intonation, approximately 50-80 percent of the time

Grope for high-frequency words and often have to rephrase to be understood, approximately 50-80 percent of the time

Mid-Intermediate   *[50%-80% proficiency]* '

Understand everyday speech fairly well, 20-50 percent, though English-speakers often have to choose words carefully or restate ideas

Make many significant grammatical errors of interference, approximately 20-50 percent of the time

Speak with many significant distortions of words and intonations, approximately 20-50 percent of the time

Usually grope for high-frequency words so that speakers must rephrase to be understood, approximately 20-50 percent of the time

High Intermediate   *[80%-90% proficiency]*

Understand extensively, approximately 50-80 percent, but English-speakers occasionally need to restate ideas

Make occasional significant grammatical errors of interference approximately 10-20 percent of the time

Speak with occasional significant distortions of words and intonation, approximately 10-20 percent of the time

Occasionally grope for high-frequency words and English-speakers may have to rephrase to be understood, approximately 10-20 percent of the time

Independent   *[90%-100% proficiency]*

Understand nearly everything a native speaker of comparable age and intelligence understands, approximately 80-100 percent of the time

Use English with few grammatical errors and can rephrase to make meaning clear, with less than 10 percent of probability of error

Speak with minor, nonsignificant distortions of pronunciation and intonation, with less than 10 percent probability of error

Use vocabulary comparable to that of native speakers of the same age and academic level, groping for words or rephrasing less than 10 percent of the time

Further standardization of the instructional program for non-English-speaking and limited-English-speaking students in the Dade County Public Schools was undertaken in the mid-seventies in response to the evaluation of the county's program by the United States Office of Civil Rights. In essence, the county needed to provide a standardized bilingual instructional program for all of the non-English-speaking and limited-English-speaking students enrolled in public schools. In addition to special English as a Second Language classes and regular curriculum content classes presented in the English language, this type of program would provide these students with bilingual curriculum content, curriculum content presented with English as a Second Language techniques, and native language arts classes.

Fundamental to this program was the recognition that the student's home language could play a major role in the instructional process in any school in Dade County, not just the 26 with bilingual school programs in operation at the time. Equally fundamental was the recognition that mastery of English and the ability to function successfully in the school setting was the ultimate goal of this extensive program. In view of this final goal, the standardized plan adopted by the county was of the transitional type (see Table 9). It was a three-year program covering 12 nine-week quinmester sessions (quins) that was designed for non-English-speaking beginners and students with limited-English-speaking skills (intermediates) whose native languages were either Spanish, Haitian-French, Vietnamese, Chinese, Italian, Hebrew, Portuguese, German, Arabic, Greek, or Korean.[54] The large majority of these students, of course, were from Spanish-speaking backgrounds, and the sample schedules provided by county school officials presented the time requirements in terms of Spanish-speakers (see Tables 10 and 11).

This standardized plan was initiated at the beginning of the 1976-77 school year in certain grade levels at the elementary and junior high schools in Dade County with the highest concentrations of non-English-speaking students. Some resentment was expressed by local school personnel and community members because the standards had been imposed by the federal government rather than by local policy makers. Representatives of the United States Government could not require the local school system to implement this type of countywide program, but they could refuse to appropriate additional federal funds until the Dade County Public Schools were found to be in compliance with standards that the United States Supreme Court had judged appropriate for public schools throughout the nation. This was a powerful incentive to comply, because the federal government provided approximately $40,000,000 annually in revenue to the local school system at that time. The level of federal funding allotted for the bilingual instructional program alone had risen to almost $3,000,000 in 1976, the largest amount in a history of federal support for bilingual education in Dade County that dated back to the early 1960's.

Table 9
TIME PHASING BY LANGUAGE IN TRANSITIONAL PROGRAMS

	Quin 1	Quin 2	Quin 3	Quin 4	Quin 5	Quin 6	Quin 7	Quin 8	Quin 9	Quin 10	Quin 11	Quin 12
Number of minutes in home language	150	150	120	120	90	90	90	60	60	60	60	30
Percent of time in home language	42%	42%	33%	33%	25%	25%	25%	17%	17%	17%	17%	8%
Number of minutes in English	210	210	240	240	270	270	270	300	300	300	300	330
Percent of time in English	58%	58%	67%	67%	75%	75%	75%	83%	83%	83%	83%	92%

Source: Division of Elementary and Secondary Education, *Plan for Meeting the Instructional Needs of Students of Limited-English-Speaking Ability: 1976-1979,* Miami: Dade County Public Schools, Feb. 18, 1976, p. 20.

Table 10
A SCHEDULE FOR BEGINNING STUDENTS

Quinmester 1	Quinmester 2	Quinmester 3	Quinmester 4	Summer Quin (Optional)
Spanish Language Arts (Spanish-S)	Spanish Language Arts (Spanish-S)	Spanish Language Arts (Spanish-S)	Spanish Language Arts (Spanish-S)	Spanish Language Arts (Spanish-S)
Spanish Language Arts (Spanish-S)	Spanish Language Arts (Spanish-S)	Spanish Language Arts (Spanish-S)	Spanish Language Arts (Spanish-S)	Spanish Language Arts (Spanish-S)
Curriculum Content in Spanish	Curriculum Content in Spanish	Curriculum Content in Spanish	Curriculum Content in Spanish	Curriculum Content using ESOL
Curriculum Content in Spanish	Curriculum Content in Spanish	Curriculum Content in Spanish	Curriculum Content in Spanish	Curriculum Content using ESOL
Curriculum Content in Spanish	Curriculum Content in Spanish	ESOL Language Arts	ESOL Language Arts	Curriculum Content using ESOL
ESOL Language Arts	ESOL Language Arts	ESOL Language Arts	ESOL Language Arts	ESOL Language Arts
ESOL Language Arts	ESOL Language Arts	ESOL Language Arts (Reading)	ESOL Language Arts (Reading)	ESOL Language Arts
ESOL Language Arts	ESOL Language Arts	ESOL Language Arts (Reading)	ESOL Language Arts (Reading)	ESOL Language Arts
Curriculum Content using ESOL	Curriculum Content using ESOL	Curriculum Content using ESOL	Curriculum Content using ESOL	ESOL Language Arts
Curriculum Content using ESOL	Curriculum Content using ESOL	Curriculum Content using ESOL	Curriculum Content using ESOL	ESOL Language Arts
Curriculum Content using ESOL	Curriculum Content using ESOL	Regular English Curriculum	Regular English Curriculum	Each block represents approximately 30 minutes
Regular English Curriculum	Regular English Curriculum	Regular English Curriculum	Regular English Curriculum	

Source: Division of Elementary and Secondary Education, *Plan for Meeting the Instructional Needs of Students of Limited-English-Speaking Ability: 1976-79,* Miami: Dade County Public Schools, Feb. 18, 1976, p. 19.

Table 11
A SCHEDULE FOR INTERMEDIATE STUDENTS

Quin 5	Quin 6	Quin 7	Quin 8	Quin 9	Quin 10	Quin 11	Quin 12
HL	HL	HL	HL	HL	HL	HL	HL
							ESOL
						ESOL	CCE-ESOL
				ESOL	ESOL		
			ESOL			CCE-ESOL	
ESOL	ESOL	ESOL					
				CCE-ESOL	CCE-ESOL		
			CCE-ESOL				
CCE-ESOL	CCE-ESOL	CCE-ESOL					CCE
						CCE	
					CCE		
				CCE			
CCE	CCE	CCE	CCE				

KEY TO MEDIUMS OF INSTRUCTION IN EDUCATIONAL PROGRAM:

HL - Study of Spanish or other Home Language and/or Use of That Language for Curriculum Content Instruction.

ESOL - Language Arts Instruction in English for Speakers of Other Languages

CCE-ESOL - Curriculum Content Instruction in English Using ESOL Techniques

CCE - Regular Curriculum Content Instruction in English

Source: Adapted from Division of Elementary and Secondary Education, *Plan for Meeting the Instructional Needs of Students of Limited-English-Speaking Ability: 1976-79,* Miami: Dade County Public Schools, Feb. 18, 1976, pp. 21-23.

Notes

1. Mae Walters, South Beach, Southside, Miami Gardens, Rockway, Springview, and Caribbean Elementary Schools.
2. Within the Dade County Public Schools System at that time, the instructional program at a specific grade level was considered to be organized for bilingual schooling when both language arts instruction and all or part of the academic program were presented in both the English and the Spanish languages for both English-speaking and Spanish-speaking students. An elementary school (kindergarten and grade levels one through six), a junior high school (grade levels seven through nine), or a senior high school (grade levels ten through twelve) was often identified as a complete Bilingual School Organization when this two-way, bilingual schooling program was offered at all grade levels in that particular school.
3. Rosa G. Inclan, Coordinator of Bilingual Education, "Report on Survey of Spanish-Speaking Pupils". Dade County Public Schools, Miami, Fla., Mar. 11, 1969.
4. Edgar W. Hooper, Jr., Principal, "Report of Plans for School Improvement, 1966-67", Mae Walters Elementary School, Hialeah, Fla., Oct. 15, 1966, p. 1.
5. Paul W. Bell.
6. Supra Note 3
7. Department of Administrative Research, *Spanish-Speaking Pupils in the Dade County Public Schools: 1969-70,* vol. XVII, no. 11. Dade County Public Schools, Miami, Fla., 1970, p. 20.
8. Von N. Beebe, "A Process Description and Evaluation of the Programs for Bilingual Education within Three Bilingual Elementary Schools in Dade County Public Schools, Florida". Miami, Fla., 1970, pp. 36, 43, 44.
9. Department of Administrative Research, *Spanish-Speaking Pupils in the Dade County Public Schools: 1970-71,* vol. XVIII, no. 11. Dade County Public Schools, Miami, Fla., 1971.
10. Department of Administrative Research, *Desegregation: September 1972,* vol. XX, no. 2. Dade County Public Schools, Miami, Fla., 1972, pp. 28, 46, 58, 94-95.
11. Department of Administrative Research, *Desegregation: September 1971,* vol. XIX, no. 2. Dade County Public Schools, Miami, Fla., 1971, pp. 8, 26.
12. Supra Note 9
13. Rosa Inclan became the county's Coordinator of Bilingual Education in 1969.
14. Supra Note 2
15. Supra Note 10
16. Supra Note 3
17. Supra Note 11
18. Ibid.
19. This organizational feature was similar to the county's third model for bilingual schooling at the elementary school level. See Figure 14.
20. This organizational feature was similar to the county's second model for bilingual schooling at the elementary school level. See Figure 13.
21. This organizational feature was similar to the county's first model for bilingual schooling at the elementary school level. See Figure 12.
22. Although not required by the State of Florida at that time, special classes in English as a Second Language also were offered.
23. Another alternative course, Foreign-Born Math, was also available for students in the school who were just beginning to learn English.
24. "Typical Schedules for Students in the Bilingual Program," Shenandoah Junior High School. Dade County Public Schools, Miami, Fla., 1970.
25. Spanish-S was designed for students who already spoke Spanish. Some of the native English-speakers in the bilingual program found this course, which emphasized reading, writing, and literature skills in Spanish, to be too difficult. The option of attending Spanish as a Second Language (Spanish-SL) classes, therefore, became available.

26. "Seventh Grade Program of Studies, 1972-73", Ida M. Fisher Junior High School. Dade County Public Schools, Miami, Fla., 1972.
27. Supra Note 3
28. Supra Note 10
29. Supra Note 9
30. Dade County Public Schools, *Program Budget for Fiscal Year 1972-73*, Miami, Fla., 1972, p. 38.
31. Supra Note 2
32. The quinmester courses produced in Spanish were not direct translations of the parallel courses in English, but the same basic skills and content were developed.
33. *The Miami News*, April 15, 1974 (editorial).
34. Supra Note 10
35. "Spanish Language Origin Student Survey (Oct. 2, 1972)", revised as of Nov. 8, 1972. Dade County Public Schools, Miami, Fla., 1972, p. 1.
36. Department of Program Evaluation, *Evaluation of Programs for Spanish Language Origin Students: 1970-71*. Miami: Dade County Public Schools, 1972, pp. 52-65.
37. Department of Planning and Evaluation, *Evaluation of Dade County Public School Bilingual Programs: 1973-74*. Miami: Dade County Public Schools, 1975, pp. 3-10.
38. Ibid.
39. Ibid.
40. Ibid.
41. In 1975, the title of the English as a Second Language (ESL) program was changed to English for Speakers of Other Languages (ESOL) at the request of some citizens who objected to possible interpretations of the word "second" in the original title.
42. J. Gonzalez, "The Coming of Age of Bilingual, Bicultural Education" in *Inequality in Education*, No. 9. Cambridge: Harvard University Center for Law and Education, 1975.
43. Division of Elementary and Secondary Education, *Plan for Meeting the Instructional Needs of Students of Limited-English-Speaking Ability: 1976-79*. Miami: Dade County Public Schools, Feb. 18, 1976.
44. Ralph F. Robinett.
45. Supra Note 43
46. Von N. Beebe, "Anglos on la Isla Caribe", *Hispania*, September, 1976, pp. 499-501.
47. W. E. Lambert and R. C. Tucker. *The Bilingual Education of Children*. Rowley: Newbury House, 1972.
48. D. Cohen. *Sociolinguistic Model of Bilingual Education*. Rowley: Newbury House, 1975.
49. Department of Program Evaluation, *Summary of Evaluation Reports: 1970-71*. Miami: Dade County Public Schools, 1971, Part C. p. 1.
50. The authors of this text selected to use the term "Spanish-speaking" students because of its wide acceptance throughout the world. Although the term "Spanish language origin" students is often more inclusive, it is not as familiar to the general public (see Introduction).
51. J. L. Jones, Deputy Superintendent, Dade County Public Schools, Memorandum to All Associate, Area and Assistant Superintendents, Department Heads, and School Principals, "Revision of Official Racial/Ethnic Designations for Use in All School System Surveys, Data Collection Activities, and Reports", Oct. 1, 1975.
52. Division of Instruction, *Procedures Manual: Bilingual Education Program*. Bulletin 1C, Revised, Miami: Dade County Public Schools, 1971.
53. Division of Elementary and Secondary Education, *Procedures Manual: Bilingual Programs*. Bulletin 1C, Revised, Miami: Dade County Public Schools, 1975.
54. Supra Note 43

8

Support for Bilingual Schooling

Without the necessary support, the initiation, expansion and generalization of public bilingual schooling in a democratic society are impossible. This support must include sufficient public backing and some degree of educational initiative at the school level.

PUBLIC SUPPORT

Public support for bilingual schooling begins with a change in cultural attitudes and educational opinion, and this is often a slow and gradual process. In order to initiate bilingual schooling, therefore, private rather than public support and financing are frequently necessary. Subsequently, public policies concerning education are adapted or modified, and, as part of the politics of accommodation, new public policies concerning bilingual schooling are created that legitimize the search for public funding for these programs in the schools.

Public Opinion

During the 1960's, the support of the general public in Dade County for the bilingual education programs in the area's public schools can best be described as nonexistent or passive. Bilingual education in the English and Spanish languages had been fairly common in Cuban schools, therefore, most of the Spanish-speaking residents did not view the programs as a startling innovation. Instead, many Spanish-speakers perceived the public schools' bilingual programs as a gesture of respect and friendship by their American hosts. They supported the concepts of bilingualism, but few Spanish-speakers were politically active during the sixties and their support remained passive. Many English-speaking residents were apathetic because they also viewed the public schools' bilingual programs as a temporary accommodation that would only involve Cuban refugee children prior to their return to their Spanish-speaking homeland. In fact, the countywide programs in English as a Second Language and Spanish for Spanish-Speakers were basically just that in the early 1960's; and, with the exception of English-speaking children attending the county's four bilingual schools during the sixties, the children of English-speaking residents were not directly involved in bilingual education. Participation in the new programs at the bilingual schools generally was on a voluntary basis at the time, and most of the English-speaking parents at these schools felt that learning a second language would be a nice addition to their children's education.

During the early 1970's, bilingual education spread rapidly in the area's public schools. It directly affected English-speaking students in the form of additional bilingual school programs and a countywide program in Spanish as a Second Language; and, some English-speaking residents began to attack the concept. They were usually monolinguals themselves, as were the large majority of native English-speakers in the Miami area, and their reasoning generally was similar to that discovered elsewhere by Lambert and Tucker. "For someone who knows just one language, bilingualism may seem to be a mysterious, essentially alien process. Because of his own limited linguistic experience, the monolingual tends to link language inseparably with both thinking and learning. He wonders whether a person can 'think' equally well in two languages." [1] As one would expect, some of these citizens claimed that bilingual education was "anti-American". They explained that the "melting pot" philosophy had been a stabilizing force in the United States and that the exclusive use of English for instructional purposes in public schools was one of the crucial factors in the success of the Americanization process.

Many Cuban refugees, realizing that their residence in the United States was probably permanent, became American citizens and politically active during the early 1970's. At this point, their support for the public schools' bilingual programs was heard loud and clear. Many English-speaking residents also became active supporters of bilingual education. The major reason for the support of the latter group, perhaps, was that bilingualism had become a desirable attribute, if not a prerequisite, for employment in many large and small businesses throughout Dade County. After all, businessmen of both English and Spanish-speaking backgrounds were competing for the billion dollar market of the local Spanish-speaking population.

In addition to having their children pursue bilingual education in school, a large number of English-speaking adults started to learn Spanish themselves in the 1970's. Approximately 6,000 adults participated in public and private Spanish classes as well as informal neighborhood study groups. To respond to the demand and encourage the trend, the adult education branch of the Dade County Public Schools provided sixteen-week courses in Spanish at a cost of only five dollars. Some 12,000 adults enrolled. In addition, about 2,800 people studied Spanish at a local community college and some 1,000 at the University of Miami. The total number of adults studying Spanish in Dade County surpassed 20,000 in the mid-seventies. [2] Many of these adults had found that fluency in the Spanish language had become a valuable new job skill in the area's two-language economy.

The extraordinary success of local Cuban refugees in various realms of business and the professions and the resultant benefits to the economy of the Miami area also had a positive effect upon the public's opinion of bilingual schooling. [3] In fact, in 1973, a local survey indicated that almost 70 percent of the residents of Dade County supported the school's bilingual education program for both English and Spanish-speaking students, feeling that it had become an essential component of the overall program for public education. [4] Later that year, the Dade County Public Schools conducted a survey of public opinion on a representative cross-section of the area's adult population, and the results revealed that 88 percent of those interviewed favored the public schools providing bilingual education on a voluntary basis for all students. Requiring English-speaking students to learn Spanish, however, was opposed by 66 percent of the respondents, indicating the majority's opposition to forced bilingualism for native English-speaking children. [5]

In sum, by the mid-seventies, public opinion concerning bilingual schooling in Dade County ranged from those who would prohibit it for all students to those who would require it for all students. Some believed that Dade County would eventually return to a basically monolingual, English-speaking area and that bilingual schooling was merely postponing this natural outcome. Others believed that Dade County would soon become predominantly Spanish-speaking and that the public schools would be negligent if they did not prepare the area's youth for this type of community. The opinion of the majority of the residents fell somewhere between these two extremes and leaned strongly toward preparing students for a society that would continue to be bilingual and bicultural. This consensus had already permitted significant changes in public policy.

Public Policy

With the exception of some unofficial courtesies provided for wealthy businessmen, shoppers, and tourists from Latin America, no public policies concerning bilingualism, biculturalism, or bilingual schooling existed in Dade County prior to the initial influx of Cuban refugees in 1960. The status quo was maintained during the 1960's, and, with the exception of the public school system, there were no significant changes in public services or policies. When Spanish-speakers began to actively participate in local politics in the early 1970's and the economic power of this group was recognized, however, major changes occurred.

Perhaps the most significant event happened in April, 1973, when the county's top elected officials declared Dade County a bilingual and bicultural community and Spanish the area's second official language (see Appendix C). This new statement of public policy led to additional changes in governmental services that had always been provided on an "English only" basis; for example, county court forms and traffic tickets were printed in Spanish as well as English, bilingual personnel were assigned to answer the emergency telephones for the police and fire departments, information concerning taxes and marriage licenses was provided in both languages, and election ballots were printed in both English and Spanish.

It was apparent to all local residents by the early 1970's, often on a daily basis, that Dade County had become a bilingual and bicultural community. The official resolution and accompanying accommodations in public services that encouraged knowledgeable involvement in government and provided for the safety of the area's Spanish-speaking residents seemed to meet with the approval of the majority of citizens. There were some residents, of course, who claimed that these changes were unnecessary and "un-American", and others who stated that they were not sufficient or not being truly implemented. The latter group were predominantly native Spanish-speakers and they revived the Spanish-American Coalition in order to apply political pressure on local government leaders to further enforce the concepts of bilingualism and biculturalism in the county. The coalition's priorities included: 1) upgrading the bilingual capabilities of county departments serving the public; 2) increasing employment for Spanish-speakers in local government offices; and 3) providing for a better understanding of Latin-American culture within the total community. [6]

Although Dade County's huge Spanish-speaking population, as well as its emerging role as the commercial bridge between English-speaking and Spanish-speaking America, caused changes in the area's local policies concerning bilingualism and biculturalism, no such changes had occurred by the mid-seventies in official policies at the state level. In terms of public education, Florida State Statutes still stated that "the basic language of instruction will be English", and the United States Constitution assigned the responsibility for public education to the governments of each state. Historically, most states had required that this public education be presented in the English language. Following passage of the Bilingual Education Act by the national government in 1967, a number of states began to repeal these laws. By 1972, only ten states still prohibited public school instruction in any language other than English. Public policies in all of the other states permitted local school boards to institute instructional programs where curriculum content was presented in languages other than English.[7] In fact, the state of Massachusetts enacted a law that *required* every school district within the state to provide bilingual instruction "whenever there are twenty or more children who share the same native language other than English." [8] At about the same time, six other states enacted similar legislation, some allocating state funds to support program implementation.[9]

By the middle of the 1970's, national public policy, based upon the United States Supreme Court's findings in what was commonly referred to as the *Lau Decision*, supported use of the native languages of non-English-speaking students in public instructional programs. The federal government's Civil Rights Task Force examined the appropriateness of existent programs in public schools and found that more than 229 school districts in 21 states, including five county school systems in the State of Florida, appeared to be in violation of this new national policy.[10] Bilingual education was not exactly prohibited in the State of Florida, but it was not until more than ten years after bilingual instructional programs had been pioneered in Dade County that there were some signs of adaptation or change in public policies at the state level.

In 1973, three significant events occurred. For the first time, the Florida State Department of Education agreed to include textbooks for English as a Second Language instruction on the list of approved textbooks provided at a reduced cost by the state to local school systems. Textbooks for instruction in Spanish for Spanish-Speakers, Spanish as a Second Language, and Curriculum Content in Spanish, however, were still not included on this list at the time. The second event indicating an adaptation of state level policies was the distribution by the Florida State Department of Education of a position paper on foreign language study that included, for the first time, Spanish as a Second Language (at the elementary school level) and English as a Second Language courses as part of the state's recommended foreign language program. The position paper also encouraged every community within the state "to go beyond a second-language program into bilingual experiences and/or bilingual school organizations".[11] And finally, the Florida State Legislature seriously considered enacting a Florida Bilingual Education Act of 1973 that would have required school systems throughout the state with more than 400 non-English-speaking students: "1) to teach basic subjects such as mathematics and history in the native language of the students, until the students learn to speak English; 2) to accelerate the program of instruction in English as a Second Language; 3) to provide continuing education in the native language of the student, in grammar and in the history of the mother country."[12] The act was not passed by the Florida State Legislature that year, and, by 1976, no legislation of this nature had changed the state's policies concerning bilingual schooling.

In summary, the major modifications and changes in public policies concerning bilingual schooling had occurred at the local and national levels, but not at the state level where the nation's constitution had delegated responsibility for public education. In addition to the efforts of public school leaders in Dade County to design and implement bilingual education programs, governmental officials at the local level had declared the county bilingual and bicultural, naming Spanish as the area's second official language. National leaders had enacted a Bilingual Education Act to support the initiation of these programs throughout the country and had begun investigations to ensure that non-English-speaking students were receiving instruction in a language that they understood. In turn, these changes in public policies legitimized the financing of bilingual education from public funds at the national and local levels; however, back in the early 1960's, local school leaders relied primarily upon a non-public funding source to introduce a biethnic model for bilingual schooling.

Finding the Funds

Although the first source of funding related to bilingual education in Dade County came from the federal government's Cuban Refugee Program, these funds were not allocated in the beginning to directly support bilingual education but to reimburse the local school system for the costs of educating large numbers of Cuban refugees. As in other parts of the world, private funds were needed to develop the first experimental program in bilingual schooling. When local and national policies began to change in the late 1960's and early 1970's, financial support was sought and obtained from the budgets of the local school system and the United States Office of Education.

As relatively large numbers of Cuban students suddenly enrolled in the public schools of Dade County at the beginning of the 1960's, it soon became apparent that local taxpayers and the financial structure of the school system would not be able to provide the monetary resources necessary to meet the large demand for more classroom space, more teachers, and special language programs.[13] Supplementary support for educating the refugee students had not been received from the State of Florida, therefore there was a need for assistance from the federal government. After all, as the Florida State Superintendent of Public Instruction noted at the time, "only an accident of geography [its proximity to Cuba] made Florida the center of the refugee problem..." [14] During the early months of 1961, an assistant superintendent of the Dade County Public Schools met with representatives of the President of the United States, representatives of both local and national groups, and representatives of the newly-established Cuban Refugee Center in Miami. It was agreed that federal relief was justified because the Cuban influx into the public schools in Dade County was a result of federal policy, that is a decision by the nation's leaders to accept all refugees from Cuba. The relief took the form of agreements between the United States Commissioner of Education and the Dade County School Board, and was one of the major components within the overall Cuban Refugee Program in the United States. The funds were provided as a general reimbursement to the Dade County Public Schools, based upon the exact number of Cuban refugee children and adults that were served, and was not categorically tied to the funding of specific programs that served only Cuban refugees.

The first agreement was approved on March 8, 1961. Its terms provided for federal reimbursement to the county's taxpayers for increases in current operating expenses caused by the presence of Cuban refugee children in the regular instructional program of grades one through twelve. Additional expenses for special summer school programs in conversational English for Cuban refugee students and special educational and vocational programs (including an English Language Institute) for Cuban refugee adults were also to be refunded by the federal government as part of the agreement.[15] A portion of these funds were applied to the new English as a Second Language program that had been initiated in the county during the 1960-61 school year. The following year, some of these reimbursement funds were similarly applied to the Spanish for Spanish-Speakers program initiated in the county at that time.

A continued need for this type of federal assistance was apparent almost from the start, and, in the summer of 1962, Public Law 87-510 was passed by the United States Congress authorizing yearly appropriations by the Department of Health, Education, and Welfare to the Dade County School Board for a Cuban Refugee Program.[16] As the school years passed and the Cuban refugees continued to immigrate to Dade County, school officials became more aware of the actual costs involved in educating non-English-speaking students within the local public schools: additional textbooks, new instructional materials, curriculum development projects and staff development workshops. Consequently, the allocation formula in the agreements with the United States Commissioner of Education became more specific and, at the same time, more complex.

This form of financial reimbursement to the Dade County Public Schools was maintained throughout the 1960's and into the seventies. By the middle of the 1970's, as indicated in Table 12, total funds received from the Cuban Refugee Program had grown to more than $150,000,000. On the other hand, the allocations had been gradually diminished each year during the seventies, and there was serious question as to how much longer the federal government would provide funds through this program to the Dade County Public Schools.

To obtain financial assistance to directly support bilingual schooling back in the early 1960's, local educators found that it was prudent first to convince leaders of a private foundation of the need. This was achieved and, in 1963, The Ford Foundation awarded a three-year grant to the Dade County School Board for the implementation of specific projects for the bilingual education of Cuban refugee students.[17] One of these projects included English-speaking students in a bilingual school program. This project was successful and Coral Way Elementary became the nation's first public school to offer a two-way, bilingual program for English-speaking and Spanish-speaking students. The project's leaders were also successful in completing one other project to support bilingual education locally, the development of a beginning-reading program in the English language for Spanish-speaking students.[18]

Funding from The Ford Foundation, as planned, was terminated in 1966; and the bilingual school program at Coral Way Elementary was maintained and funded by the local school system, along with some financial assistance from the Cuban Refugee Program. These same two funding sources supported

Table 12
THE CUBAN REFUGEE PROGRAM
(Federal Funding for the Dade County Public Schools: 1960-1975)

School year	Program in Grades 1-12	Vocational & Adult Program	Summer Program	Total
1960-61	$ 623,500	$ 50,000	$ 26,078	$ 699,578
1961-62	$ 3,076,284	$ 882,740	$ 30,187	$ 3,989,211
1962-63	$ 5,953,586	$1,651,457	$ 80,317	$ 7,685,360
1963-64	$ 5,763,669	$1,140,315	$ 44,858	$ 6,948,842
1964-65	$ 5,261,318	$1,154,386	$ 81,987	$ 6,497,691
1965-66	$ 5,832,646	$1,039,727	$102,390	$ 6,974,763
1966-67	$ 9,427,135	$ 990,786	$100,374	$10,518,295
1967-68	$13,000,819	$ 891,995	$158,718	$14,051,532
1968-69	$13,519,220	$ 904,623	$160,000	$14,583,843
1969-70	$15,588,598	$ 876,667	$159,997	$16,625,262
1970-71	$13,512,238	$ 935,204	$159,914	$14,607,356
1971-72	$12,814,069	$ 919,177	$ 99,471	$13,832,717
1972-73	$12,638,552	$ 833,195		$13,471,747
1973-74	$12,399,987	$ 167,327		$12,567,314
1974-75	$12,400,000	$ 98,843		$12,498,843
	$141,811,621	$12,536,442	$1,204,291	$155,552,343

Source: Department of Planning and Evaluation, *The Cuban Refugee in the Public Schools of Dade County, Florida, Report No. 14,* Dade County Public Schools, Miami, Florida, 1976, p. 2.

new bilingual school programs that were implemented subsequently, as well as the countywide English as a Second Language, Spanish for Spanish-Speakers, and new Spanish as a Second Language programs. As national policy concerning bilingual education changed in the late 1960's, local school officials applied for supplemental funds from the federal government to support additional special programs in bilingual education plus teacher-training and materials-development projects for bilingual education.

SCHOOL SUPPORT

Local school support for bilingual schooling was highlighted in October, 1971, when the Superintendent of the Dade County Public Schools issued five directives:

1. That each school provide instruction in English as a Second Language for those students entering the school who are either "non-independent" or "intermediate".
2. That every school provide the opportunity for Spanish language origin and bilingual English language origin students to be involved in an instructional program in Spanish for Spanish-Speakers.
3. That a Spanish as a Second Language pilot program be implemented by the [local] Division of Instruction in one or more [local administrative] districts in schools not functioning within a Bilingual School Organization for the 1971-72 school year; and that, based on the success of the Spanish SL pilot program or programs during the 1971-72 school year, a supplemental budget appropriation request be submitted for 1972-73 to provide funds for the expansion of the program to all schools that identify the need for such a program.
4. That each district, in cooperation with the Division of Instruction, develop a plan during the 1971-72 school year for establishing within the district a K-12 Bilingual School Organization.
5. That an internal certification program in second-language teaching and in Spanish-S for teachers and para-professionals be developed by the Division of Instruction, in cooperation with the Personnel Division. This certification program is to be developed since the state has no certification program for English SL, Spanish-S, or Bilingual Education.[19]

These directives were operationalized in Dade County during the early 1970's, and, beginning with the 1972-73 school year, the improvement and expansion of bilingual programs was established as one of the school system's educational priorities.

Financial support for bilingual education within the budget of Dade County's public school system was difficult to isolate, however local funds had always been provided in the form of classroom space, furniture, utilities, supervision, teacher-training, and some instructional materials. As budgeting procedures became more sophisticated in the early seventies, school officials were better able to trace various expenses and to ascertain the overall cost of instruction for specific programs (instructors' salaries, fringe benefits, equipment, materials, etc.). During the 1975-76 school year, school officials determined that the basic cost of the bilingual education program for that school year was $7,500,000 of which a little more than half, $3,800,000 constituted locally-generated funds. The remaining funds were allocated directly to the bilingual education program from the $12,400,000 educational budget of the Cuban Refugee Program. The complete bilingual education budget represented less than 2 percent of the total school system budget of approximately $500,000,000 that year. In addition to those basic finds, $900,000 was allocated at the time by the federal government, under the nation's Emergency School Aid Act, to help improve cross-cultural understanding through bilingual programs for both English and Spanish-speaking students. Various other federally-funded projects established in Dade County during the 1970's also made direct and indirect contributions that supported the efforts of the local school system to implement programs, train teachers, and develop materials for bilingual education.

The Programs

The key factor in the school system's support for bilingual schooling in Dade County was the initiation of four special programs: English as a Second Language, Spanish for Spanish-Speakers, Spanish as a Second Language, and curriculum content courses presented bilingually or in Spanish. By the early 1970's, the first three of these programs were no longer perceived as "special" by most community members. They had attained the status of regular offerings in Dade County's public education program. A number of schools presented all four courses in addition to the normal instructional program in the English language.

The English as a Second Language (ESL) program was initiated during the 1960-61 school year at a few schools in Dade County that were enrolling large numbers of non-English-speaking students from the first wave of Cuban refugees migrating to the United States. By 1975, the ESL program had become mandatory for the increased numbers of non-English-speaking or limited-English-speaking students and had spread with these students to 127 of the county's 172 elementary schools, to 35 of the 39 junior high schools, and to 17 of the 20 senior high schools. At that time, the goal of this program was:

> To enable the other-than-English-speaking student and the limited-English-speaking student to acquire the linguistic skills and cultural understanding necessary to participate fully in the regular school program and in all pertinent areas of his community within the United States in accordance with his age, interest level, and ability.[20]

The Spanish for Spanish-Speakers (Spanish-S) program was initiated one year after the ESL program in a few schools with large numbers of Cuban refugees to help these students maintain their Spanish language skills for, what many people believed would be, their quick return to Cuba. Within a few years, Spanish-S classes were offered on a voluntary basis to other Spanish-speaking students, as well as Cuban refugees, to enable them to maintain or improve their native language skills for use within Dade County or in any other location. By 1975, Spanish-S classes were offered at 136 elementary schools, 32 junior high schools, and 16 senior high schools, and the program's goal was stated in the following manner:

> To meet the educational needs of the Spanish language origin students and bilingual or independent level other-than-Spanish language origin students by enabling them to preserve and acquire skills in utilizing Spanish as a native language. The Spanish-S program is also designed to facilitate the Spanish language origin students' acquisition of communication skills in English through the application of what they learn in their vernacular, and to enhance their self-image through the acquisition of knowledge of their original culture. [21]

The Spanish as a Second Language (Spanish-SL) program originated in the county's first bilingual school in 1963 in the form of second-language classes for English-speakers that would enable these students to understand instruction in Spanish in curriculum content areas. It was included in each of the later bilingual school programs, and, in the early 1970's, was initiated as a countywide program in most elementary schools. Spanish-SL classes were presented as an option for non-Spanish-speaking students rather than as a requirement and were coordinated with the long-established foreign language program in Spanish at the secondary school level. In 1975, 162 of the county's 172 elementary schools, 36 of the 39 junior high schools, and all 20 of the senior high schools offered classes in Spanish-SL or Spanish as a Foreign Language. The goal for this program in the elementary schools at that time was:

> To enable students of non-Spanish language origin to communicate in Spanish and to interact successfully on the cultural and conceptual levels with their Spanish language origin peer groups. [22]

Instruction in this program at the elementary school level was intended to provide students who participated for a number of years with sufficient mastery of Spanish to permit eventual enrollment in Spanish-S classes or curriculum content classes presented in the Spanish language. The goal for this program in secondary schools was stated differently:

> To provide for students of non-Spanish origin a continuum of programs from which they may choose those which will enable

them to develop skills and understandings of the Spanish language and cultures. [23]

The Curriculum Content in Spanish (CCS) program also appeared for the first time in Dade County in the first bilingual school program in 1963. These courses were designed to provide first-language instruction in curriculum areas (for example, social studies, mathematics, and science) for Spanish-speaking students and to reinforce and enrich in the Spanish language the instructional concepts in these courses that were introduced in English to native English-speaking students. These courses were modified, being presented bilingually rather than only in Spanish in some cases, and introduced in all of the bilingual school programs at both the elementary and secondary school levels (see Tables 6 and 7). In 1975, the goal of this program was stated as aiming "to develop cross-cultural understandings and attitudes as well as concepts and skills in curriculum areas". [24]

The establishment of a number of bilingual schools at both the elementary and secondary school levels, offering all four of these bilingual education programs, was also a clear demonstration of local school officials' support for bilingual education. By 1975, the goal for this special type of program organization at the elementary school level had been refined into this statement:

The bilingual school organization is designed to enable students of other-than-Spanish language origin and Spanish language origin to master listening, speaking, reading, and writing skills in both English and Spanish, which are commensurate with their experiential and educational levels, ages, and interests, and to interact more comfortably and more effectively with either linguistic or culture group within the school and within the community. [25]

Another indication of local school leaders' initiative in the area of bilingual education was their record of successfully obtaining supplemental grants for bilingual instructional programs as funds became available from the federal government during the 1970's. One of these grants was related to the national policy for desegregating racially-identifiable public schools. Since 1971, financial assistance had been provided by the United States Office of Education to public school systems throughout the country (under the Emergency School Assistance Program) to help in solving problems encountered during the process of desegregating student populations on a racial basis. In 1973, the United States Congress revised this program to the more extensive, yet more specific, Emergency School Aid Act (Public Law 92-318) that included a section providing for "the needs of minority group children who are from an environment in which a dominant language is other than English and who, because of language barriers and cultural differences, do not have equality of educational opportunity".[26] In the spring of 1972, officials of the Dade County Public Schools appointed a Bilingual Advisory Committee of parents, students, teachers, and representatives of civic organizations and other community groups to generate a list of needs for special funding under the Emergency School Aid Act.[27] The needs identified by the advisory committee were incorporated by school officials into a Bilingual Proposal that was formally submitted to the United States Office of Education in April, 1973.

Five components were outlined in the Bilingual Proposal:

Component One - Curriculum Implementation, Reading and English as a Second Language. This component was designed to improve reading proficiency in the English language by Spanish-speaking students, including migrants, in three elementary schools and two junior high schools and to improve verbal proficiency in the English language by Spanish-speaking students at one senior high school.

Component Two - Bilingual School Organizations. This component was designed to introduce a bilingual school program for both English-speaking and Spanish-speaking students in kindergarten, first grade, and second grade at three elementary schools.

Component Three - Spanish as a Second Language. This component was designed to improve communication between Spanish-speaking and English-speaking students by providing second-language instruction in Spanish (Spanish-SL) for English-speaking students in a number of elementary schools with racially-integrated student populations.

Component Four - Cultural Arts. This component was designed to improve communication and understanding among Spanish-speaking students, black English-speaking students, and Caucasian English-speaking students at an integrated elementary school by developing an appreciation among all students for the art, music, literature, social history, etc. associated by many with each of the three groups.

Component Five - TABA Teaching Strategies. This component was designed to improve overall academic achievement of English-speaking and Spanish-speaking students (including migrant students) at five elementary schools and one junior high school by training teachers to implement TABA strategies (discovery, inquiry approaches) in their daily instructional programs.[28]

$752,396 was requested under the Emergency School Aid Act for the Bilingual Proposal. It was approved by the United States Office of Education in the summer of 1973, as were continuation proposals during subsequent years. A number of other federal grants to support the training of teachers and development of materials for bilingual education also were obtained by officials of the Dade County Public Schools during the 1970's.

The Teachers

The task of finding teachers to present the Spanish language portion of the bilingual program had not been a problem within Dade County. Since the early sixties, many trained educators were among the Cuban refugees that settled in the Miami area, and school officials first employed some of these as Cuban aides. As the years passed, a number of the Cuban aides completed the educational requirements for teacher certification in the State of Florida by attending colleges and universities in the evenings and during the summers. Subsequently, these aides were employed as teachers, psychologists, and counselors in the Dade County Public Schools.

The percentage of teachers and administrators from Spanish-speaking backgrounds employed by the Dade County Public Schools in the mid-seventies was still less than 10 percent, much lower than the percentage of Spanish-speaking students enrolled (see Figure 7, 8 and 9). Some community members claimed that this represented discrimination against native Spanish-speaking educators, while other English-speaking teachers and applicants for teaching positions said that it was more difficult for monolinguals to secure a position or a promotion than it was for bilinguals. At that time, some of the bilingual Spanish-speaking teachers earned appointments to the position of school principal and a few of the Spanish-speaking educators obtained higher positions within the administrative hierarchy of the Dade County Public Schools. In 1973, a Bilingual Education Coordinating Committee was established to supervise the activities of seven administrators responsible for coordinating local bilingual education programs, only one administrative position having been assigned this responsibility during the sixties. The purpose of this committee was to ensure efficient operation of the overall bilingual education program and to maintain support for that program from within the Dade County Public Schools.[29]

In order to train educators involved in bilingual schooling at all levels of the public school system and to coordinate the instructional objectives in the bilingual school programs at the elementary and secondary school levels, school officials submitted a proposal to the federal government for a special project under the Education Professions Development Act. The project, titled Teacher Training Coordinating Capability for Bilingual School Organizations, was approved, and $39,563 was awarded by the United States Office of Education for implementation during the 1971-72 school year. In order to complete the project's objectives, continuation proposals were funded at approximately the same level during the next few years.

Another federally funded bilingual teacher-training project, called Career Development for Bilingual-Bicultural Education, was initiated during the early 1970's. It consisted of a special study program at local universities that was designed to improve the skills of employed aides and teachers who were not native English-speakers while they simultaneously earned credits toward certification or advanced degrees. The program was conducted after regular school hours and funded with a federal grant of $100,000 under the Bilingual Education Act, Title VII, of the nation's Elementary and Secondary Education Act. The long-range goal of the program was to increase the number of qualified teachers for bilingual education and to upgrade the quality of this instruction in local schools. The program continued to receive federal funding into the mid-1970's.

In addition to securing these and other special, federally-funded projects, local school officials demonstrated their support for bilingual education by designing and providing in-service programs within the school system to train native Spanish-speaking instructors, as well as English-speaking instructors, in the techniques of first and second-language instruction within a bilingual-bicultural setting. At the time, the need for a local certification program for teachers in bilingual programs also became apparent. Although some other states had added such special certification programs to the qualification standards set at the state level, the State of Florida had no guidelines in this field. In their absence, the Dade County Public Schools established their own criteria for certifying all teachers working in bilingual school organizations plus teachers of English as a Second Language, Spanish for Spanish-Speakers and Spanish as a Second Language. Teachers could fulfill these criteria through the school system's own in-service training program or by successfully completing specific courses at local universities. Much of this training focused upon proper selection and use of instructional materials for bilingual education.

The Materials

Some appropriate materials were available for English as a Second Language instruction during the 1960's, including the *Fries American English Series* and the locally-developed *Miami Linguistic Readers*, however teachers generally had to rely on homemade items and commercial materials published in Spanish-speaking countries for the other facets of the bilingual education program. The bindings and printing of the foreign-produced materials were frequently not up to the standards that teachers and librarians were accustomed to in the United States, and the contents often were not appropriate for instruction in Dade County's bilingual programs. By 1970, the need to develop appropriate instructional materials for teaching in the Spanish language became critical. This   need also was recognized by many other school systems throughout the country that had initiated bilingual programs within the previous three years with financial assistance from the nation's Bilingual Education Act. The executive director of the Division of Instruction in the Dade County Public Schools,[30] therefore, contacted his former co-worker in the county's Ford Foundation Projects in Bilingual Education.[31] The latter returned to Miami to prepare a proposal for the Bilingual Education Programs Branch of the United States Office of Education to establish a national Spanish Curricula Development Center in Dade County. The proposal[32] was approved for a four-year period and approximately $2,000,000 was allocated.

A Project Advisory Council for the Spanish Curricula Development Center was established to represent the ethnic and linguistic groups involved throughout the United States—primarily Mexican-Americans, Puerto Ricans, and Cubans, as well as native speakers of English—and the geographic areas to be served.[33] An appropriate ethnic and linguistic balance was established among the staff employed at the Center; and, the following year, a Curriculum Adaptation Network for Bilingual Bicultural Education was organized to ensure that the curricular materials would be appropriate for students participating in bilingual programs in all sections of the United States. [34]

The objectives of the Spanish Curricula Development Center were:

> To produce, field test, and revise 48 multidisciplinary, multimedia Spanish curricula kits, of which 16 will be for first grade, 16 for second grade and 16 for third grade. Each kit will be designed as a two-week unit and will contain materials for teachers and materials for pupils conducive to the development of six strands in Spanish: 1) Spanish Language Arts-vernacular, 2) social science, 3) fine arts, 4) science, 5) mathematics, and 6) Spanish as a Second Language. The materials for each strand will be designed so that they may be used independently or in combination with the materials for other strands in the kit.[35]

The project was successful and additional funds were received in subsequent years for producing similar materials for grades four, five and six. In addition to fulfilling its nationwide obligations, the Spanish Curricula Development Center supported bilingual schooling in the Dade County Public Schools by providing appropriate instructional materials in the Spanish language, by presenting workshops for classroom teachers in the county who were using these materials, and by training local personnel to become skilled producers of curriculum for bilingual education.

While the Spanish Curricula Development Center was providing materials for bilingual education at the elementary school level, the need persisted for similar materials at the secondary school level, especially in the area of Spanish as a Second Language instruction. It was noted in the early 1970's that one of every five residents in Dade County was from a Spanish-speaking background, yet only about 10 percent of the area's English-speaking students that were enrolled in junior and senior high schools participated in Spanish language courses. The inability of the majority of English-speaking students to communicate in the Spanish language and their lack of awareness of Latin American cultural heritage and customs prevented many of these students from interacting comfortably with some Spanish-speaking peers and adults. During vacation periods and upon graduation from senior high school, these monolingual English-speaking students also were handicapped in their efforts to obtain employment within the bilingual business community of Dade County.[36] In order to improve Spanish as a Second Language instruction and to provide English-speaking students with the necessary skills for living and working in a bilingual-bicultural community, school officials decided to revise portions of this language program in secondary schools.

A proposal for a planning grant was written by local school officials requesting federal funds to finance the organization of a special curriculum development and teacher-training project in the Dade County Public Schools entitled Individualizing Spanish for Speakers of English. The proposal was submitted to the Florida State Department of Education which had been delegated the responsibility in the state for awarding federal grants from Title III of the nation's Elementary and Secondary Education Act. The proposal was approved and $156,624 was allocated for project planning during the 1972-73 school year. At the beginning of the 1973-74 school year, $200,914 was awarded for implementation of the special project,[37] and a larger amount of federal funding was requested and obtained for subsequent years.

The product was a series of 225 "learning packages", sub-divided into numerous *cursillos* (minimal steps of learning), incorporating the audio-lingual approach to second-language instruction. The *cursillos* were designed for English-speaking students and adults desiring job-oriented fluency in the Spanish language for careers in the areas of auto repair, barber and beauty services, food services, health services, radio and television repair, or retail services.[38] These locally-developed materials, coupled with newly-produced materials from commercial publishing firms, provided support for more effective bilingual instruction in the county's secondary schools. The demand for additional materials for bilingual education at both the elementary and secondary school levels in Dade County and other areas of the United States, however continued to be voiced by educators during the mid-1970's.

THE SUPPORT IN PERSPECTIVE

Support for bilingual schooling in Dade County began in the early 1960's; but, as the numbers of native Spanish-speaking students grew from only one in every 20 students in 1960 to almost one in every three students in the mid-seventies and public policies concerning bilingualism and biculturalism were changed at the local and national levels, the sources of support shifted somewhat and became more widespread.

During the 1960's, three individuals[39] who were not leaders of the local school system supplied the educational initiative and operationalized the concepts of bilingual education in Dade County. Subsequently, school principals and other local educators assisted in the implementation of bilingual programs. Consequently, countywide programs in English as a Second Language and Spanish for Spanish-Speakers were established, bilingual schools were organized, and native Spanish-speaking personnel were employed and trained. External funds were solicited to initiate and maintain bilingual education programs, and the United States Government's Cuban Refugee Program and the private Ford Foundation provided financial support. Local educators were clearly the leading advocates in the movement for bilingual education in Dade County during the sixties. The rationale for their personal commitments was based upon philosophical concepts, educational theory, and previous experiences outside of Dade County.

During the early and mid-1970's, school officials continued to support bilingual education; but, for the first time, a significant portion of the local community began to demand that bilingual instructional programs be provided for more native Spanish-speaking and native English-speaking students throughout the county. Their demands were understandable. It had become an economic disadvantage to be a monolingual English-speaker or a monolingual Spanish-speaker in the bilingual business community of Dade County. Local citizens became a primary force in the movement for bilingual education, and their rationale at the time was based on practical concepts, economic realities, and current experiences within Dade County.

Notes

1. Wallace E. Lambert and G. Richard Tucker, "The Benefits of Bilingualism". *Psychology Today,* Vol. 7, no. 4, September, 1973, p. 89.
2. *The Miami Herald,* July 14, 1975, p. 16-H.
3. Edward J. Linehan, "Cuba's Exiles Bring New Life to Miami". *National Geographic,* Vol. 144, no. 1, July 1973, pp. 68-95.
4. "How Do You Rate Your Public Schools?" *The Miami News,* Aug. 25, 1973, p. 14-A.
5. Dade County Public Schools, "How Dade County Residents View Their Schools". Miami, Fla., 1973, pp. 24-25.
6. *The Miami Herald.* June 3, 1974, p. 21-A.
7. Jeffrey W. Kobrick, "The Compelling Case for Bilingual Education". *Saturday Review: Education,* Apr. 29, 1972, pp. 57-58.
8. Ibid.
9. Stewart Dill McBride. "Bilingual Classes in U.S. - the Debate Rages", *The Christian Science Monitor,* Oct. 6, 1973, p. 6.
10. Louise Blanchard, "Bilingual Program Violates Law, Official Says", in *The Miami News,* Apr. 16, 1974, p. 5-A.
11. General Education Specialists Section, Bureau of Curriculum and Instruction, "Foreign Language Study: A Position Paper". Department of Education, Tallahassee, Fla., May, 1973.
12. "School Panel OKs Bilingual Programs". *The Miami News,* Apr. 6, 1973, p. 5-A.
13. Department of Administrative Research and Statistics, *The Cuban Refugee: First Report, Early 1960 to December 1961.* Dade County Public Schools, Miami, Fla., 1962, pp. 1-12.
14. Ibid.
15. Ibid.
16. Department of Administrative Research, *The Cuban Refugee: Second Report, January 1962 to October 1962.* Dade County Public Schools, Miami, Fla., 1962, pp. 8-9.
17. Pauline M. Rojas, "Final Report: Ford Foundation Projects in Bilingual Education". Miami, Fla., Aug. 31, 1966, p. 1.
18. These materials were published under the title *Miami Linguistic Readers* and employed as the basic reading program for young children in English as a Second Language (ESL) classes throughout Dade County and in many other sections of the United States.
19. E. L. Whigham, Superintendent of Schools, Dade County Public Schools, Memorandum to the Associate Superintendent for Instruction and the District Superintendents, Dade County Public Schools, "Issuance of Directives Related to the Bilingual Education Program", Oct. 18, 1971.

20. Division of Elementary and Secondary Education, *Procedures Manual: Bilingual Programs,* Bulletin 1-C, Revised. Dade County Public Schools, Miami, Fla., 1975, pp. 7, 21, 34, 43, 51.
21. Ibid.
22. Ibid.
23. Ibid.
24. Ibid.
25. Ibid.
26. School Board of Dade County, "Bilingual Proposal", an application for assistance under the Emergency School Aid Act. Submitted to the United States Office of Education from Miami, Fla., Apr. 23, 1973, pp. 1-7, 26-62, 111-113.
27. "Bilingual Advisory Committee Appointed for ESAA". *The Miami Times,* Mar. 23, 1973, p. 3; "Audiencia Pública Comité Asesor de la Sección Bilingüe de ESAA", *Diario Las Americas,* Mar. 22, 1973, p. 1.
28. Supra Note 26
29. Paul W. Bell, Executive Director, Division of Instruction, Dade County Public Schools, Memorandum to Mrs. Elizabeth Alonso, Consultant, Foreign Languages, Mrs. Rosa Inclan, Consultant, Bilingual Education, and Mr. Ralph Robinett, Project Manager, Spanish Curricula Development Center, "Bilingual Education Coordinating Committee", July 13, 1973.
30. Paul W. Bell.
31. Ralph F. Robinett.
32. School Board of Dade County, "Spanish Curricula Development Center", an initial plan for a program under the Bilingual Education Act, Title VII of the Elementary and Secondary Education Act (as amended). Submitted to the United States Office of Education from Miami, Fla., May 22, 1970.
33. Ralph F. Robinett, "The Spanish Curricula Development Center". *The National Elementary Principal,* Vol. 1, no. 2, November, 1970, p. 63.
34. Ralph F. Robinett, "Developing Curriculum for Bilingual Education", in W. F. Mackey & Theodore Andersson, *Bilingualism in Early Childhood.* Rowley: Newbury House, 1977.
35. Supra Note 33
35. Supra Note 31
36. School Board of Dade County, "Individualizing Spanish for English Speakers", an initial application for funding under Title III of the Elementary and Secondary Education Act (as amended). Submitted to the United States Office of Education from Miami, Fla., Dec. 16, 1971, pp. 15-17.
37. School Board of Dade County, "Individualizing Spanish for Speakers of English", a continuation application for funding under Title III of the Elementary and Secondary Education Act (as amended). Submitted to the United States Office of Education from Miami, Fla., June 1, 1973, p. 3.
38. Supra Note 36
39. Pauline M. Rojas, Ralph F. Robinett, and Paul W. Bell.

Summary and Conclusion

Although various forms of bilingual education were relatively common in a number of other countries, they were rare within the continental United States until the mid-20th Century when the movement for cultural pluralism began to replace the prevalent philosophy of cultural assimilation. At about the time that the trend toward asserting racial, ethnic and linguistic diversity began, many Cubans left their homeland, for political reasons, and regrouped in nearby Florida.

Use of the Spanish language preceded use of the English language in the peninsula that eventually became the State of Florida. It was doubtful, however, that bilingual education, employing these two languages, would have been initiated as early as it was if the large majority of Cuban refugees had not selected the Miami (Dade County) area in the southern corner of Florida as their new homeland. As a result of this choice and the sudden large enrollments of Cuban refugee children in the area's schools, the Dade County Public Schools started bilingual education programs, including the nation's first biethnic model for bilingual schooling, almost a decade before other school systems in the United States.

The number of Spanish-speaking students, mostly children of Cuban refugees, continued to grow by the thousands in the local school system, and bilingual education programs spread throughout the county at both the elementary and secondary school levels (see Appendix E).

The economic power of the Spanish language in the Miami area paralleled the growth of bilingual programs in the public schools during the 1960's and stimulated further growth of these programs in the seventies. This gain in power was primarily a result of the continued influx of Cuban refugees and their industriousness. In the mid-seventies, local Spanish-speaking residents represented more than a billion dollar market, and their annual family incomes had risen slightly above the average for other residents of Dade County. There was also a simultaneous growth in political power at the local level as evidenced by the election of bilingual Spanish-speakers to the position of Mayor of the City of Miami and to one of the city commissioner positions.

In retrospect, the brief fifteen-year history of bilingual education in Dade County was remarkable. It grew from a concept that was unfamiliar to most of the area's educators and other residents in 1960 to a comprehensive county-wide program by 1975 and a major objective of the area's massive school system serving nearly a quarter of a million students. It began as a special program for Cuban refugee children, but it soon became available for all Spanish and most English-speaking students. The unique emphasis on bilingual programs that included students from both the majority as well as the principal minority language group was eventually supplemented by bilingual programs designed for local students from all language backgrounds.

Local economic and political factors seemed to ensure continued support for bilingual education, and projections of the language backgrounds of future student populations indicated that it would be desirable for local school officials to maintain their national leadership in this area. Within a democratic society, however, the general community would determine the future of bilingual education. In Dade County, many of these community members seemed to be convinced, as citizens in other countries had been for generations, that developing mastery of more than one language was a desirable goal for the community's public education program.

Appendix A

**A CHECK-LIST OF VARIABLES
IN EVALUATING BILINGUAL EDUCATION**

Some Relevant Questions
1. WHAT is being evaluated?
    1.1   The binguality of the program
        1.1.1   Language distribution
        1.1.2   Demographic equity
    1.2   Its Effects
        1.2.1   On the languages
            1.2.1.1   Replacement
            1.2.1.2   Maintenance
            1.2.1.3   Restoration
            1.2.1.4   Standardization
            1.2.1.5   Bilingualization
        1.2.2   On the Community
            1.2.2.1   National unity
            1.2.2.2   Interethnic harmony
            1.2.2.3   Ethnic equity
        1.2.3   On the Individual
            1.2.3.1   Intellectual development
            1.2.3.2   Emotional stability

1.2.3.3   Cultural development
1.2.3.4   Scholastic achievement
1.2.3.5   Language development
      i)   In the home language
      ii)   In the second language

2. WHY does the program exist?
  2.0   Objectives
      2.0.1   Type of objectives
      2.0.2   Their feasibility
      2.0.3   Their relative value
      2.0.4   Who was responsible for them?
  2.1   Relation to priorities of language policy
      2.1.1   Integration
      2.1.2   Diversity
  2.2   Relation to priorities of education policy
      2.2.1   Literacy in the home language
      2.2.2   Literacy in the national languages
      2.2.3   Equality of educational opportunity
  2.3   Areas of policy jurisdiction
      2.3.1   Over language and culture
      2.3.2   Over education
  2.4   Policy Convergence
      2.4.1   Between regions
      2.4.2   With national policy
      2.4.3   Resolution of policy conflicts
  2.5   Policy Implementation
      2.5.1   Who implements the policy
         2.5.1.1   A national body
         2.5.1.2   A regional authority
         2.5.1.3   A local authority
      2.5.2   Using what priorities
         2.5.2.1   National
         2.5.2.2   Regional
         2.5.2.3   Local
            i)   Community Priorities
            ii)   The parents' priorities
            iii) The educators' priorities

3. WHO is being evaluated?
  3.1   Who are the students?
      3.1.1   How many?
      3.1.2   How old?
      3.1.3   Where were they born?

3.1.4   Where have they lived?
3.1.5   Where were they educated?
3.1.6   How stable is the group?

3.2   What languages do they speak?
3.2.1   At home?
3.2.2   Among themselves?
3.2.3   How well do they know their home language?
3.2.4   How well do they know the second language?
3.2.5   How much do they use each language out of school?

3.3   What do they use their languages for?
3.3.1   At home (dialect used)?
3.3.2   How often?
3.3.3   How consistently?
3.3.4   How well?
3.3.5   What languages do they hear and read?
3.3.5.1   On television and radio?
3.3.5.2   In magazines and newspapers?
3.3.5.3   From parents and relatives?
3.3.6   What languages do they speak and write?
3.3.6.1   To parents?
3.3.6.2   To other relatives and friends?

3.4   What sort of homes do they come from?
3.4.1   Do the parents intend to preserve a language?
3.4.2   What is their social and income level?
3.4.3   How long have they been at that level?
3.4.4   How long have they been in the area?
3.4.5   How much education do they have?
3.4.6   How much education do they want their children to get?
3.4.7   How active are they in the community?
3.4.8   Do they attend school activities?

3.5   How do they feel?
3.5.1   About their home language?
3.5.2   About the second language?
3.5.3   About the school?
3.5.4   About learning in general?
3.5.5   About their ethnic group?
3.5.6   About their future?

3.6   How do they behave?
3.6.1   With their teachers?
3.6.2   With other students?
3.6.3   With their own group?

3.7   How alike are the students?
3.7.1   Linguistically
3.7.2   Socially

      3.7.3   Economically
      3.7.4   Ethnically
      3.7.5   Psychologically

4.   WHERE are they?
   4.1   Where is the program located?
      4.1.1   Size of community
      4.1.2   Density and isolation
   4.2   How independent is it?
      4.2.1   What sort of political unit is it?
      4.2.2   What does it control itself?
      4.2.3   What is controlled from elsewhere?
   4.3   How do the people live?
      4.3.1   How do they make a living?
      4.3.2   Are they divided into social classes?
      4.3.3   How rigid and stable are the classes?
      4.3.4   Is there any class rivalry?
      4.3.5   Are many leaving or settling in?
      4.3.6   How many are out of work?
      4.3.7   How many need to learn another language to get a job?
   4.4   What sort of people are they?
      4.4.1   How many languages are used and by how many people?
      4.4.2   How many ethnic organizations are there and of what strength?
      4.4.3   Are some of the jobs in the hands of certain ethnic groups?
      4.4.4   What sort of ethnic organizations are there: church, school, social, political?
      4.4.5   Do some have special political or social status?
      4.4.6   Are some more bilingual than others?
      4.4.7   How much contact is there between the ethnic groups?
   4.5   How many in each ethnic group can read and write?
      4.5.1   In one language
      4.5.2   In more than one language
   4.6   What facilities do they have?
      4.6.1   How many public and ethnic libraries?
      4.6.2   How many radio and television programs in each of the languages?
      4.6.3   How many newspapers and magazines?
   4.7   How do the ethnic groups get along?
      4.7.1   Who is prejudiced against whom and to what extent?
      4.7.2   Do members of some ethnic groups have difficulty getting certain jobs?
      4.7.3   What are the priorities of each ethnic group?
      4.7.4   Is there rivalry between groups, and how is it expressed?

4.7.5   What is the attitude toward bilinguals and mixed marriages?

5.   WHICH LANGUAGES are involved?
5.1   How many languages are involved?
5.2   How different are they?
5.3   How important are they?
 5.3.1   Economically
 5.3.2   Politically
 5.3.3   Socially
 5.3.4   What can be done with them?
5.4   How standardized are they?
5.5   What dialects are used and in what way?
 5.5.1   How close are they to the standard?
 5.5.2   How are they considered in the community?
 5.5.3   How are they used in education?
 5.5.4   Is one dialect used for one thing and another for something else?
 5.5.5   How intermixed are the languages?
 5.5.6   Do more and more people tend to use one language rather than the other?

6.   WHICH SCHOOLS are used?
6.1   Where are the buildings and what are they like?
 6.6.1   In what sort of area are they located?
 6.1.2   How much workspace is there for the program?
  6.1.2.1   How many classrooms and what are they like?
  6.1.2.2   How much library space is there per child?
  6.1.2.3   Is there a materials room?
  6.1.2.4   Is there a language laboratory?
 6.1.3   What sort of accommodations are there?
  6.1.3.1   For recreational activities and sports
  6.1.3.2   For eating and drinking: cafeterias, canteens and dining rooms
  6.1.3.3   For social activities: common rooms and project rooms.
 6.1.4   How accessible is the school?
  6.1.4.1   Distance travelled to school
  6.1.4.2   Public transportation
  6.1.4.3   School transportation
6.2   What are the aims of each school?
 6.2.1   Does it have a religious, social or political ideology and which sort?
 6.2.2   Does it operate under a particular educational ideology (Montessori, *ecole active*, open classroom, etc.)

6.2.3   Is it operated for any ethnic group?

6.2.4   How does it relate to the community the parents organization or the church group?

6.2.5   Do its aims have the cooperation of the school board?

6.2.6   Does it operate under certain administrative criteria?

6.2.7   What is its policy on extra-curricular activities?

6.3   How is it organized and administered?

6.3.1   Who has the authority?

6.3.2   Who pays for the school and its programs?

6.3.3   Who determines choice of language to be used?

6.3.4   What sort of director does it have and what are his contacts with the program, with its teachers and with the community?

6.4   How are the students grouped?

6.4.1   By which criteria?

6.4.1.1   By age?

6.4.1.2   By level?

6.4.1.3   By language comprehension?

6.4.1.4   By home-language?

6.4.2   How many groups are there?

6.4.3   How many students per class?

6.4.4   What is the home language distribution in each?

6.4.5   What teaching languages are used in each?

6.4.6   How many teachers per class?

6.4.7   How are the students seated?

6.4.7.1   In home-language blocks?

6.4.7.2   Alternately by languages?

6.4.7.3   By which seating pattern?

6.5   How is the school day divided?

6.5.1   How are the groups scheduled?

6.5.2   How do students advance from one level to the next?

6.6   What sort of teaching materials are there?

6.6.1   What is available in each of the languages?

6.6.1.1   Textbooks

6.6.1.2   Visuals (including films)

6.6.1.3   Audio (including tapes)

6.6.2   How accessible are these?

6.6.2.1   How available are they?

6.6.2.2   How are they distributed?

6.6.3   How suitable are they?

6.6.3.1   For whom were they first published?

6.6.3.2   How much do they cost?

i)   For individual students

ii)   For the school

6.6.3.3   How much of the teaching can they do?

6.6.4 How much of the teaching material is there for each of the subjects and in what language is it?

6.7 How many people have jobs at the school and what do they do?

6.7.1 How many program coordinators?

6.7.2 How many curriculum development persons?

6.7.3 How many librarians - bilingual and unilingual?

6.7.4 How many language advisors?

6.7.5 How many language assistants (adult and pupil)?

6.7.6 How many volunteer parent aids?

6.7.7 How many office staff - bilingual and unilingual?

6.7.8 How many specialists and master-teachers?

7. WHICH TEACHERS participate?

7.1 How well do they know the languages they use?

7.1.1 Their second language

7.1.2 Their home language

7.2 How do they use them in their teaching?

7.2.1 How many teach in their home language?

7.2.2 How many teach in their second language?

7.2.3 How many teach in two languages?

7.3 How competent are they as teachers?

7.3.1 How many years of schooling do they have?

7.3.2 Which professional diplomas do they hold?

7.3.3 How many years of experience?

7.3.4 How much experience in bilingual teaching?

7.3.5 How many specialist courses have they completed?

7.3.6 How much training in bilingual education?

7.3.7 How much experience with certain age-groups?

7.3.8 How versatile are the teachers?

7.3.9 Did they volunteer for the program?

7.4 How do they teach languages and other subjects?

7.4.1 How do they stage the primary language skills: listening, speaking, reading and writing?

7.4.2 How do they correct errors and how often?

7.4.3 How do they use the materials, including the visuals, and how often?

7.4.4 How do they use the materials, including the visuals, and how often?

7.4.5 How do they present new concepts in various subjects?

7.4.5.1 In one language only?

7.4.5.2 In both languages—alternately, consecutively?

7.4.6 How much interaction is there in the classes?

7.5 How do they feel about the program?

7.5.1 How committed are they to it?

      7.5.2   Do they understand its objectives?
      7.5.3   What do they think about bilingual education?
      7.5.4   Do they work as a team?
      7.5.5   What sort of support do they have?
           7.5.5.1   From the administration
           7.5.5.2   From the parents
           7.5.5.3   From the community
   7.6   How do they rate in the profession?
      7.6.1   How are they chosen?
      7.6.2   What is their salary range?
      7.6.3   What work space are they given?
      7.6.4   Is there much competition for their position?

8.   HOW does the program operate?
   8.1   How are the languages distributed?
      8.1.1   In relation to the national and area languages?
      8.1.2   By time and subject?
      8.1.3   According to the curriculum objectives?
      8.1.4   What basic type of bilingual education predominates?
   8.2   What sort of classes have been organized?
      8.2.1   How do they related to the type of program?
      8.2.2   Is the instruction unilingual or bilingual?
      8.2.3   Are the materials unilingual or bilingual?
      8.2.4   Are the students unilingual or bilingual and to what extent?
      8.2.5   What type of classes are treated by the grouping of students, materials and teaching methods according to language?
   8.3   What level of attainment is to be reached?
      8.3.1   In each language
      8.3.2   In each subject
   8.4   How is the attainment determined?
      8.4.1   Unilaterally or comparatively?
      8.4.2   By which methods?
           8.4.2.1   Examinations
           8.4.2.2   Special tests
           8.4.2.3   Special inventories
      8.4.3   What have been the results and how are they judged?

Appendix B

LANGUAGE POLICY, BILINGUAL SCHOOLING, AND BICULTURAL CLASSES

Making or keeping people bilingual through formal schooling depends ultimately on what happens in the classroom. This in turn depends to a greater or lesser extent on language policies and programs at various levels of the hierarchy of political and educational organization within which the school functions.

Introduction

We can distinguish three levels—local, regional and national—in the hierarchy of political organization within which bilingual schooling may be authorized. Each of these levels may be officially bilingual or unilingual in one of the official languages—trilingual, quadrilingual, and other plurilingual situations being simply numerical variations. At each of these levels the policy may be to promote the second language, to tolerate it, or to discourage its use. Implementation of the policy in the schools may include various types and degrees of bilingual education: compulsory second-language learning, the toleration of private ethnic schools, or the non-recognition of minority languages. Bilingual education may be provided for unilinguals and/or bilinguals; or unilingual education may be imposed on all. The degree of bilingual schooling provided may vary according to the distribution of languages in the curriculum throughout the length of the school career. What is taught in each of the languages, when and for how long, will determine which language is to become dominant in education and whether both languages are to be maintained at equal or comparable levels. The effects of the distribution at any given moment will depend on the learning and teaching at the classroom level, the linguistic quality of the teaching, the materials used, and the language mix in the group of pupils which comprises each class.

In other words, in analyzing any particular situation for evaluative or comparative purposes, we are dealing with hierarchies and levels of policy, usage, and jurisdiction, types of implementation, degrees of bilinguality, language distribution, and cultural grouping. What is needed, therefore, is a systematic and quantitative analysis of the following: 1) the language policy, 2) the levels of jurisdiction, 3) the types of policy situations which result, 4) the types of implementation, 5) the language patterns of curriculum and 6) the types of classes in the school. Let us see what each of these implies.

Language Policy

It is important at the outset to understand what the language policy specifies, what it implies and what it leaves unstated. The policy may be to promote the second or minority language, to tolerate it, or to discourage its use.[1] The policy may not necessarily be the same in all regions of the country. For example, in Canada the policy has been to promote individual bilingualism, since both English and French have equal status as official languages. In the different regions (provinces), however, language policies are divergent; in Quebec, French only is official, although English has special status; in most of English-speaking Canada, however, the situation is de facto the reverse; whereas in the bilingual regions (New Brunswick and Northern Ontario) both languages are officially promoted. Promotion, toleration and discouragement, however, are matters of degree. In practice they constitute a continuum along which there may be borderline or evolving situations in which it is sometimes difficult to decide, in the absence of quantitative criteria, whether the policy at a given moment is one of toleration or of promotion.

Since language policy, especially in complex industrial societies, may touch so many of the daily activities of the population—schooling, transportation, public administration, the courts, the trade unions, and the police—it is important for each of these domains to know what level of government holds jurisdiction.

Levels of Jurisdiction

In the application of language policy in the schools what matters most is the extent to which each level of government holds jurisdiction in matters of education. Although both Britain and France, for example, are each officially unilingual nation-states, differences in educational jurisdiction account for the remarkable divergences in matters of public bilingual schooling. When education is purely a local matter, as it traditionally has been in the United Kingdom where the power was vested in the local educational authorities, accommodations were possible at the local level to encourage the survival of such important Celtic languages as Welsh and Gaelic through the organization of bilingual schooling for the children of native speakers. Their Celtic cousins in France, however, could not be thus accommodated because all power in educational matters was centralized at the national level. The Bretons could not use their language for purposes of education, since in all fairness, the other regional languages like Basque, Provencal, and the Allemaic dialects had likewise been excluded as part of the national language policy. [2]

In sum, the potential and possibilities for any type of bilingual schooling depend in the first instance on the policy situations within which all education must take place.

Types of Policy Situations

According to the area of jurisdiction, situations are created at each level of government by the divergence or convergence of language policies. In the field of education, for example, the language policy of a bilingual country may be the promotion of national bilingualism to the extent that every citizen learns something of the other official language, yet the effectiveness of such a policy depends on the control which the national administration may exercise over what is taught in the schools. If this control, as we have seen, remains in the hands of regional or local authorities, the learning of the second language may be optional in one region and compulsory in the other or it may even be excluded entirely from the curriculum.

In other words, each of the three levels may have a common policy of promoting one of the languages—Language X, for example, locally (L), regionally (R), and nationally (N), in brief LRN: XXX; or all levels may promote both (B) languages, creating a BBB type of language policy situation. For example, in Japan where only one language may be recognized as being official locally, regionally, and nationally, an XXX policy situation exists which does not allow for the use in education of the home language of any minority. It is to be expected, then, that nothing in the line of public bilingual education would be provided. Contrariwise, the minority may enjoy official status at all levels--local (B), regional (B), and national (B)--as do the inhabitants of certain Acadian towns where both French and English have official status in the town, the province (new Brunswick), and the nation (Canada). Such a fully bilingual policy situation, however, does not necessarily imply the existence of bilingual schools for the benefit of the minority. On the contrary, the official status of the minority may be so high as to permit the operation of its own unilingual schools, bilingual schooling being reserved as an (immersion) option for the children of the majority group. Between these two extremes----XXX and BBB--there exists a range of about a dozen other types. In Miami, for example, although both Spanish and English are official at the municipal and county level (B), only English (X) is official at the state, as it is at the federal level. This policy situation (BXX) is the context within which the future of bilingual education in Miami must be considered. It poses problems quite different from those arising from the converse situation (XXB) such as exists in Zurich where German is the official language at the municipal and cantonal levels, while both French and German (and to a lesser extent Italian and Romansch) enjoy official and/or national status at the federal level.

It is therefore important at the outset to identify the policy situation context within which language education in the schools must take place. Convergence or divergence at the local (L), regional (R), and national (N) levels may create any of the following types:

LRN	LRN	LRN
XXX	XXB	BXB
XXY	XYB	XBB
XYX	XBX	BBX
XYY	XBY	BBB
	BXX	
	BXY	

Types of Implementation

A policy can be effective only when it is implemented. The same policy may be implemented in a variety of different ways and to different degrees. For example, the implementation of a promotion policy may range from the compulsory study of the second language in secondary school to the active support of immersion programs for the unicultural majority whereby all subjects are taught to them in the minority language.

Within this range there exists a number of different culture/education language varieties—the culture being the one (or ones) to which the learner belongs when he enters school, distinguished chiefly, as it must be, by the language of the home, which may be distinct from the language or languages of formal instruction in the school (school language). For each of the language groups (X and Y) one may have separate unicultural (U-) schools for learners speaking the same home language or mixed, bicultural (B-) schools. Each of these types, (U-) and (B-), may be either unilingual (-U) or bilingual (-B) in so far as one or both languages are to be used as media of instruction. On the basis of this culture/education dichotomy, one can distinguish four main types of schools in the implementation of language policy in education:

unicultural and unilingual (U-U)
unicultural and bilingual (U-B)
bicultural and unilingual (B-U)
bicultural and bilingual (B-B)

Within each of these main types, the unilingualism or bilingualism may be the lot of the culturally dominant or majority (M) group, and/or that of the culturally dependent or minority (m) group, majority and minority roles being subject to potential variation and reversal from one region to the other. The following types are possible:

$$U\text{-}U_M \qquad U\text{-}U_m \qquad U\text{-}U_{Mm}$$
$$U\text{-}B_M \qquad U\text{-}B_m \qquad U\text{-}B_{Mm}$$
$$B\text{-}U_M \qquad B\text{-}U_m \qquad B\text{-}U_{Mm}$$
$$B\text{-}B_M \qquad B\text{-}B_m \qquad B\text{-}B_{Mm}$$

The implementation of a language policy at any level may involve the use of any or all of these types. In Miami, for example, Types ($B\text{-}U_{Mm}$) and ($B\text{-}B_{Mm}$) were promoted during the sixties, while Types ($U\text{-}U_m$) and ($U\text{-}B_m$) (mostly private schools for Cuban refugees) were tolerated. The language policy may make certain types more appropriate for one stage in the school career of the population. It may, for instance, tolerate and even promote diversity at the elementary and intermediate levels, that is, up to and including the ninth grade (k-9), but require uniformity at the senior levels of high school and college where integration may be important. The formula used in Miami in the early and mid-sixties may be summarized thus:

$$B\text{-}U_{Mm}^{k\text{-}9} \ \& \ B\text{-}B_{Mm}^{k\text{-}9} \ \& \ U\text{-}U_m^{k\text{-}6} \ \& \ U\text{-}B_m^{k\text{-}6} \ > \ B\text{-}U_{Mm}^{10\text{-}12}$$

This includes only the bicultural-bilingual groupings and not the biracial ones. Superimposed upon the first two types of bicultural public education was the creation of biracial groupings through the federal requirements for racial integration in public schools. Some of the B-B schools, however, were already biracial within both cultural groups since they included black Cuban pupils and teachers whose home language was Spanish, as well as black American pupils and teachers whose home language was English.

The way each of the above types is made operative through curriculum and program development at the school level may vary greatly from one region to the next.

Languages in the Curriculum

Each of these culture/education types may include different dosages of each of the languages in the curriculum at any given period (term, grade or level) of the course. The distribution of languages throughout the course in a dual-medium (D) school, however, may follow certain patterns. The two languages may be maintained (M) at an equal (E) level in that one is used as much as the other in the same context, or they may be maintained for different (D) but equivalent purposes—dual-medium differential maintenance (DDM). Contrariwise, one of the languages may assume a more and more important place in the curriculum at the expense of the other language tending to produce a transfer (T) of the main language of instruction. If the duration of the course or phase (e.g. four grades, one grade, or even a term) is represented horizontally and the subjects in the curriculum are represented vertically, shading the intersecting areas to represent the use of the other language (x or y), we can visualize all the possible types of language distribution throughout the curriculum. For example, in a bicultural-bilingual school, during the first four grades (B-B $^{1-4}$) the curriculum having the above DDM (dual-medium differential maintenance) pattern can be seen as quite different from the one with a DEM (dual-medium equal maintenance) pattern (See Figure 18).

A school or school system may be characterized by one or more of these patterns according to which languages are distributed throughout the curriculum.[3] In the final analysis, however, it is the way these types and patterns are applied at the classroom level which will determine whether or not the policy is effectively implemented. In this respect, the cultural make-up of the class may be decisive.

Types of Bicultural Classes

Within the time-span covered by a curriculum pattern, learners and teachers from each culture group may be assembled together in different ways, for different purposes and for varying periods of time. For the entire duration, the grouping may be stable or it may vary from term to term, or even from hour to hour.

The three language-related components of any class are the home languages of the learners, the language or languages of instruction, and the language or languages of the teaching materials. Each of these home languages (small circles), school languages (large circles) and languages of the teaching materials (triangles) come together, as it were, and meet in the classroom, where they may interact (See Figure 19). Each learner enters the class with a certain degree of competence in one or more languages. These may include an oral and/or reading competence in one or more languages of instruction (x and y). The learner may be unilingual in x, unilingual in y, competent in both (b) or unilingual or bilingual in neither (0) (See Figure 20). Likewise, instruction may be given in either or both languages (x/y) orally or in writing (See Figure 21). Materials, oral and written, may also be in either or both of these languages (See Figure 22).

If we choose not to refine the distinction between bilinguals and biliterates, the basic language-related components of the classroom therefore remain the languages of instruction—either x or y, or a dosage or mixture (m) of both the languages of the materials (x,y, or m) and the home languages of the learners. The latter may be grouped according to home language (x or y), they may be linguistically mixed according to the same criteria (m) comprising learners of different home languages, they may all be from bilingual homes (b), or there may be representatives from all of these categories to form a linguistically heterogeneous (h) class (See Figure 23).

The possible class types generated by the various possible combinations of these basic components, numbering 45, may exist within the types of bilingual

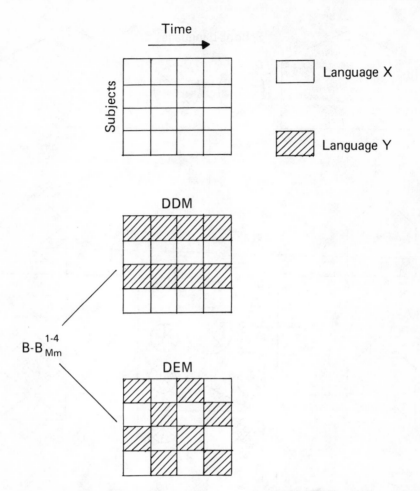

Maintenance of two home languages through bicultural-bilingual schooling for both cultural groups in Grades 1 to 4 (B-B$_{Mm}^{1-4}$), organized in the first example into a dual-medium differential pattern (DDM) designed for use of both languages in different subject areas, and in the second example (below) into a dual-medium equalization pattern (DEM) designed for the use of both languages in the same subject areas.

Figure 18   Two Maintenance-Oriented Patterns of Bilingual Schooling

schools classified according to curriculum patterns (See Figure 24). For example, the dual-medium differential maintenance (DDM) type of bilingual curriculum may be implemented through two complementary types of classes, (xyx) for mathematics and the type (xxx) for geography, whereas dual-medium equal maintenance types (DEM) may have two overlapping classes of the (mmx) type, both for mathematics and for geography (See Figure 25).

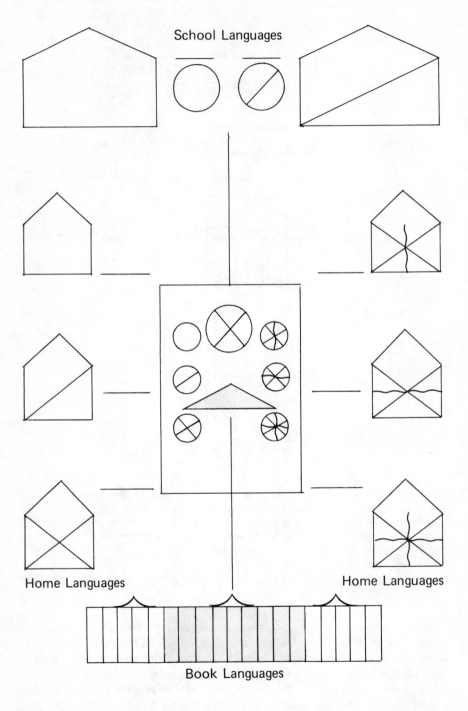

Figure 19   Languages in the Bicultural Classroom

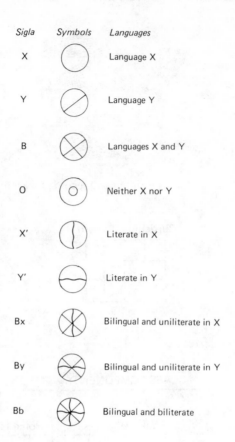

	Sigla	Symbols	Languages
	X		Language X
	Y		Language Y
	B		Languages X and Y
	O		Neither X nor Y
	X'		Literate in X
	Y'		Literate in Y
	Bx		Bilingual and uniliterate in X
	By		Bilingual and uniliterate in Y
	Bb		Bilingual and biliterate

Figure 20   Home Languages

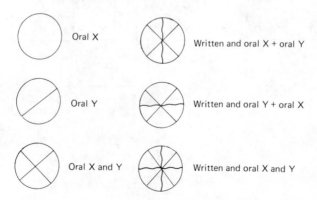

Oral X

Oral Y

Oral X and Y

Written and oral X + oral Y

Written and oral Y + oral X

Written and oral X and Y

Figure 21   School Languages

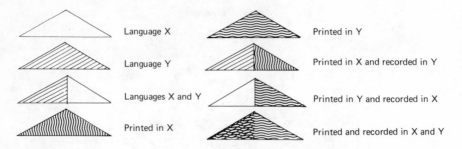

Figure 22   Book Languages (printed and recorded teaching materials)

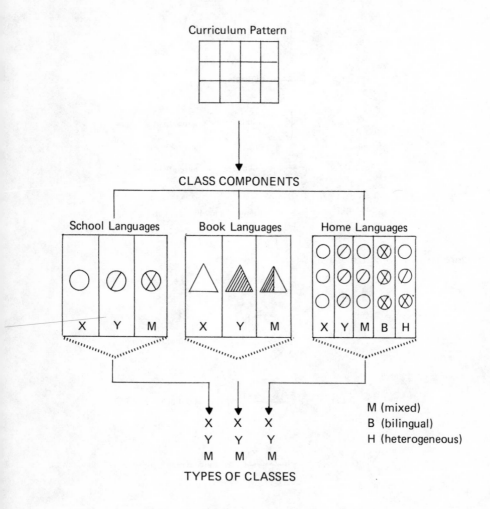

Figure 23   Basic Components of Bicultural Classes

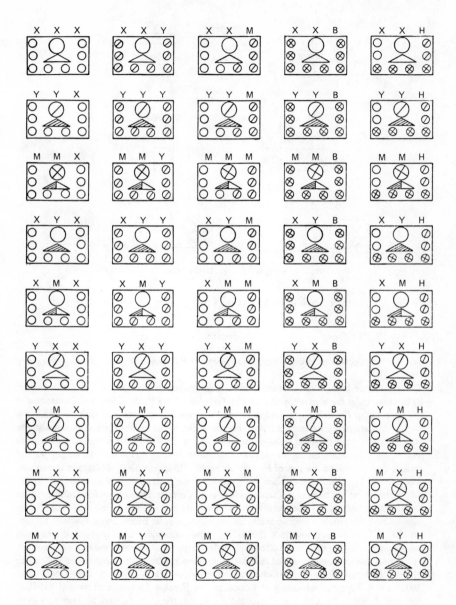

Figure 24   Basic Class Types

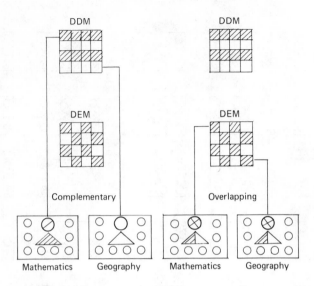

Figure 25   From School-Type to Class-Type

Notes

1. See the Introduction to Heinz Kloss, *The American Bilingual Tradition*, Rowley: Newbury House, 1977.

2. The policy has been a long-standing one. It originated in the early days of the French Revolution under the inspiration of l'abbe H. Gregoire of the Public Education Committee of the Constituent Assembly who had grouped all regional languages and dialects under the somewhat derogatory heading of *patois*. He had difficulty reconciling their existence with the integrative and egalitarian principles of the new republic. In 1794 the National Assembly gave legal status to his report on the necessity and means of irradicating the regional languages and dialects and of making the use of French universal   (*Rapport sur la nécéssité et les moyens d'anéantir les patois et d'univérsaliser l'usage de la langue francaise*). The complete text of this influencial report has been reproduced by Michel de Certeau, Dominique Julia, and Jacques Revel in their study of the fate of the regional languages and dialects during the French Revolution, *Une politique de la langue: la Revolution francaise et les patois*, Paris: Gallimard, 1975, pp. 300-317. In the mid-seventies (1974-75), some concessions were made to the regional languages by allowing them to be offered as the language requirement of the baccalaureate.

3. For a more complete treatment of curriculum patterns in bilingual schooling, see William F. Mackey, *Bilingual Education in a Binational School* (Appendix A), Rowley: Newbury House, 1972, or A Typology of Bilingual Education, in *Foreign Language Annals* 3 (1970): 596-608. Reprinted in Vol. 2 of *Bilingual Schooling in the United States* by Theodore Andersson and Mildred Boyer, Washington: U.S. Government Printing Office, 1970; also in *Advances in the Socioloy of Language 11*, edited by Joshua A. Fishman, Paris/The Hague: Mouton, 1973.

Appendix C

THE MIAMI DECLARATION OF OFFICIAL BILINGUALISM

Resolution Declaring Dade County a Bilingual and Bicultural County

Whereas, the history of Dade County has been beneficially and inextricably interlaced with that of our Spanish-speaking population; and

Whereas, a large and growing percentage of the population of Dade County is of Spanish origin; and

Whereas, Dade County is legally, morally and historically obligated to aid our Spanish-speaking population in achieving the goals they have traveled so very far to share; and

Whereas, it is the welcome responsibility of Dade County to aid the Spanish-speaking community in their efforts to enter more easily the mainstream of the American way of life; and

Whereas, the Spanish-speaking population of Dade County, many of whom have retained the culture and language of their native lands, encounter special difficulties in communicating with governmental agencies and officials; and

Whereas, our Spanish-speaking population has earned, through its ever increasing share of the tax burden, and active participation in community affairs, the right to be serviced and heard at all levels of government; and

Whereas, Dade County has a need to expand its communications with the

Spanish-speaking segment of its population in order to promote a mutually prosperous interchange of ideas as well as a closer affinity with these citizens:

Now, therefore, be it resolved by the Board of County Commissioners of Dade County, Florida:

Section 1: That the Board of County Commissioners of Dade County Florida hereby declares Dade County a bilingual and bicultural County, where Spanish language is considered the second official language.

Section 2: That a department or division named "Division of Bilingual and Bicultural Affairs" be created in the Office of the County Manager for the purpose of the implementation of this Resolution. *

Agenda Item No. 7 [g] [3] 4-16-73
The foregoing resolution was offered by Commissioner John B. Orr, Jr., who moved its adoption. The motion was seconded by Commissioner Mike Calhoun and it was unanimously passed by the commission members.
The Mayor thereupon declared the resolution duly passed and adopted the 16th day of April, 1973. This document was signed by the Deputy Clerk of Dade County Board of Commissioners, Florida.

Appendix D

SURVEY OF PRIVATE SCHOOLS

In May, 1974, Von N. Beebe sent questionnaires to 53 private schools in Dade County serving Spanish-speaking children or located in predominantly Spanish-speaking neighborhoods. Responses were received from 17 schools, 32 percent of those surveyed.

Of the schools responding, 53 percent already were serving the community in the early 1960's. The remaining 47 percent opened in the late 1960's or early 1970's in response to a need that their directors had identified within their growing communities. Approximately 75 percent of the schools presented bilingual programs, using both English and Spanish for instructional purposes. Three-fourths of the schools also used both English and Spanish for administrative purposes, the others employing only the English language.

Appendix E

HIGHLIGHTS OF DADE COUNTY'S BILINGUAL PROGRAM: 1974-75

THE COUNTYWIDE BILINGUAL EDUCATION PROGRAM

Program Definition

Four components are offered in elementary and secondary schools:

1. English for Speakers of Other Languages (ESOL)
2. Spanish for Spanish-Speakers (Spanish-S)
3. Spanish as a Foreign/Second Language (Spanish FL/SL)
4. Curriculum Content in Spanish (CCS)

Elementary Schools that offer all four components, in addition to the regular instructional program in English, are classified as bilingual school organizations (BISO).

Program Goal

To offer Spanish language origin and non-Spanish language origin students the opportunity to become bilingual and bicultural.

Program Cost

$7,251,076.

Local Program Support

Bilingual education has been identified by the county's school board and administration as one of the school system's top program priorities.

State Program Support
No state funds have been allocated or state legislation enacted to support bilingual education in Dade County or the State of Florida.

National Program Support
Upon the request of local school officials, the United States Office of Education and a private foundation have provided financial support for bilingual education in Dade County.

Countywide Program Supervision
A Department of Bilingual Programs has been established within the county school system's Division of Elementary and Secondary Education. It is staffed by a director, one consultant for bilingual education, one consultant for foreign languages, one coordinator of bilingual education, a number of coordinators of special projects supporting bilingual education, and some teachers on special assignment for bilingual education.

Countywide Support Personnel
In each of the six administrative areas of the county's school system, there is one teacher on special assignment to facilitate implementation of bilingual education programs. In addition, there are 13 bilingual psychologists, 23 bilingual visiting teacher counselors, and 95 bilingual support aides distributed throughout the county.

Support of Regular Instructional Program
All four components of the countywide bilingual education program are directly related to and support the goals of the county's regular instructional program in the English language.

THE COUNTYWIDE ENGLISH FOR SPEAKERS OF OTHER LANGUAGES [ESOL] PROGRAM

Program Definition
A full American English language arts and culture program, based on contrastive analyses of language systems and cultures, provided for all children who do not speak English fluently.

Program Goal
To enable the student to acquire English language skills and cultural insights necessary for effective participation in a regular school program and community within the United States.

Schools Involved
127 of the 172 elementary schools, 35 of the 39 junior high schools, and 17 of the 20 senior high schools provide formally structured ESOL programs.

Determination of Pupil Involvement
Upon enrollment in school, students who are not of English language origin are diagnosed by school personnel and, if they are not linguistically independent (fluent) in the English language, they are assigned to one of the following

ESOL classes: nonindependent, low intermediate, mid-intermediate, or high intermediate.

Number of Pupils Involved

elementary	junior high	senior high	total
11,923	2,884	1,289	16,096

Time Devoted

ESOL class periods range from approximately two hours daily for non-independent students to approximately one hour daily for high intermediate students.

Average Program Cost

$112.59 in salaries, per student.

Expected Progress

Students are expected to achieve linguistic independence in English within three school years.

Grading and Promotion

Students are graded in terms of individual progress in ESOL rather than in terms of grade level standards for English language origin students. In elementary and junior high schools, the students' language handicap is not used as a basis for denying the student promotion to a higher grade level.

Special Staff Allocations

In elementary schools, one ESOL teacher is allocated for every 150 student hours of ESOL instruction. In secondary schools, one ESOL teacher may be allocated for every 300 student hours of ESOL instruction.

Other Special Allocations

When available, two dollars per ESOL student in active membership is allocated to schools for the purchase of special instructional materials and equipment.

Requirements for ESOL Teachers

1) Florida State Certification in elementary education or, at the secondary school level, in English or foreign language teaching; 2) Dade County internal certification in teaching ESOL; 3) native proficiency in English.

Basic Textbooks

Elementary schools: Miami Linguistic Readers (D. C. Heath and Co.) and American English Series, Books I, II, and III (D. C. Heath and Co.) Secondary Schools: English for Today Series, Revised, Books I-IV (McGraw-Hill Book Co.).

Formal Evaluation Results

Irregular but consistent growth in English reading skills has been associated with participation in the county's ESOL program. No countywide assessments of participants' growth in oral communication skills in English or the extent of their participation in school and community activities have been undertaken.

Program Direction
Maintain program countywide and improve procedures for placement and promotion of students within the program.

THE COUNTYWIDE SPANISH FOR SPANISH-SPEAKERS [SPANISH-S] PROGRAM

Program Definition
A full Spanish language arts and culture program for any student that speaks Spanish.

Program Goal
To enable the student to preserve and acquire Spanish language skills, to gain further insight into the cultures of Spanish-speaking people, and, by association, to improve communication skills in English.

Schools Involved
136 of the 172 elementary schools, 32 of the 39 junior high schools, and 16 of the 20 senior high schools provide Spanish-S programs.

Determination of Pupil Involvement
Upon request, students who speak Spanish are diagnosed by school personnel and placed in a Spanish-S class at any of the 12 grade levels.

Number of Pupils Involved

elementary	junior high	senior high	total
32,474	6,048	3,328	41,850

Time Devoted
Spanish-S class periods are presented for a minimum of 30 minutes daily or 150 minutes weekly in elementary schools and approximately 45 minutes daily in secondary schools.

Average Program Cost
$54.67 in salaries, per student, at elementary schools.

Grading and Promotion
Students are graded and promoted according to the same standards established in the school for other academic areas. In senior high schools, Spanish-S course credits count as foreign language credits toward graduation.

Special Staff Allocations
In elementary schools, one teacher or paraprofessional aide is allocated for every 150 students enrolled in Spanish-S classes. In secondary schools, Spanish-S classes are presented by members of the school's regular foreign language staff.

Other Special Allocations
When available, two dollars per Spanish-S student in active membership is allocated to schools for the purchase of special instructional materials and equipment.

Requirements for Spanish-S Teachers and Para-Professionals
1) Florida State Certification in elementary education or, at the secondary

school level, in Spanish; 2) Dade County internal certification in teaching Spanish-S; 3) native proficiency in Spanish; 4) ability to conduct school business in English. Paraprofessional aides (elementary schools only) must have a high school diploma (or its equivalent) and fulfill requirements two, three, and four above.

Resource Materials

Numerous series, individual books, and other materials in Spanish are used for Spanish-S instruction. Among the more popular resources are the *Language Arts Strand* of the Spanish Curricula Development Center (Miami, Fla.), *SISDELE-Sistema de diagnóstico y evaluación para la lectura* (Dade County Public Schools, Miami, Fla.), *Por el mundo del cuento y la aventura* (Laidlaw Brothers, Inc.), *Lengua española* (editorial Vasco Americana), and *Senda* (Santillana, S.A.).

Formal Evaluation Results

Consistent gains in Spanish (as well as English) reading skills have been associated with participation in the county's Spanish-S program. No countywide assessments of participants' growth in oral communication skills in Spanish or acquisition of knowledge about the cultures of Spanish-speaking people have been undertaken.

Program Direction

Maintain program countywide and emphasize individualized reading instruction in Spanish.

THE COUNTYWIDE SPANISH AS A FOREIGN/SECOND LANGUAGE [SPANISH FL/SL] PROGRAM

Program Definition

A Spanish language arts and culture program, presented with foreign/second language instructional techniques, for students who do not speak Spanish.

Program Goal

To enable the student to acquire the Spanish language skills and cultural insights necessary for successful interaction with Spanish language origin peers and effective participation in classes presented in the Spanish language.

Schools Involved

162 of the 172 elementary schools, 36 of the 39 junior high schools, and all 20 of the senior high schools provide Spanish FL/SL programs. Although some of the elementary schools already offered Spanish FL/SL in grades 1 through 6 during the 1974-75 school year, the countywide Spanish FL/SL program that year included only grades 1 and 2. The plan was to add one grade level to the program countywide each year until grades 1-6 were included.

Determination of Pupil Involvement

Upon request, students who do not speak Spanish well are diagnosed by school personnel and placed in a Spanish FL/SL class designed for their ability level.

Number of Pupils Involved

elementary	junior high	senior high	total
29,895	4,706	6,162	40,763

Time Devoted
Spanish FL/SL class periods are presented for 30 minutes daily or 150 minutes weekly in elementary schools and approximately 45 minutes daily in secondary schools.

Average Program Cost
$42.23 in salaries, per student, at elementary schools

Grading and Promotion
Students are graded and promoted according to the same standards established for other academic areas. In secondary schools, Spanish FL/SL course credits are foreign language credits toward graduation.

Special Staff Allocations
In elementary schools, one teacher or paraprofessional aide is allocated for every 150 students enrolled in Spanish FL/SL classes. In secondary schools, Spanish FL/SL classes are presented by members of the school's regular foreign language staff.

Other Special Allocations
When funds are available, recommended textbooks are purchased for schools by the county school system's Department of Bilingual Programs.

Requirements for Spanish FL/SL Teachers and Para-Professionals
Secondary school teachers must have Florida State Certification in Spanish. Elementary school teachers must fulfill the following requirements: 1) Florida State Certification in elementary education; 2) Dade County internal certification in teaching Spanish FL/SL; 3) native proficiency in Spanish; 4) ability to conduct school business in English. Paraprofessional aides (elementary schools only) must have a high school diploma (or its equivalent) and fulfill requirements two, three, and four above.

Resource Materials
Among the more popular resources are the Spanish SL Strand of the Spanish Curricula Development Center (Miami, Fla.), Let's Speak Spanish (McGraw -Hill), and Audio-Lingual Materials (ALM)-Spanish (Harcourt, Brace & World, Inc.).

Formal Evaluation Results
Consistent gains in Spanish (as well as English) reading skills have been associated with participation in the county's Spanish FL/SL program. No countywide assessments of participants' growth in oral communication skills in Spanish, knowledge of the cultures of Spanish-speaking people, interaction with Spanish language origin peers, or participation in classes presented in the Spanish language have been undertaken.

Program Direction
Maintain program in secondary schools, expand program in elementary schools throughout the county from grades one and two to grades one through six, and provide for more individualized instruction at all grade levels.

Other Foreign Languages
Instruction in the following foreign languages also is offered in secondary schools: French, German, Hebrew, Italian, Latin, and Russian.

THE ELEMENTARY BILINGUAL SCHOOL ORGANIZATION [BISO] PROGRAM

Program Definition
An organization for instruction which, in addition to the regular elementary school program in English, offers classes in ESOL, Spanish-S, Spanish FL/SL, plus Curriculum Content in Spanish (CCS).

Program Goal
To enable Spanish language origin and non-Spanish language origin students to master listening, speaking, reading, and writing skills in both English and Spanish in order to interact more comfortably and effectively with both cultural groups within the school and community.

Schools Involved
Eight elementary schools: Coral Way (K-6), Central Beach (K-6), South Beach (K-6), Southside (K-6), Springview (K-3), Miami Gardens (K-3), Rockway (K-3), and Caribbean (K-2).

Determination of Pupil Involvement
All pupils attending these eight schools and enrolled in grade levels where the program is offered (see above) are eligible for participation. In the few cases where parents request that their children not participate, these students participate only in the regular program at that school or attend a nearby school.

Number of Pupils Involved

Spanish language origin	Non-Spanish language origin	Total
2,608	1,075	3,683
(71%)	(29%)	

Curriculum Content in Spanish (CCS)
In addition to language arts classes in Spanish, participants in these eight schools receive instruction in the Spanish language in some or all of the following curriculum content areas: social studies, science and health, mathematics, fine arts.

Time Devoted
Classes with instruction in Spanish occupy anywhere from 24 percent to 47 percent of the students' school day, with an average of 31.5 percent of the school day throughout all eight schools.

Grading and Promotion

Students are graded and promoted according to the same standards established for other elementary schools. Until a student masters the second language, grades on report cards for courses presented in his second language reflect individual progress rather than mastery of the concepts and skills associated with that curriculum area.

Special Staff Allocations

In addition to the special staff allocations for ESOL, Spanish-S, and Spanish FL/SL, two teachers generally are allocated to an elementary bilingual school organization plus one paraprofessional aide for each grade level where the program is offered.

Other Special Allocations

In addition to the special allocations for instructional materials and equipment for ESOL, Spanish-S, and Spanish FL/SL, recommended textbooks for CCS are purchased for the eight schools, whenever funds are available, by the county school system's Department of Bilingual Programs.

Requirements for CCS Teachers and Para-Professionals

1) Florida State Certification in elementary education; 2) native proficiency in Spanish; 3) ability to conduct school business in English. Paraprofessional aides must have a high school diploma (or its equivalent) and fulfill requirements two and three above.

Requirements for All Instructional Staff

In addition to the requirements for their specific instructional position, all teachers and paraprofessional aides working in the eight elementary bilingual school organizations must acquire Dade County internal certification in bilingual schooling.

Resource Materials for CCS

Various textbooks and resource materials are used for teaching social studies, science and health, mathematics, and fine arts in Spanish. There is no common program in these curriculum areas in Spanish in the eight schools; however, in the lower grades, the curricula kits produced by the Spanish Curricula Development Center (Miami, Fla.) for social studies, science, and fine arts are quite popular.

Formal Evaluation Results

Countywide assessments of this organization for instruction indicate that adding ESOL, Spanish-S, Spanish FL/SL plus some CCS classes to the instructional program in an elementary school does not interfere with the Spanish language origin or the non-Spanish language origin participants' performance on standardized achievement tests in English. Results concerning mastery of reading skills in Spanish have been mixed, and no countywide assessments of growth in listening, speaking or writing skills in Spanish have been undertaken. Similarly, there have been no formal evaluations of the degree to which the participants interact within the two cultural groups in their school and community.

Program Direction
Pending further evaluations of this type of organization for instruction, no additional elementary schools will become bilingual school organizations.

THE SECONDARY SCHOOL CURRICULUM CONTENT IN SPANISH [CCS] PROGRAM

Program Definition
Instruction in Spanish dealing with the regular curriculum content normally taught in English in the Dade County Public Schools.

Program Goal
To enable Spanish language origin and non-Spanish language origin students to master the concepts and skills in curriculum areas and to develop cross-cultural understandings and attitudes.

Schools Involved
Eight junior high schools: Fisher, Hialeah, Brownsville, Kinloch Park, Robert E. Lee, Ada Merritt, Shenandoah, and Homestead
Three senior high schools: Miami, Miami Beach, Coral Park

Determination of Pupil Involvement
All students attending these 11 secondary schools are eligible to participate if they have mastered Spanish language skills to the extent that they can benefit from curriculum content instruction in Spanish.

Number of Pupils Involved
Class rosters reveal that 1,943 students are enrolled in all of the CCS classes in the 11 secondary schools, and 188 of these enrollees are not of Spanish language origin. A number of the students are enrolled in more than one CCS class at their school, therefore there is no accurate count of the total number of program participants.

Curriculum Content in Spanish
The regular curriculum courses taught in Spanish in the 11 schools are social studies, science, mathematics, music, typing, and a few others.

Time Devoted
Each CCS class lasts as long as the regular class in English, approximately 45 minutes.

Grading and Promotion
Students are graded and promoted according to the same standards established for the regular curriculum content classes in English.

Special Staff Allocations
No special allocation of teachers should be required if the school's instructional staff includes bilingual personnel; however, temporary allocations of 13 teachers were provided by the county to some of the schools during the 1974-75 school year to provide CCS instruction.

Other Special Allocations
When funds are available, recommended textbooks for CCS are purchased for the 11 secondary schools by the county school system's Department of Bilingual Programs.

Requirements for CCS Teachers
1) Florida State Certification in the curriculum area to be taught; 2) native proficiency in Spanish; 3) ability to conduct school business in English.

Resource Materials for CCS
Various textbooks and resource materials are used for teaching social studes, science, mathematics and other curriculum areas in Spanish.

Formal Evaluation Results
No countywide assessments have been undertaken to determine the degree to which secondary school students master curriculum concepts and skills presented in Spanish rather than in English. Similarly, there have been no formal evaluations of the extent to which CCS classes develop cross-cultural understandings and attitudes.

Program Direction
Extension of CCS program to other secondary schools enrolling large numbers of Spanish language origin students.

Some Other Books on Bilingual Schooling

ANDERSSON, Theodore & Mildred Boyer, *Bilingual Schooling in the United States*. 2 Vols. Washington: U. S. Government Printing Office, 1970.

BUREAU of Indian Affairs, *Bilingual Education for American Indians*. Office of Education Programs, Curriculum Bulletin No. 3. Washington: Bureau of Indian Affairs, 1971.

COHEN, Andrew D., *A Sociolinguistic Approach to Bilingual Education*. Rowley: Newbury House, 1975.

DEPARTMENT of Education and Science, *Bilingualism in Education*. London: H. M. Stationery Office, 1965.

FISHMAN, Joshua et al., *Bilingualism in the Barrio*. Bloomington: Indiana University Press, 1971.

JOHN, Vera P. & Vivian M. Horner, *Early Childhood Bilingual Education*. New York: Modern Language Association, 1971.

JONES, W. R., *Bilingualism in Welsh Education*. Cardiff: University of Wales Press, 1966.

KLOSS, Heinz, *The American Bilingual Tradition*. Rowley: Newbury House, 1977.

LAMBERT, Wallace E. & G. Richard Tucker, *The Bilingual Education of Children* Rowley: Newbury House, 1972.

MACKEY, William F., *Bilingual Education in a Binational School*. Rowley: Newbury House, 1972.

MACKEY, William F., *L'écologie éducationnelle du bilinguisme* (publication B-46 du CIRB). Quebec: International Center for Research on Bilingualism, 1974.

MACKEY, William F. & Theodore Andersson (eds.), *Bilingualism in Early Childhood*. Rowley: Newbury House, 1977.

MACNAMARA, John, *Bilingualism in Primary Education*. Edinburgh, Edinburgh University Press, 1966.

MALHERBE, E. G., *The Bilingual School*. London: Longmans, 1946.

PIALORSI, Frank (ed.), *Teaching the Bilingual*. Tuscon: Arizona University Press, 1974.

SPOLSKY, Bernard (ed.), *The Language Education of Minority Children*. Rowley: Newbury House, 1972.

SPOLSKY, Bernard & Richard Cooper (eds.), *Current Trends in Bilingual Education* (2 Vols.). Rowley: Newbury House (to appear).

STERN, H. H. (ed.), *Languages and the Young School Child*. London: Oxford University Press, 1969.

SWAIN, Merrill (ed.), *Bilingual Schooling: Some Experience in Canada and the United States*. Toronto: Ontario Institute for Studies in Education, 1972.

TITONE, Renzo, *Bilinguismo precoce e educazione bilingue*. Rome: Armando, 1972.

WIECZERKOWSKI, Wilhelm, *Bilinguismus im fruhen Schulalter*. Helsinki: Societas Scientiarum Fennica, 1963.

Bibliographies

AFENDRAS, E. A. & A. Pianarosa, *Child Bilingualism and Second Language Learning: A Descriptive Bibliography* (CIRB Publication F-4). Quebec: Laval University Press, 1975.

BRANN, C. M. B., *Language in Education and Society in Nigeria* (CIRB Publication B-52). Quebec: International Center for Research on Bilingualism, 1974.

CHIU, Rosaline, *Lanquage Contact and Language Planning in China (1900-1967)* (CIRB Publication F-2). Quebec: Laval University Press, 1970.

HAUGEN, Einar, *Bilingualism in the Americas: A Bibliography and Research Guide*. University of Alabama: American Dialect Society, 1956.

HAUGEN, Einar, Bilingualism, Language Contact and Immigrant Languages in the United States. A Research Report 1956-70. *Current Trends in Linguistics*, Vol. 10 (505-591). The Hague: Mouton, 1973.

MACKEY, William F. (ed.), *International Bibliography on Bilingualism*, 2 Vols. (CIRB Publication F-3). Quebec: Laval University Press. Vol. 1 (11,000 titles) 1972; Vol. 2 (9,000 titles) (to appear).

MACKEY, William F., *Le bilinguisme canadien: bibliographie analytique et guide du chercheur* (5,000 titles limited to French-English bilingualism in Canada) (CIRB Publication B). Quebec: International Center for Research on Bilingualism (to appear).

Glossary of Terms

This list includes not only the key terms used in this book, but also the most usual ones employed in the study of bilingual education.

A

Abstand language A superseded language, often with a rich cultural and literary past, having been politically degraded to the status of a "dialect" but retaining all the characteristics of a "language" in its own right. It is a "language by distance". Example: Provencal (i.e. Occitan) in France and Catalan in Spain. (Compare *ausbau language*).

Acculturation The learning of social behavior from another culture. It may include language, and when only this is considered the study may be limited to what has been called *linguistic acculturation*.

Adstratum The elements of the language and culture of peoples in a situation of language contact, neither dominating the other. When some of these elements enter the other language there is an *adstratum* influence. Example: Spanish words in French and French words in Spanish. (Compare *substratum* and *superstratum*).

Alternation The change from one language to another in speech or writing. The change may vary in the frequency and the duration of the use of each of the languages. (See *code switching*).

American The term is used in its more limited definition in this text to refer to a citizen of the United States of America. It is recognized that the term "American" also refers to any native or inhabitant of the

North, Central, or South American continents, especially in Spanish-speaking countries where citizens of the United States are often referred to as "North Americans" (*norte americanos*).

American school   "A term applied to schools outside the boundaries of the United States for children of United States citizens living in foreign countries.

Amerindian (American Indian) "A person having origins in any of the original peoples of the Western Hemisphere." (Memorandum on *Racial and Ethnic Designations* circulated to the elementary school principals of Dade County on Jan. 19, 1976.

Anglo   North American not classified as either black or of Spanish language origin. (Memorandum on *Racial and Ethnic Designations* circulated to the elementary school principals of Dade County on January 19, 1976).

Asian   "A person having origins in any of the original peoples of the Far East, Southeast Asia, or the Pacific Islands." (Memorandum on *Racial and Ethnic Designations* circulated to the elementary school principals of Dade County on Jan. 19, 1976).

Audio-lingual   An approach to foreign language instruction that stresses oral and auditory skills in the initial stages of instruction and progresses from listening and speaking to reading, and finally to the writing skills.

Ausbau language   A dialect that has been politically or socially upgraded to the status of a different language. It is a "language by elaboration." Example: Gallego is linguistically a dialect of Portuguese; but in Spain it was regarded as a separate language. (Compare *abstand language*).

Avoidance strategy   Technique used by bilinguals to refrain from having to employ words and structures in their other language of which they are unsure, while at the same time correctly conveying what they mean. Example: Unsure ot the right superlative to thank his hostess (*delicious, delightful, tasty, tasteful . . .?*), Pedro sticks to what he knows, *"That was a very good meal"*.

B

Balanced bilingualism   Equal capacity in two languages for concept formation and word association in a given field. Example: Within the same limit of time, Pedro can think of as many English words associated with *house* as he can Spanish words associated with *casa*.

Batistianos   Cubans alleged to be supporters of Cuban Dictator F. Batista whose regime was overthrown by the Leftist revolution of Fidel Castro.

BEA (Bilingual Education Act) This act was Title VII in a series of amendments, labeled *Public Law 90-247*, attached to the Elementary and Secondary Education Act of 1965. Passed by the United States Congress in December, 1967, this act was designed to provide federal financial support to schools with large enrollments of non-English-speaking students.

Bicultural   Participating in two cultures. The participation may include any or all of the cultural components—language, religion, manners, customs, social behavior, and morals. The extent to which each of these is shared is a matter of degree. Example: Pedro speaks Spanish better than he does English, but his behavior is more English than it is Spanish. (Compare *biethnic, biracial, and bilingual*).

Bidialectalism   The alternate use of two dialects of the same language, such as Castilian Spanish and Texmex.

Biethnic   Shared by two ethnic groups, each of which has a sense of belonging to a community by virtue of one or many cultural or racial traits—language, religion, customs, or racial origin—language being the most distinctive and isolating of these traits. Example: Miami is a biethnic city insofar as it is shared by English-speaking and Spanish-speaking groups, each with its sense of belonging; but if racial criteria are superimposed, the term *triethnic* might be considered more appropriate.

Bilingualism   The basic term refers to the alternate use of two or more languages or dialects. Trilingualism, quadrilingualism, and quinelingualism are simply numerical variations of the phenomenon of using more than one language. (See *multilingualism, plurilingualism, bidialectalism;* see also under types such as *receptive, recessive,* and *reciprocal bilingualism*). For a fuller definition, see W. F. Mackey "Bilingualism" in the *Encyclopedia Britannica*.

Bilingual Advisory Committee   A committee of parents, students, teachers, and representatives of civic organizations and other community groups established in Dade County in 1973 to generate a list of needs for special funding under the Emergency School Aid Act.

Bilingual by combination   At a given level of analysis (e.g. the word-level), the introduction into the speech of a bilingual of an item (in this case, a word) composed of elements from two languages. Example: *blufista*, from English *bluff* and Spanish-*ista*. (Compare *bilingual by modification*).

Bilingual by modification   An item in bilingual speech (e.g. a word) which has been modified to fit the pattern of the other language. Example: The modification of the English *landlord* to the Spanish-sounding word *lamlor*. (Compare *bilingual by combination*).

Bilingual education   The use of two languages in an educational program, with instruction in those two languages and study of their corresponding cultures.

Bilingual Education Coordinating Committee   A committee of school administrators established in the Dade County Public Schools in 1973 to ensure efficient operation of the school system's overall-bilingual education program and to maintain support for the program from within that school system.

Bilingual description   A parallel account of the grammar, phonology, and lexicon of two languages for the purpose of discovering their differences and similarities. (*See dialinguistics, contrastive* and *differential linguistics*).

Bilingual neighborhoods or communities   Specific areas that are inhabitated by speakers of two different languages. The inhabitants may be speakers of only one or both of the languages.

Bilingual program   A program that provides language arts and curriculum content instruction in two languages.

Bilingual school   A school that offers language arts and curriculum content instruction in two languages for some or all students.

Bilingual school component One of the four parts of Dade County's bilingual education program: English as a Second Language (ESL), Spanish for Spanish-Speakers (Spanish-S), Spanish as a Second Language (Spanish-SL), and Curriculum Content in Spanish (CCS).

BISO (Bilingual School Organization)   An organization for instruction in elementary schools which, in addition to the regular instructional program in the English language, offers all four components of Dade County's bilingual education program: ESL, Spanish-S, Spanish SL, and CCS.

An elementary school offering the bilingual education program at all grade levels is sometimes referred to as a complete bilingual school organization. A partial bilingual school organization offers the program at only some grade levels.

Bilingual state   A polity (nation, state, province) within which two or more languages have legal status. Bilingual states exist, not to promote individual bilingualism, but to protect the right to remain unilingual in one's native language. State bilingualism may be founded either on the principle of personality or the principle of territoriality. (*See personality principle, territoriality principle* and *institutional bilingualism*).

Biracial   Shared by two races. A biracial school includes students from two different racial groups. Race is exclusively hereditary and is distinct from culture which is entirely acquired. A person of any race may belong to any culture, since both are mutually exclusive. (Compare *bicultural* and *biethnic*).

Black (non-Hispanic)   "A person having origins in any of the peoples of sub-Saharan Africa." (Memorandum on *Racial and Ethnic Designations* circulated to the elementary school principals of Dade County, on Jan. 19, 1976).

Borrowing   The process of adding to one language elements belonging to another language. Example: The Spanish words *beisbol* and *futbol* have been borrowed from English. (*See* also *integration* and *loans*).

C

Calque   A substitution of elements of an expression in one language for their equivalent in the other language. Example: Spanish *rascacielos* modeled on the English *skyscrapers*.

CANBBE (Curriculum Adaptation Network for Bilingual Bicultural Education)   A project jointly sponsored by the Bilingual Education Programs Branch of the United States Office of Education and the private Randolph Hearst Foundation in 1971 to employ Spanish-speaking educators throughout the United States to ensure that the curricular materials produced by the Spanish Curricula Development Center in Miami would be appropriate for students in all sections of the United States.

CCE (Curriculum Content in English)   The regular curriculum subjects offered in the English language. As with the Curriculum Content in Spanish program, these subjects are often presented to mixed groups of students. In some cases, however, the program is offered for separate groups of native Spanish-speaking students (CCE-S) and in other cases to separate groups of native English-speaking students (CCE-E).

CCS (Curriculum Content in Spanish)   A subject area program (or segment of a program) of the regular school curriculum offered in Spanish. In some cases, this program is offered separately for native Spanish-speaking students (CCS-S), in other cases it is offered separately for native English-speaking students (CCS-E). In many cases, it is offered for combined groups of students that generally represent these two language backgrounds.

Clean switching   Abrupt and complete change-over from one language to another in the speech of bilinguals. (Compare *ragged switching*).

Code switching   Change-over from one language to another in speech or writing. (See *alternation*).

Complementary bilingualism   The alternate use of two languages according to their function in a speech community—e.g. one is used at home, another at school. (See *functional bilingualism* and *diglossia*).

Compound association   The merging of languages, or the subordination of one language to another in the mind of the bilingual. More precisely, the association of a single concept with equivalent words in two different languages. Example: Pedro associates his idea of church with both the words *iglesia* and *church* (*iglesia = church*). This applies to single one-meaning word-relations, not to entire semantic or grammatical systems. Some writers suggest that "compound bilinguals" have learned both languages within the same context; others claim that they are the products of the 'translation method"; still others say that they are pre-school bilinguals. Whether or not there exist such types as "compound bilinguals" remains to be established. (Compare *coordinate association*).

Constitutional right   In the context of public education, the right of parents to exclude their children from participation in courses which are not essential to citizenship and the general welfare of the state.

Contrastive linguistics   The study of the differences between two languages, especially in the juxtaposition of descriptions of their phonology and grammar. (Compare *differential linguistics*).

Coordinate association   The separation of language in the mind of the bilingual into two distinct but co-existing systems. More precisely, the parallel association of a given concept with a given language. Example: Pedro associates the word *church* with one idea and the word *iglesia* with another idea of church. For him *iglesia* is not exactly the same as *church*. This applies to single one-meaning word relations, not to entire semantic and grammatical systems. Some writers have suggested that "coordinate bilinguals" have learned their two languages in different contexts or became bilingual after starting school. Whether or not the dichotomy "coordinate" or "compound" can be used to classify all bilinguals is debatable. (Compare *compound association*).

Coordinator   An administrator who is responsible for organizing programs within the Dade County Public Schools.

County   The largest territorial division for local government within a state of the United States. Dade County is located in the southeastern section of the State of Florida.

County public school system   A public school system that is established and organized by individual counties within a state, rather than by cities, townships, or other regional bodies.

Creole language   Due to imperfect learning or rarity of native speakers, this is usually a mixed and imported language which has displaced other languages as the mother tongue of an ethnic group. There are various types of creoles such as *plantation creoles* learned and adopted by slave labor populations and *settler creoles* adopted by colonists. Examples of creoles are the Spanish-based Papiamentu of Curacao and the English-based Taki-taki of Surinam. (Compare *lingua franca, interlanguage* and *pidgin*).

Cuban   Citizen of Cuba, an island in the West Indies located some 200 miles south of the State of Florida.

Cuban aide   Teacher assistants of Cuban heritage whose position in the Dade County Public Schools is funded by the Cuban Refugee Program.

Cuban refugee   Citizen of Cuba who left that country after 1959 because of disagreement with the philosophy and practices of the Leftist revolutionary regime.

Cuban Refugee Center   A center opened at the Freedom Building in downtown Miami early in 1961. This center was to be the base for program operations of the nation's Cuban Refugee Program, including registration of incoming Cuban refugees and determination of Cuban refugees' eligibility for federal support and services. Administrators of the program were directed to coordinate the activities of all federal and private agencies in the United States that were providing assistance to Cuban refugees.

Cuban Refugee Program   A national program established in February, 1961, under the supervision of the United States Department of Health, Education, and Welfare to provide financial assistance and aid to Cuban refugees within the United States. During the summer of 1962, the United States Congress passed *Public Law 87-510* which authorized yearly appropriations under this national program to the Board of Instruction of the Dade County Public Schools providing financial support for educational programs for the large number of Cuban refugee students enrolled.

Cuban Teacher Retraining Program   A program initiated in February, 1963, at the University of Miami and funded by the Cuban Refugee Program to prepare Cuban refugees who had been teachers in Cuba, but were not citizens of the United States, for teacher certification and teaching positions in public schools within the United States.

Cubanos exilados   Cubans who went into exile following the controls imposed by the Leftist Revolutionary Government in Cuba. (See *Cubanos residentes*).

Cubanos residentes   Cubans who had part or full-time residence status in the United States prior to the Leftist Revolution in Cuba.

Cursillos   Minimal steps of learning. The *cursillos* were designed for English-speaking students studying first or second-year Spanish Lan-

guage Arts in junior and senior high schools and English-speaking children and adults desiring job-oriented fluency in the Spanish language for career purposes.

D

Deceptive cognate   A word in one of the bilingual's languages so similar in form to a word in his other language as to lead to the assumption that the meanings are always identical. The French term, *faux amis* (false friends) indicates the effect that such words have on the incidence of semantic interference. Example: The Spanish word *oficina* is a specific term which refers to one type of office. The presence of the generic word *office* in the bilingual's repertoire leads him to use *oficina* also as a generic term. (Compare *pillow words*).

Demonstration teacher   A teacher assigned to travel from school to school and demonstrate instructional techniques and materials to other teachers.

Desegregation   The process of eliminating the practice of isolating members of particular races, especially when the isolation was formerly practiced on an official basis. In Dade County, desegregating the student populations in the Dade County Public Schools began in September, 1959. In 1971, the courts determined that the desegregation of student populations was adequate. In February, 1970, approximately 2,000 teachers were transferred between schools in Dade County to establish in each school a racial balance among the classroom teachers comparable to the one prevailing among classroom teachers employed throughout the county's school system. (Compare *racial segregation* and *racial integration*).

Dialinguistics   The study of the similarities and differences between two languages. (See *bilingual description*, *contrastive* and *differential linguistics*).

Dialinguistic identification The assumption of identity of meaning on the basis of similarity of form. Example: The identification of English *buffet* with Spanish *bufete*.

Diamorph   The identification of two morphemes of one language with one in the other language. Example: The treatment of Spanish *frio* (cold temperature) as if it were the same as English *cold* (temperature) and *cold* (infection).

Diaphone   Two or more speech sounds (phonemes or allophones) in the second language perceived by the bilingual as identical to a single speech sound of his first language. Example: Since English has three final nasal consonants and Spanish only one /-n/ the English words *sun*, *sung* and *some* may sound identical to the Spanish-speaker who may reproduce them all as "sun"

Differential linguistics   The study of the differences between two languages, especially as regards different means used to express the same concept. Includes differential grammar, differential stylistics, differential semantics, differential lexicology, and differential phonetics. (Compare *contrastive linguistics*).

Diglossia   The function distribution of languages in a bilingual community. Example: The use of Spanish is limited to the family, whereas the use of English is limited to the office or factory. Spanish is the language of the home; English, the language of work.

District   The public school system of Dade County was decentralized for administrative purposes into six geographical districts—northeast, north central, northwest, southwest, south central, and south—each with its own district superintendent and staff. In the early 1970's, each county in the State of Florida was referred to as a school district, therefore, the six decentralized sections of Dade County were renamed areas.

Dominance configuration   A profile of individual competence and use of two or more languages for the purpose of determining in which respects one of them is dominant. The profile is composed of such variables as use of each language in communication, age and order of learning each of the languages, their literary and cultural value, their relative function in social advance and their emotive functions.

Dual-medium   Using two languages to teach school subjects. A dual-medium school may have equivalent or complementary distribution; that is, all subjects may be taught in both languages or some, such as history and geography, may be taught in one language, and others, such as science and social studies, may be taught in the other language. (Compare *single medium*).

E

ELA (English Language Arts)
A language arts program designed to teach English Language Arts skills both to native English-speaking students and to all others who have achieved linguistic independence in English. (See *independent*).

Elementary school   A school generally organized into a seven-year sequence comprising kindergarten and six one-year grade levels for children from the age of four or five to age eleven or twelve.

English language origin   Persons considered by themselves, by the school, or by the community to be of English-speaking ancestry or what may arbitrarily be considered as the equivalent.

English-speaking   One who can communicate orally and with native fluency in the English language. The term *native English-speaker* is also used and is often limited to students who speak English as their home language.

Equilingualism   Comparable competence in two languages or dialects within a given field. Example: Ability to count equally well in English and Spanish.

ESAA (Emergency School Aid Act)   A public law (92-318) passed by the United States Congress in 1973 (revising the Emergency School Assistance Act of 1971). The law provides for federal financial assistance to public school systems to help solve problems encountered during the process of desegregating student populations on a racial or language-origin basis.

ESEA (Elementary and Secondary Education Act)   This was the title for *Public Law 89-10* which was a series of amendments attached to the Federally Impacted Areas Legislation (*Public Law 874*) in 1965. These amendments were designed to provide federal financial support for schools with large enrollments of educationally disadvantaged students.

ESL (English as a Second Language)   A program designed for students of all ages whose native language is other than English. It was a full language arts and culture program. At the beginning of 1975, the name of this course in Dade County was changed to English for Speakers of Other Languages (ESOL).

ESOL (English for Speakers of Other Languages)   See *English as a Second Language [ESL]*.

Ethnocentrism   The identification of one's life with that of an ethnic group. Ethnic groups in which a majority of members have a high degree of ethnocentrism are characterized by a superior level of ethnicity and group cohesion based on the sharing of such distinguishing features as language, religion, education, law, customs, diet, dress, manners, social behavior, personal beliefs, and group attitude.

Ethnolinguistic intersection
The grouping of people belonging to different ethnic groups speaking different languages, as in biethnic marriages whereby at least one party must learn the language of the other.

Express power   Authority to prescribe a course of action. The Florida state legislature has delegated to itself the express power to prescribe and proscribe courses of study, textbooks, and content.

Expressive switching   Changeover from one language to another in the discourse of bilinguals as a result of their internal needs.

F

Federal aid   Financial assistance provided by the United States Government.

Federally Impacted Areas Legislation   This national legislation (*Public Law 874*) of 1950 provided federal financial relief to public schools that were "impacted" with students whose parents did not pay local property taxes to support their community's public schools because they lived or worked on property owned by the federal government.

Federal programs   Programs financed by the United States Government. These include projects involving bilingual education for adults, migrant workers, and other students; Titles I, II, and IV of the Elementary and Secondary Education Act; programs of the U.S. Office of Economic Opportunity; etc.

FLES (Foreign Languages in the Elementary School)   A program employed in many elementary schools in the United States in the 1960's. New techniques were used, such as radio and television broadcasts to schools, as part of an audiolingual approach to foreign language instruction.

Ford Foundation Projects in Bilingual Education   Initially titled Project in Bilingual Education of Cuban Refugee Pupils—Ford Foundation Grant, this was a three-year grant (1963-1966) of $278,000 to the Dade County Public Schools from the private Ford Foundation for: 1) The preparation of language and reading materials for non-English-speaking pupils entering first grade; 2) The revision or adaptation of the books of the *Fries American English Series* for non-English-speaking bilingual pupils who can read and write their vernacular; 3) The preparation of guides and audio-visual materials for teachers of bilingual pupils; 4) The establishment of a bilingual school. Projects 1 and 4 were initiated and implemented throughout the three-year period. Due to a lack of time and personnel, Project 2 was initiated but later abandoned and Project 3 was never initiated.

Freedom Flights   An airlift started on Dec. 1, 1965, between Varadero Beach in Cuba and Miami International Airport. Until these flights were stopped on Apr. 6, 1973, Cuban citizens who chose to leave Cuba, with the exception of males of military age (15 through 26 years), were able to fly to Miami with the permission of Cuban authorities. Cuban-American Day was celebrated in Miami on the first of December each subsequent year to commemorate the initiation of these Freedom Flights.

Functional bilingualism   The phase in the evolution of a bilingual community where each language has a specific role. (See *complementary bilingualism* and *diglossia*).

G

Geolinguistics The study of the geographic and demographic distribution of languages in relation to the power, attraction, and pressure which each of them exerts on the population. (See *language power, language attraction* and *language pressure*).

Grade-level One of 12 sequenced stages in elementary and secondary education in the United States. Generally, students are promoted to the next higher grade level at the beginning of each school year. (See *elementary school, junior high school, senior high school*.)

H

High-intermediate pupil Other-than-English language origin student who: 1) Understands extensively, approximately 50-80 percent of the time (English-speakers occasionally need to restate ideas to them); 2) Makes occasional significant grammatical errors of interference, approximately 10-20 percent of the time; 3) Speaks with occasional significant distortions of words and intonation, approximately 10-20 percent of the time; 4) Occasionally gropes for high-frequency words, approximately 10-20 percent of the time (English-speakers may have to rephrase to be understood). (Compare *mid-* and *low-intermediate, independent* and *non-independent*.)

Hilfssprache A language learned for occasional needs. Example: A Spanish doctor may learn English for the purpose of reading the medical literature in that language.

Hispanic "A person of Mexican, Puerto Rican, Cuban, Central or South American or other Spanish culture or origin, regardless of race." (Memorandum on *Racial and Ethnic Designations* circulated to the elementary school principals of Dade County on Jan. 19, 1976.)

Hybrid creation The use of a loanword as a base for deriving a new word with the native suffix: Example: Spanish *cranquiar* (to act cranky).

I

Immersion Schooling in a language unknown in the home. The term *immersion course* has been applied mostly to the type of bilingual schooling whereby children from unilingual homes that use the majority or dominant language are taught in the minority or less dominant language. According to the proportion of teaching done in the other language, a distinction is made between *total immersion* and *partial immersion*. According to the grade-levels in which such teaching takes place, we must distinguish *primary* or *elementary immersion* and *secondary immersion*.

Implied power Indirect authority to legislate. For example: the power of a local board of education to add, delete, or change courses of study, textbooks, and supplementary instructional materials which do not violate state requirements.

Importation The introduction into the speech of a bilingual of items from his other language without changing their form or meaning.

Example: *Frankfurter* in the Spanish sentence *No quiero comer el frankfurter.* (Compare *substitution*).

Inceptive bilingualism The introduction into a speech community of the occasional use of a second language. (See *supplementary bilingualism*).

Incipient bilingualism A limited knowledge of a second language sufficient for the minimal needs of a community or an individual.

Independent pupil Other-than-English language origin student who:1) Understands nearly everything a native speaker of comparable age and intelligence understands, approximately 80-100 percent of the time; 2) Uses English with few grammatical errors and can rephrase to make meaning clear, with less than 10 percent of probability of error; 3) Speaks with minor, nonsignificant distortions of pronunciation and intonation, with less than 10 percent probability of error; 4) Uses vocabulary comparable to that of native speakers of the same age and academic level, groping for words and rephrasing less than 10 percent of the time. (Compare *non-independent, high-, low-* and *mid-intermediate*.)

Institutional bilingualism The official use of two languages within an institution. This does not necessarily require that individuals in the institution be bilingual, since institutional bilingualism may be maintained by two unilingual groups working within the institution. (See *bilingual state*).

Integration The degree to which an element from another language has been accepted and used. Some foreign words are used by only part of the population, others are limited to bilingual communities. (See also *borrowing* and *loans*. For the social meaning of integration, see *racial integration*).

Interference The use of elements from one language while speaking or writing another. These elements may include words, expressions, structures, or even sounds. Example: *What means this word?* and *She said me goodbye* are instances of structural and grammatical interference.

Interlanguage A stage in the development of individual bilingualism whereby the speaker uses his new language fluently with a high level of interference from his other language which has become habitual. It is characteristic of certain types of immigrant speech, and it may eventually apply to the native language, so that some adult immigrants are able to speak two interlanguages, but no other. (Compare *creole* and *pidgin*).

Interlingual distance Measures of the degrees of differences between languages. These can reveal the extent to which, for example, Spanish is closer to Italian than it is to English.

Interlinguistics The comparative study of two or more languages, especially as regards semantic and grammatical equivalence. (See *differential* and *contrastive linguistics*).

Internal certification A plan for Dade County teachers and teacher aides working in English as a

Second Language, Spanish as a native or foreign language, Curriculum Content in Spanish, or within a bilingual school organization that required their participation in training sessions designed to improve their teaching competence in these areas. This local certification program was initiated by the Dade County Public Schools because no standards had been established for these instructional areas by the State of Florida.

Irridentism   A policy of restoring a former status. In bilingual schooling, this may imply giving more and more time to a language which is declining in use. For example, in bilingual areas where Spanish is no longer the home language of the younger generation, schools may be organized where most of the instruction is in Spanish.

J

Junior high school   A school generally organized into a three year sequence of seventh, eighth and ninth grade-levels for children between the ages of twelve and fifteen.

K

Kindergarten   A one-year public school program for children from ages four, five, or six that directly precedes their entrance into the first grade. In the 1970's, kindergarten classes were available at all public elementary schools in Dade County.

L

Language attraction   Capacity of a language to cause certain people to adopt it. English has a greater attraction for Crees than Cree has for native-speakers of English. But for the Quechuas, Spanish has a greater attraction than has English. Determinants of language attraction involve not only the relative power of the two languages but also the interlingual distance between the languages and the territorial distance separating their speakers. (See *language power* and *interlingual distance*).

Language didactics   The study of language teaching, including the analysis of methods and materials, techniques of testing their effects, language teaching techniques, lexicometrics, lesson analysis, automated teaching, teacher training, and related topics.

Language power   The independent influence that a language is able to exert on potential users and learners. Spanish, for example, can exert greater world influence than can Indonesian. Indicators of language power include such variables as population, average per capita income, geographic distribution, mobility, ideology, and cultural production. (Compare *language attraction* and *language pressure*).

Language pressure   The relative influence exerted by each of the two languages on the population of a bilingual community. Determinants of the pressure of each language include its power, status, attraction, and local functions, such as language of schooling, the press, radio, television, church services, business, labor, industry, and government administration. (See *language power* and *language attraction*).

Lexicometrics   The quantification and measurement of vocabulary features, such as the frequency of occurrence of words, their distribution, range, degree of availability to certain sections of the population, and their coverage or amount of work they are able to perform for general purposes. The measures are used in determining the extent of the repertoire of bilinguals in their two languages as compared to the unilingual norms.

Liaison bilingualism   Communication between managements speaking different languages. The transmission of information is done through a liaison officer, a bilingual personal assistant, or a bilingual private secretary. These persons do more than translate the content of the communication; they are often responsible for the delicate cross-cultural public relations of management. Most bilingual industries rely on this type of bilingualism. (Compare *line bilingualism*).

Line bilingualism   The institutionalized transmission within an organization of instructions beyond a language barrier. For example, bilingual supervisors or foremen may be responsible for transmitting orders from management to labor. The mass production of goods and services in bilingual societies is made possible by this type of institutional bilingualism. (Compare *liaison bilingualism*).

Lingua franca   A dialect or mixed language used as an auxiliary language for purposes of communication between different speech communities. The term is based on the name of a mixture of Provencal and Italian widely used in the past as a means of communication in the ports of the Mediterranean. (Compare *pidgin* and *creole*).

Literary diglossia   The functional distribution of written languages. For example, in the Middle Ages, although popular literature was written in the national vernacular of Europe, science and philosophy were expressed in Latin.

Loan translation   See under *calque*.

Loanblend   The use of the forms of one language in the adoption of words from another language. Example: The Spanish-speaking bilingual may blend the ending -*ando* into the word *chopeando* to obtain an equivalent to the English expression *to go shopping*. (Compare *loanshift*).

Loans   Elements adopted from another language. These may include words, expressions, structures, and even sounds. Example: The American English *creole* is a loanword adopted from the Spanish word *criollo*. (See *borrowing*).

Loanshift   The effect produced by one language on the meaning of words in the other language, often as a result of similarity of form. Example: In some Spanish-English bilingual communities, the Spanish word *libreria* (bookstore) is also used for the library, instead of the Spanish *biblioteca*, because of the similarity in form with the English word *library*. (Compare *loanblend*).

Loanword phonology   What happens to the pronunciation of a word when it is imported from another language. The word is often modified to fit the phonological structure of the host language. Example: English words like *steak* and *store* appear in Spanish as *esteque* and *estor*.

Low-intermediate pupil   Other-than-English language origin student who: 1) Understands limited everyday speech, approximately less than 20 percent of the time, when speakers choose carefully or restate ideas; 2) Makes frequent significant grammatical errors of interference, approximately 50-80 percent of the time; 3) Speaks with frequent significant distortions of words and intonation approximately 50-80 percent of the time; 4) Gropes for high-frequency words so that speakers often have to rephrase in order to be understood, approximately 50-80 percent of the time. (Compare *mid-* and *high-intermediate, independent* and *non-independent*).

M

Macaronic speech (text)   A type of artificial speech mixture designed for literary or psychological effect. The term is derived from the title of the grotesquely humorous comic epic *Maccaronea* published in Italy in 1517. Its author, Teofilo Folengo, uses Italian words with Latin grammar.

Maintenance type   Distribution of teaching time designed to maintain through the school a knowledge of both the home language and the second language. The maintenance may be at equal levels or at different levels.

Example: In each grade, the time in which Spanish is used as a teaching language is equal to that devoted to English. (Compare *transfer type*).

Melting pot   Concept of American nationality whereby immigrants from all over the world, after several generations of North American schooling, social and economic interaction and intermarriage, blend into a new American ethnic type.

Mexican Americans   Citizens of the United States of America whose ancestry can be traced to the Republic of Mexico.

Mid-intermediate pupil   Other-than-English language origin student who: 1) Understands everyday speech fairly well, 20-50 percent, though English-speakers often have to choose words carefully or restate ideas; 2) Makes many significant grammatical errors of interference, approximately 20-50 percent of the time; 3) Speaks with many significant distortions of words and intonations, approximately 20-50 percent of the time; 4) Usually gropes for high-frequency words so that speakers must rephrase to be understood, approximately 20-50 percent of the time. (Compare *high-* and *low-intermediate, independent* and *non-independent*.)

Migrant worker   One who moves periodically throughout the year from place to place in order to find work, especially in the harvesting of crops. Many such workers have come from adjacent countries in Latin America, including Mexico, to work as agricultural laborers in several parts of the United States.

Missile Crisis The confrontation in the 1960's between the United States and the Soviet Union, created when the latter installed intercontinental nuclear missiles in Cuba. Under the threat of an American naval engagement, the missiles were removed.

MLA (Modern Language Association) The Modern Language Association of America is a professional organization of teachers of modern language and literature founded in the United States at the end of the 19th Century.

Model A loanword or other borrowing as used in the lending or source language. (Compare *replica*).

Monolingual Knowing or using only one language. (See *unilingual* and *bilingual*).

Multilingualism The alternate use of more than one language or dialect. (See also under *bilingualism* and *plurilingualism*).

N

NABE (National Association for Bilingual Education) A professional organization of teachers, coordinators, and administrators working in schools and programs where two languages are used as media of instruction.

Natural bilingualism Competence in two languages, each acquired in the context of social needs and pressures.

Naturalized citizen Immigrants are placed on parolee status upon their arrival in the United States. After two-and-one-half years, immigrants may apply for legal resident status. Five years of legal resident status are required before an immigrant can become a naturalized citizen.

On Nov. 3, 1966, the United States Congress passed *Public Law 89-732* that permitted Cuban refugees to apply their time as parolees toward their legal resident requirement and complete the naturalization process in a total of five rather than seven-and-a-half years.

Non-English-speaking Not able to communicate orally in the English language.

Non-independent pupil Other-than-English language origin student who: 1) Understands only very limited if any conversation, approximately less than 10 percent of the time; 2) Makes constant errors in using the most frequent and useful significant grammatical structures, approximately 80-100 percent of the time; 3) Speaks with constant significant distortions of words and intonation, approximately 80-100 percent of the time; 4) Uses extremely limited vocabulary, approximately 80-100 percent of the time. (Compare *independent*, *high-*, *low-* and *mid-intermediate*).

Non-reciprocal bilingualism The use in communication of two languages by one interlocutor and of one language by the other. Example: Pedro speaks Spanish and English to Jane, who speaks only English to Pedro. (Compare *receptive bilingualism* and *reciprocal bilingualism*).

Norm specification Detailed description of the vocabulary, grammar, and phonology of each of the languages in the normal model available to the bilingual.

North American The term is sometimes used in its more limited definition in this text to refer to a citizen of the United States of America. It is recognized that the term "North American" can also refer to any native or inhabitant of the North American continent.

O

One-way bilingualism The use of two languages by one ethnic group but not by the other. A biethnic school may have a one-way bilingual course in that only one group is expected to become bilingual. Example: A school attended by both North Americans and Cuban children, the latter taking part of their education in Spanish. (Compare *two-way bilingualism*).

Organizational Model for Bilingual Schooling The schedule established for assigning students and allocating school time to the four components of the bilingual education program: English as a Second Language (ESL), Spanish as a Second Language (Spanish-SL), Spanish for Spanish-Speakers (Spanish-S), and Curriculum Content in Spanish (CCS).

Orientation Teacher Another title for second-language teachers of English or Spanish, used in the Dade County Public Schools in the early 1960's.

Other-than-English language origin Students who (1) use a language other than English as the first language for communication at

home and (2) at the time of placement in an instructional program, are considered by themselves and their parents to be of a language ancestry other than English, and (3) still can communicate orally in that other language, regardless of their current surname.

P

Parochial schools Privately-supported religious denominational institutions of learning associated with the community or parish church.

Parolee A person on parole status. This was the first step for immigrants in the process of becoming naturalized citizens of the United States. It preceded legal resident status.

Personality principle Recognition of the right of the individual to be served by the state in the official language of his choice in any area where the principle has the force of law. The state accommodates itself linguistically to the individual. (Compare *territoriality principle*).

Pidgin Originally a makeshift language permitting communication between a dominant but transient minority and a resident majority who adopt the imperfectly-learned minority language as a basis for communication. The new language is characterized by a predominance of substratum influence on the structure of the language and a simplified grammar, since constancy of corrective pressure from the base language is lacking. Some *pidgins* become creoles and national languages. See *creole, substratum,* and *lingua franca*).

Pillow words   Words which may belong to either one of the bilingual's languages. Example: Words like *visa* and *plan* look and mean the same in English and in Spanish. (Compare *deceptive cognates* and *dialinguistic identification*).

Plurilingualism   The alternate use of more than one language or dialect. (See also under *bilingualism* and *multilingualism*).

Private schools   Institutions that provide instruction for children, and at times, for adults. These institutions are established, conducted, and primarily supported by a nongovernmental organization, a church or business enterprise.

Productive bilingualism   The use of two languages or dialects for purposes of expression—speaking and/or writing. (Compare *receptive bilingualism*).

Professional right   The right of local administrators and teachers to determine methodology for teaching of content in all courses.

Progressive bilingualism   The increasing use of two languages in a speech community. Example: In Miami, the population of bilinguals increased as more and more of the younger generation of Cubans learned English.

Proportion of interference   The number of units in a specimen of bilingual speech which, at each level of analysis—phonology, morphology, and syntax—belong to each of the languages used.

Prototype   See under *model*.

Psycholinguistic   Related to the study of language in the mind. This may include the study of such questions as language acquisition, the effects of bilingualism on intellectual and emotional development, and the storage of two languages in the memory.

PTA (Parent and Teachers Association)   A group of parents and teachers that volunteer to raise money and provide other types of support for a local school. Each local PTA is generally affiliated with the National Parents and Teachers Association. In the 1970's, students were added to this association in some schools in Dade County.

PTO (Parents and Teachers Organization)   A group of parents and teachers that volunteer to raise money and provide other types of support for a local school.

Public school   Tax-supported institution providing free instruction for children and, at times, for adults. In the United States, these institutions are established for all children from ages 4 or 5 to 17 or 18. Children usually begin their first year in kindergarten and then are promoted from year to year, as they get older, through 12 grade levels. In general, children are required to attend a public or private school until they reach the age of 16. The school year normally begins in September and ends in June.

Puerto Rican   Citizen of the United States of America whose ancestry can be traced to the island of

Puerto Rico, a self-governing Commonwealth in union with the United States.

Q

Quadrilingualism   The alternate use of four languages or dialects. (See also under *bilingualism*).

Quin (quinmester)   One of five sessions of nine weeks into which the school year is divided. Students wishing to skip vacations and take successive quins may graduate from public school at a younger age and/or at an earlier date.

R

Racial discrimination   Functional classification according to race. Whether for purposes of domination or of promotion, discrimination always implies the recognition of an operational difference. For example, the zoning of residential areas to exclude blacks and the promotion of black English are both instances of racial discrimination. Both racial segregation and racial integration imply some sort of discrimination.

Racial integration   The grouping of people from different races. In cases where races are segregated by residence, a policy of racial integration in school may imply the transporting of pupils from one area to another. This process, known as *busing*, obliges some pupils to attend school outside their community. (Compare *biracial, racial segregation,* and *desegregation*).

Racial segregation   The separating of people according to racial origin. This may imply separate schools or classrooms for children of different races. The segregation may be *de jure* or *de facto*, the former being a matter of policy, the latter being a separation of races due to the tendency of people with similar needs to congregate together. (Compare *racial integration, racial discrimination,* and *desegregation*).

Ragged switching   Gradual change-over from one language to the other in the speech of bilinguals, characterized by speech mixture at the switching point. (Compare *clean switching*).

Rate of interference   The number of times per hundred occurrences that a bilingual speaker changes languages at each level—phonological, morphological, syntactic—in a specimen of his speech.

Receptive bilingualism   The use of one language for expression and two languages for comprehension. Example: Although Jane reads and understands Spanish and English, she speaks and writes only the latter.

Reciprocal bilingualism   The use in communication of two languages by each interlocutor. Example: Pedro and Jane speak both English and Spanish to each other. (See *non-reciprocal bilingualism*).

Redistribution   (See under *substitution*).

Regressive bilingualism   The decreasing use of two languages in a speech community. Example: In Middleville, the population of bilinguals has declined, since the younger English-speaking generation has not learned Spanish and the older generation, mostly bilingual, is dying away.

Replacive bilingualism The reduction in the number of functions for which one of the languages is used. (See *residual bilingualism*.).

Replica A loanword or other borrowing as used in the receiving or target language. (Compare *model*).

Residual bilingualism The phase in the evolution of a bilingual community in which one of the languages is used only occasionally, and often by only the older generation (See *replacive bilingualism*).

S

SAC (School Advisory Committee) A group of parents, students, and other community members organized to meet regularly with school leaders to identify school-community problems and to suggest ways of solving those problems. In the Dade County Public Schools, separate advisory committees were established at each school, for each of the six administrative areas, and for the county as a whole. Most of these committees, in turn, established subcommittees for bilingual education.

SALAD (Spanish American League Against Discrimination) Organization founded in Miami in the late 1960's to protect the interests of all Spanish-speaking ethnic groups in the area.

Sandwich words See under *pillow words*.

SCDC (Spanish Curricula Development Center) A national materials production center established on Miami Beach in 1970 by the Bilingual Education Programs Branch of the United States Office of Education at the request of the Dade County Public Schools. The center produced multidisciplinary, multimedia Spanish curricula kits for use in bilingual programs in elementary schools throughout the United States.

School Board (Board of Education) A small group of citizens elected by members of the community to establish policies for the local school system. Once they are selected as school board members, these individuals become officials of the state government. Policies established by a local school board must not violate the laws of the state or those of the nation.

Second-language program A foreign language program designed to teach students a language which they do not know. In addition, instruction is presented concerning the culture associated with this foreign language.

Self-determination Claim of a people, nation, or ethnic group to the right to decide the form of government it shall have, free from the influence of any other such group. (See *separatism*).

Senior high school A school generally organized into a three-year sequence of tenth, eleventh, and twelfth grade levels for children aged 15 or 16 years to 17 or 18 years.

Separatism A policy advocating separation from an established political or religious entity. Separatist movements are often based on claims to the right of linguistic or ethnic self-determination. (See *self-determination*).

Single-medium   Using only one language to teach all school subjects. A single-medium school may use only the national language, even though it is not necessarily the home language of all of the pupils. (Compare *dual-medium* and *immersion*).

Sociolinguistic   Related to the study of language in society. This may include the functions of two or more languages in a bilingual community, the language behavior of small groups and the political coexistence of two or more languages.

Source language   The language from which a transfer (translating or borrowing) is made (Compare *target language*; see also *model* and *prototype*).

Spanish CORE and Enrichment See *Curriculum Content in Spanish (CCS)*.

Spanish FL (Spanish as a Foreign Language)   See *Spanish as a Second Language (Spanish-SL)*.

Spanish FL/SL (Spanish as a Foreign/Second Language) See *Spanish as a Second Language (Spanish-SL)*.

Spanish language origin   Persons considered by themselves, by the school, or by the community to be of Mexican, Puerto Rican, Central American, Cuban, Latin-American, or of other Spanish-speaking ancestry.

Spanish-S (Spanish for Spanish-Speakers)   Initially titled Spanish for Cuban pupils, Spanish-S is a language and culture program designed to teach Spanish language arts skills to any Spanish-speaking student.

Spanish-SL (Spanish as a Second Language)   A language and culture program designed to provide instruction in Spanish to non-Spanish-speaking students. In elementary bilingual school organizations, this program is called Spanish-SL, in other elementary schools it is called *Spanish as a Foreign/Second Language (Spanish-FL/SL)*, and in secondary schools it is called *Spanish as a Foreign Language (Spanish-FL)*.

Spanish-speaking   One who can communicate orally and with native fluency in the Spanish language. The term *native Spanish-speaker* also is used and often includes students for whom Spanish is or was the home language.

Spanish-surnamed   An individual whose family name indicates Spanish-speaking ancestry.

Special education teachers Teachers who are certified by the state and employed to instruct students with various exceptionalities, such as, the mentally retarded, the blind, and the emotionally disturbed.

Special Spanish teacher   An instructor in Dade County's bilingual education program who presents Spanish-S, Spanish-SL, or CCS instruction at elementary schools or Spanish-S instruction at secondary schools. In most cases, this position is funded by the Cuban Refugee Program.

Sprachgefühl   An acquired sense of norm permitting one to judge the extent to which certain expressions are customary in a given language and certain others are not.

State   One of the governmental units of a nation having a federal government. The United States of America is comprised of 50 states.

State certification   Each state has training qualifications for public school teachers and administrators. In most cases, individuals must prove to the state that they have fulfilled these qualifications (usually courses at colleges or universities) for a specific subject area (for example, art, elementary education, Spanish) before they can be employed by a public school in that state.

Structural resistance   Grammatical characteristics of a language which prevent it from integrating features (words or structures) from some other language. Certain highly inflected languages with a high percentage of morphologically bound forms have been found to resist the influence of other languages through highly productive mechanisms of compounding and word formation.

Substitution   The adaptation of items from one language when used in the context of another language. Example: The phonological substitution to accommodate the word *frankfurter* in the Spanish sentence: *No quiero comer la fanfurria.* (Compare *importation*).

Substratum   The elements comprising the language and culture of a dominated people in a situation of language contact. When some of these elements enter the dominant language there is a *substratum influence.* Example: Amerindian words in Spanish. (Compare *superstratum*).

Superintendent   The chief administrative official of a local public school system in the United States. The superintendent may be elected by local citizens or appointed by the school board and is responsible for implementing the policies established by the school board.

Superstratum   The elements comprising the language and culture of the dominant people in a situation of language contact. When some of these elements enter the language of the dominated, there is a *superstratum influence.* Example: Hispanisms in the Amerindian languages. (Compare *substratum*).

Supplementary bilingualism   The alternate use in a community of two languages one of which is used only as a back-up or supplement to the other. (See *inceptive bilingualism*).

Supplementary personnel   Staff members, other than classroom teachers, assigned to a school on a full-time or part-time basis. For example, music teachers, art teachers, physical education teachers, special reading teachers, and counselors are often placed in this category.

Switching   See under *code switching*; see also, under types of switching—*expressive, clean* and *ragged*.

T

Tagging   Lexical and grammatical code-marking of each linguistic element in the bilingual's memory as belonging to one of his languages and not belonging to the other language.

Target language   The language toward which the transfer (translation or borrowing) is directed. (Compare *source language*; see also *replica*).

Teacher Trainer Coordinator for Bilingual School Organizations
A position funded in 1971 by the Education Professions Development Act of the United States Office of Education to train teachers, aides, and administrators involved in bilingual education in the Dade County Public Schools and to coordinate the objectives of the local bilingual school programs at the elementary and secondary school levels.

TSA (Teachers on Special Assignment)   Teachers assigned to assist the staffs at a number of schools in organizing and implementing certain instructional programs.

Territoriality principle   Recognition of the right of a state or any of its territorial components to choose its own official language. Individuals within these territorial limits must accommodate themselves to the language requirements of the state. Swiss bilingualism is based on the territoriality principle. (Compare *personality principle*).

Transfer type   Distribution of teaching time in such a way as to phase out one of the languages of instruction. The transfer, which may be gradual or abrupt, is generally made from the mother tongue to the national language. Example: Grade one may be entirely in Spanish, more and more English being added until grade six, which is entirely in English. (Compare *maintenance type*).

Transitional bilingualism
The bilingualism of the middle generation serving to bridge the transfer from the unilingualism of one generation in language A to that of the third generation in language B. Example: The children of a Spanish-speaking Puerto Rican immigrant in the Mid-West become bilingual and their bilingualism serves as a transition to the unilingualism of their own children, who become English-speaking. The term *transitional* also is used to identify school programs of the *transfer type*.

Triggering   Cause of a changeover from one language to another in the discourse of bilinguals. The causal factor may be a change of topic, of interlocutor, word association, or the greater availability of a concept in the other language. (Compare *alternation* and *code switching*).

Trilingualism   The alternate use of three languages or dialects. (See *bilingualism*).

Two-way bilingualism   The use of two languages by both groups in a biethnic community. In a two-way bilingual school, both groups are expected to become bilingual. Example: In Coral Way School, both North American and Cuban children are schooled in both English and Spanish. (Compare *one-way bilingualism*).

Two-way bilingual program
A program that employs two languages for purposes of instruction and involves students who are native speakers of each of those languages.

U

Umgangssprache   Everyday speech. The vernacular used for daily oral communication.

Unilingualism   The regular use of only one language or dialect.

V

Vernacular bridge   The use of the home dialect in instruction as a transition to the standard language.

W

White (non-Hispanic)   A person having origins in any of the original peoples of Europe, North America, the Middle East, or the Indian sub-continent." (Memorandum on *Racial and Ethnic Designations* circulated to the elementary school principals of Dade County on Jan. 19, 1976).

X

Xenophobia   Mistrust of strangers. Groups with a high degree of ethnicity and exclusiveness have been characterized by this trait which functions as a protection against assimilation, acculturation, or absorption into the "foreign" majority.

Y

Yankee   A familiar name given to English colonists before and during the American Revolution, to Northerners during the American Civil War, to American soldiers in both World Wars, and to citizens of the United States by people of other countries.

Z

Zoning laws   Municipal regulations controlling the use of property (real estate) in a given area. Such regulations have sometimes been used to exclude certain ethnic groups from owning property or taking up residence in certain parts of town.

Index